London

WHAT'S NEW | **WHAT'S ON** | **WHAT'S BEST**

www.timeout.com/london

Contents

London by Area

Essentials

Guides

Published by Time Out
4th Floor
125 Shaftesbury Avenue
London WC2H 8AD
Tel: + 44 (0)20 7813 3000
Email: guides@timeout.com
www.timeout.com

Editorial Director Sarah Guy
Group Finance Manager Margaret Wright

Time Out Guides is a wholly owned subsidiary of Time Out Group Ltd.

© **Time Out Group Ltd**
Chairman & Founder Tony Elliott
Chief Executive Officer Tim Arthur
Chief Financial Officer Matt White
Publisher Alex Batho

Time Out and the Time Out logo are trademarks of Time Out Group Ltd.

This edition first published in Great Britain in 2014 by Ebury Publishing
A Random House Group Company
Company information can be found on www.randomhouse.co.uk
Random House UK Limited Reg. No. 954009
10 9 8 7 6 5 4 3 2 1

Distributed in the US and Latin America by Publishers Group West (1-510-809-3700)

For further distribution details, see www.timeout.com

ISBN: 978-1-84670-340-9

A CIP catalogue record for this book is available from the British Library.

Printed and bound in Germany by Appl.

The Random House Group Limited supports the Forest Stewardship Council® (FSC®), the
leading international forest-certification organisation. Our books carrying the FSC label are
printed on FSC® - certified paper. FSC is the only forest-certification scheme supported by
the leading environmental organisations, including Greenpeace. Our paper procurement
policy can be found at www.randomhouse.co.uk/environment

MIX
Paper from
responsible sources
FSC® C004592
www.fsc.org

London Shortlist

The **Time Out London Shortlist 2015** is one of a series of annual guides that draws on Time Out's background as a magazine publisher to keep you current with everything that's going on in town. As well as London's key sights and the best of its eating, drinking and leisure options, it picks out the most exciting venues to have opened in the last year and gives a full calendar of annual events. It also includes features on the important news, trends and openings, all compiled by locally based editors and writers. Whether you're visiting for the first time in your life or the first time this year, you'll find the *Time Out London Shortlist* contains all you need to know, in a portable and easy-to-use format.

The guide divides central London into five areas, each containing listings for Sights & Museums, Eating & Drinking, Shopping, Nightlife and Arts & Leisure, and maps pinpointing their locations; a further chapter rounds up the best of the rest. At the front of the book are chapters rounding up these scenes city-wide, and giving a shortlist of our overall picks. We also include itineraries for days out, plus essentials such as transport information and hotels.

Our listings give phone numbers as dialled within London. To dial them from elsewhere in the UK, preface them with 020; dial 08… and 07… numbers as they are given. From abroad, use your country's exit code followed by 44 (the country code for the UK), 20 and the number given, dropping the initial '0'; for 08… and 07… numbers just use 44 and drop the initial '0'.

We have noted price categories by using one to four pound signs (**£-££££**), representing budget, moderate, expensive and luxury. Major credit cards are accepted unless otherwise stated. We also give **Event highlights**.

All our listings are double-checked, but places do sometimes close or change their hours or prices, so it's a good idea to call a venue before visiting. While every effort has been made to ensure accuracy, the publishers cannot accept responsibility for any errors that this guide may contain.

Venues are marked on the maps using symbols numbered according to their order within the chapter and colour-coded as follows:

1 Sights & Museums
1 Eating & Drinking
1 Shopping
1 Nightlife
1 Arts & Leisure

Map Key

Major sight or landmark	▬
Railway or coach station	▬
Underground station	⊖
Park	▬
Hospital	▬
Casualty unit	✚
Church	✚
Synagogue	✡
District	MAYFAIR
Theatre	●

Time Out **London** Shortlist

EDITORIAL
Editor Simon Coppock
Deputy editor Ros Sales
Additional editorial Carol Baker, Yolanda Zappaterra
Proofreader Marion Moisy

DESIGN & PICTURE DESK
Senior Designer Kei Ishimaru
Group Commercial Senior Designer Jason Tansley
Picture Editor Jael Marschner
Deputy Picture Editor Ben Rowe
Freelance Picture Researcher Lizzy Owen

ADVERTISING
Account Managers Deborah Maclaren, Helen Debenham at the Media Sales House

MARKETING
Senior Publishing Brand Manager Luthfa Begum
Head of Circulation Dan Collins

PRODUCTION
Production Controller Katie Mulhern-Bhudia

CONTRIBUTORS
This guide was researched and written by Simon Coppock, Ros Sales and the writers of *Time Out London*, with assistance from James Bristow and Daisy Snooks.

About **Time Out**

Founded in 1968, Time Out has expanded from humble London beginnings into the leading resource for those wanting to know what's happening in the world's greatest cities. As well as our influential what's-on weeklies in London and New York, we publish nearly 30 other listings magazines in cities as varied as Beijing and Mumbai. The magazines established Time Out's trademark style: sharp writing, informed reviewing and bang up-to-date inside knowledge of every scene.

Time Out made the natural leap into travel guides in the 1980s with the City Guide series, which now extends to over 50 destinations around the world. Written and researched by expert local writers and generously illustrated with original photography, the full-size guides cover a larger area than our Shortlist guides and include many more venue reviews, along with additional background features and a full set of maps.

Throughout this rapid growth, the company has remained proudly independent, still owned by Tony Elliott four decades after he started Time Out London as a single fold-out sheet of A5 paper. This independence extends to the editorial content of all our publications, this Shortlist included. No establishment has been featured because it has advertised, and no payment has influenced any of our reviews. And, for our critics, there's definitely no such thing as a free lunch: all restaurants and bars are visited and reviewed anonymously, and Time Out always picks up the bill.

For more about the company, see www.timeout.com.

WHAT'S BEST
Sights & Museums

We were pleased, but not entirely surprised, to read that some experts reckon London will be the world's most visited city in 2014, with approaching 19m visitors. London has an amazing – and very visible – history. It is blessed with four UNESCO World Heritage Sites: the **Tower of London** (p143), the fine buildings round Parliament Square in **Westminster** (p66), soothing **Kew Gardens** (see box p154) and the many attractions of **Greenwich** (the National Maritime Museum, the *Cutty Sark* and the Old Royal Naval College, pp164-166); and, at a micro-level, the city's very fabric traces centuries-old alleys and byways.

This is a city of memories, too. With the centenary of the start of World War I just gone, and the 70th anniversary of the end of World War

II due in 2015, there's no better time to visit London's plethora of war museums: from the grand – the **IWM** (p53) has had a major renovation – to the bijou (Guards Museum, p72; Household Cavalry Museum, p72; National Army Museum, p86). Those interested in military aviation will find a visit to north London's **RAF Museum** (Grahame Park Way, NW9 5LL, 8205 2266, www.rafmuseum.org.uk/london) especially rewarding: there are 100 aircraft on display, with lots of interactives.

But this is a restless city too, always seeking to accommodate the new within the old: the suddenly dominant **Shard** (p59) is symbolic of a brazenly commercial side of London often overlooked in tourist guides – the Emirates Air Line's sponsorship of a river **cable car** (p163) is another aspect of this. And

few museums seem able to resist updating and improving their material fabric: those listed (right) are just a selection.

We seem to have entered a period when the city's grand projects, long in planning, all come to fruition: out east, the **Olympic Park** (p163) has reopened to the public; in the north, the transformation of a post-industrial wasteland is nearly done with the completion of **Granary Square** (p106); in the City, a copse of skyscrapers has grown up around the '**Gherkin**' (30 St Mary Axe; p140), with the '**Cheesegrater**' (p140) and the '**Walkie-Talkie**' (p143) only the most prominent.

A whistle-stop tour

The **South Bank** remains London's key tourist destination. The principal attractions are well established: **Tate Modern** (p59), **Shakespeare's Globe** (p56) and **Borough Market** (p62), the **London Eye** (p56) and the lively **Southbank Centre** (p65). The Shard now looks down on all of them from London Bridge, and the **London Dungeon** (p53) has upped sticks to County Hall to join the Eye, the **Sea Life London Aquarium** (p56) and, probably arriving in summer 2015 and also run by Merlin Entertainments, **Shrek's Far Far Away Adventure**. Even here there are discreet joys to be found: take the time to explore minor highlights such as the **Garden Museum** (p52).

Across the river, the **City** authorities have made a concerted effort to alter the reputation of the most ancient part of London as a place just for finance workers. It's a pretty easy sell, given the number of historic attractions – the Tower of London and **St Paul's** (p141) are the best known – and easy access from the South Bank over the Millennium Bridge. St Paul's and the **Monument** (p140) have been vividly renovated,

SHORTLIST

New attractions
- British Postal Museum & Archive (see p134)
- Design Museum (see p75)
- Garden Bridge (see p52)
- House of Illustration (p108)
- Museum of Comedy (p105)

Welcome returns
- Cast Courts, V&A (p80)
- Imperial War Museum (p53)
- Grand Gallery, Wallace (p91)
- Wellcome Collection (see p108)

Best views
- Emirates Air Line cable car (p163)
- London Eye (p56)
- Shard (p59)
- Heritage Routemaster bus (p70)

Finest for free
- British Museum (p104)
- Museum of London (p141)
- National Gallery (p69)
- Tate Britain (p70)
- Victoria & Albert Museum (p80)

Unsung places
- Grant Museum of Zoology (p105)
- Old Operating Theatre, Museum & Herb Garret (p56)
- Trinity Buoy Wharf (p164)

Best late events
- Science Museum (p79)
- Sir John Soane's Museum (p135)
- Tate Britain (p70)
- Victoria & Albert Museum (p80)

Best outdoor
- Swimming in the ponds on Hampstead Heath (p154)
- Royal Botanic Gardens (p154)
- Watching the pelicans in St James's Park (p72)

TAKE YOUR IMAGINATION
INTO UNCHARTED
TERRITORY!
WADLOW
FAMILY ALBUM
Ripley's
Believe It or Not!®
LONDON
DISCOVER THE UK'S MOST
EXTRAORDINARY ATTRACTION
RIPLEYSLONDON.COM
NO. 1 PICCADILLY CIRCUS

British Museum

while a trip to the **Museum of London** (p141) is essential to get a grip on the bewildering history of this city.

The other essential visits are **South Kensington** for its cluster of three brilliant Victorian museums – the **V&A** (p80), the **Natural History Museum** (p79) and the **Science Museum** (p79) – and **Bloomsbury** for the world-class **British Museum** (p104), at which a new extension is now open to the public. North of the British Museum, the ghoulish animal remains at the **Grant Museum** (p105) are an atmospheric treat, while the **Wellcome Collection** (p108) – having carved itself a special niche for arrestingly themed science and culture exhibitions – has embarked on a £17.5m expansion, due for completion in late 2014/early 2015.

And we haven't yet visited the geographical centre of London: just south of **Trafalgar Square** (p70),

behind an equestrian statue, a plaque marks the official centre of the city. Nearby you'll find Nelson's Column supported by its weary lions, contemporary art on the Fourth Plinth, and – along the pedestrianised northern edge – two brilliant art collections: paintings from every era and part of the world at the **National Gallery** (p69) and the oddly compelling historical portraiture of the **National Portrait Gallery** (p70); it will be interesting to see what happens to them both after the departure of their respective directors, Nicholas Penny and Sandy Nairne, in 2015.

The problem with a visit to London is – as it always has been – how to fit it all in. The truth is, you can't… not in a single trip, not in a single lifetime. So relax and do whatever you most fancy. And if you've only a couple of days at your disposal, consider following our **itinerary** (pp44-45).

FASHION RULES

**EXHIBITION
NOW OPEN**

**DRESS FROM THE COLLECTION
OF HM THE QUEEN,
PRINCESS MARGARET AND
DIANA, PRINCESS OF WALES**

Exhibition sponsor

ESTĒE
LAUDER
COMPANIES

**Members go free
hrp.org.uk/fashion**

© William Hustler and Georgina Hustler / National Portrait Gallery, L

Hampton Court Palace

Doing the geography

This book is divided by area. The **South Bank** primarily covers riverside Bankside, home of Tate Modern, and the Southbank Centre. Over the river, **Westminster & St James's** cover the centre of UK politics, while the impressive Victorian museums of **South Kensington**, the famous Knightsbridge department stores, and the boutiques and eateries of **Chelsea** lie to the west.

The **West End** includes most of what is now central London. We start north of **Oxford Street**, in the slightly raffish shopping district of **Marylebone**. South is **Mayfair**, as expensive as its reputation but less daunting, with fine mews and pubs. Eastward are **Fitzrovia**, its elegant streets speckled with restaurants and shops; the squares and Georgian terraces of literary **Bloomsbury**, home of the British Museum; and up-and-coming **King's Cross**.

Head south for **Covent Garden**, so popular with tourists that locals often forget its many charms, and **Soho**, notorious centre of fun.

The **City** comprises the once-walled Square Mile of the original city, now adjoined by the bars and clubs of **Shoreditch; Holborn & Clerkenwell** have wonderful food.

Around these central districts, London's **neighbourhoods** have clusters of fine restaurants, bars and clubs, while further afield still lie lovely Kew Gardens and grand **Hampton Court Palace** (see box p154), both of them worth a day trip in their own right.

Making the most of it

Don't be scared of London's public transport: it's by far the best way of getting around town. Invest in an **Oyster travel smartcard** (p182) on arrival and roam cashless through the city by bus, tube (underground

Stunning ceremonials

Can anywhere touch London when it comes to pageantry?

Changing of the Guard

On alternate days from 10.45am (www.royal.gov.uk/RoyalEventsand Ceremonies/ChangingtheGuard/ Overview.aspx has the details), one of the five Foot Guards regiments lines up in scarlet coats and bearskin hats in the forecourt of Wellington Barracks; at exactly 11.27am, the soldiers march to Buckingham Palace (p72) with their regimental band to relieve the sentries in a 45min ceremony for the **Changing of the Guard**.

Not far away, at Horse Guards Parade in Whitehall, the Household Cavalry mounts the guard daily at 11am (10am on Sunday). Although this ceremony isn't as famous as the one at Buckingham Palace, it's more visitor-friendly: the crowds aren't as thick as they are at the palace, and spectators aren't held far back from the action by railings. After the old and new guard have stared each other out in the centre of the parade ground, you can nip through to the Whitehall side to catch the departing old guard

perform their hilarious dismount choreography: a synchronised, firm slap of approbation to the neck of each horse before the gloved troopers all swing off.

As well as these near-daily ceremonies, London sees less frequent but grander parades. The most famous is **Trooping the Colour**, staged to mark the Queen's official birthday in June (her real one's on 21 April). At 10.45am, the Queen rides in a carriage from Buckingham Palace to Horse Guards Parade to watch the soldiers, before heading back to Buckingham Palace for a midday RAF flypast and a gun salute.

Also at Horse Guards, on 4-5 June, **Beating the Retreat** (7414 2271, tickets 7839 5323) is a pageant of military music and precision marching. It begins at 7pm, when the Queen (or another royal) takes the salute of 300 drummers, pipers and musicians of the Massed Bands of the Household Division.

trains) and train, especially the excellent London Overground – which is treated as part of the underground network, but listed as 'rail' in our listings.

The tube is the easiest mode of transport for newbies (avoid rush hour: 8-9.30am, 4.30-7pm Mon-Fri), but buses are best to get a handle on the city's topography. Some good sightseeing routes are RV1 (riverside), 7, 8 and 12, but hop on a **Routemaster Heritage bus** (p70) to enjoy a classic red bus. Note that no London buses accept cash anymore – if you don't have an Oyster, you'll have to use a contactless debit or credit card.

The Barclays bike hire scheme (universally known as **'Boris Bikes'**) isn't very useful to commuters unless they're pretty enterprising, but given good weather is a lot of fun, and inexpensive; for more on **cycling** the city, see p185.

Crime in central London is low, so walk whenever you can to get a feel for the character of different areas of the city. No one thinks any the less of someone consulting a map – so long as they duck out of the stream of pedestrian traffic while doing so. And, despite Londoners' not entirely undeserved reputation for being unhelpful, most of us are quietly delighted to show off the breadth of our local knowledge by assisting with directions.

To avoid the worst of the crowds, avoid big attractions at weekends and on late-opening nights, and aim to hit blockbuster exhibitions in the middle of a run; January to March are the quietest months for visiting attractions, July to September the busiest. Last entry can be up to an hour before closing time (we specify when it is more than an hour before), so don't turn up at the last minute and expect to get in. Some sights close at Christmas and Easter – ring ahead to confirm opening hours.

Chiltern Firehouse

Eating & Drinking

London's restaurateurs seem to have put the recession behind them with a giddying number of high-profile openings or roll-outs of successful brands. The **Chiltern Firehouse** (p91), with Nuno Mendes in residence producing sometimes artistic and delicate, sometimes bold dishes, has quickly become a celeb magnet. Mendes was formerly at Viajante, which has now been transformed into the **Typing Room** (p159), east London's home of high-fashion food with a nod to New Nordic. There's **Hixter** (9A Devonshire Square, EC2M 4AE, 7220 9498, www.hixter.co.uk) from Mark Hix, a retro bar and grill with City prices, the first in a chain, for which **Tramshed** (p147) was the prototype. Meanwhile, having won plaudits for his pretty, daring and

tiny dishes at **Pollen Street Social** (8 Pollen Street, W1J 1NG, 7290 7600, www.pollenstreetsocial.com) and the **Social Eating House** (p116), Jason Atherton has been behind more hot openings, among them glamorous **Berners Tavern** (p102) and the newest sibling, **City Social** (p144). It doesn't stop there: Gordon Ramsay is due to reopen a restaurant on the site of his first London endeavour, Aubergine, in August 2014. And one of the most lauded recent openings is modern Indian restaurant **Gymkhana** (p96), with chef-patron Karam Sethi's take on regional dishes.

Down and dirty

The popularity of 'dirty food' shows no signs of abating – burger, pulled

SHORTLIST

Best new restaurants
- Barnyard (see p102)
- Berners Tavern (p102)
- City Social (p144)
- Typing Room (p159)
- Gymkhana (p96)

Best of British
- Albion (p156)
- Lyle's (p19)
- Poppies (p157)
- St John (p137)

Food & drink with a view
- Duck & Waffle (p144)
- Gong (p145)
- Paramount (p126)
- Sushisamba (p144)

Best no-bookings restaurants
- 10 Greek Street (p117)
- Barnyard (p102)
- Burger & Lobster (p96)
- Pitt Cue Co (p115)

Best ice-cream
- Gelateria 3bis (p61)
- Scoop (p126)

Best gastropubs
- Anchor & Hope (p61)
- Eagle (p137)

Best pubs
- Cock Tavern (p160)
- Ye Olde Mitre (p138)

Best for wine
- Terroirs (p126)
- Vinoteca (p138)

Best cocktails
- 69 Colebrooke Row (p151)
- Purl (p93)
- White Lyan (p159)

Best Indian
- Gymkhana (p96)

pork, chicken, barbecue and Creole places continue to flourish, with the likes of **Spuntino** (grungy Italian-American with big bold flavours, p116), **Pitt Cue Co** (a trailblazing rib joint, p115) and **Burger & Lobster** (just as the name says, with the lobster roll a favourite, p96) continuing to pack them in. Exciting opening **Barnyard** (p102), from the haute cuisine stable of **Dabbous** (39 Whitfield Street, W1T 2SF, 7323 1544, www. dabbous.co.uk) but nothing like it, does a riff on canteen cooking with a superbly flavoured sausage roll, chicken in a bun, cauliflower cheese and so on, in a rural-industrial setting.

No bookings taken

The trend for quality dining at the lower end of the scale continues, led by a surprisingly large number of places that don't take bookings: diners have shown themselves willing to eschew this luxury and

instead queue for good food at good prices at restaurants like **Burger & Lobster**, **Pitt Cue Co**, **10 Greek Street** (p117) and new opening **Barnyard**.

Ethnic eats

The other way to eat well for less in London is long-established: try something different. Everyone says it – and we really believe it's true: the whole world's food can be found in this city. Recently Peruvian food has become a real presence – **Lima London** (p103) and **Ceviche** (p111) are stand-outs. A branch of the former, **Lima Floral** was about to open in Garrick Street, Covent Garden, at the time of writing. Japanese ramen noodles are having a real resurgence; as if to show off, we also have a terrific exponent of the rarer udon noodles in the ever-popular **Koya** (p115). Chinese and Indian cooking styles are strong presences, with newcomer Indian restaurant **Gymkhana** a noteworthy addition , but you'll

also find Middle Eastern just off Oxford Street at **Comptoir Libanais** (65 Wigmore Street, W1U 1PZ, 7518 8080, www.busaba. com), Vietnamese in Shoreditch (**Song Que**, p157), Turkish in Dalston, and burritos just about everywhere (**Benito's Hat**, p102, is our favourite).

Brit bites

What about Brit dishes? The high point of the trend for old-fashioned English cooking is past, which has left only the key exponents and the more serious new contenders. Following the lead set by the pioneering and still wonderful **St John** (p137), avatars like the **Anchor & Hope** (p61) are now well established. St John was the game-changer in modern British cooking in the 1990s and continues to serve brilliantly simple, classic combinations of gutsy, carefully sourced ingredients. New opening **Lyle's** (Tea Building, 56 Shoreditch High Street, E1 6JJ, 3011 5911,

Lyle's

www.lyleslondon.com) follows this model too.

The British nostalgia trend is exemplified at Sir Terence Conran's Boundary Project by **Albion** (p156), a casual ground-floor café that serves unpretentious dishes, from kedgeree to welsh rarebit. A new branch, **Albion Neo Bankside** (p59) opened recently next to Tate Modern. By Spitalfields Market, **Poppies** (p157) is a fun retro setting for fish and chips, produced by a fryer who learned his trade in the 1950s on the Roman Road – proper East End, in other words.

Drinking it all in

London's top-end cocktail venues are drawing the capital's drinking scene ever closer to the quality of New York or Sydney – **Mark's Bar** (p115) has been joined by the new, super-creative **White Lyan** in Hoxton (p159), which eschews the use of ice. But beer is the new thrill. Microbreweries and craft-beer bars seem to have sprung up everywhere, from Hackney's **Cock Tavern** (p160) to Camden's swaggering **Brewdog** (p161). Again, variety is the key: Shoreditch is home to both the events-driven **Book Club** (p149) and 'secret' bars such as the **Mayor of Scaredy Cat Town** (p146); Covent Garden has the 'natural' wines of **Terroirs** (p126); **Purl** (p93) and **69 Colebrooke Row** (p151) focus on inventive cocktailing.

Gastropubs have contributed hugely to the revolution in modern British dining, their ambition to turn out top nosh in relaxed surroundings becoming a key part of the city's culinary repertoire, despite pale imitations. Pay homage at the **Eagle** (p137), widely seen as the pioneer of the genre.

Neighbourhood watch

The **South Bank**, close to foodie-magnets Borough Market (p62) and Maltby Street (p64), offers plenty of quality chain options on the riverside but **Soho**, just across the river, is probably the best place in London for eats, both cheap and chic: canteen-style **Busaba Eathai** (p91) and **Herman ze German** (p115) do a brisk trade near upmarket neighbours such as **Arbutus** (p111) and **J Sheekey** (p126), and some of London's most fashionable restaurants like **10 Greek Street** and the **Social Eating House**. Also in the West End, **Covent Garden** remains a busy tourist trap, but some very decent options have emerged, from Mexican at **Wahaca** (p126) to tapas at the **Opera Tavern** (p125). Expense-account eats are concentrated in **Mayfair**: top-name chefs here include Richard Corrigan at **Bentley's Oyster Bar & Grill** (p96) and Atherton's **Pollen Street Social**, while celebrity executive chefs populate the posh hotel dining rooms. Further west, **Marylebone** is another foodie enclave, replete with top-notch delis and cafés. Options here include **Fischer's** (p91) and **La Fromagerie** (p91). Both **South Kensington** and **Chelsea** do expensive, special-occasion destinations, such as **Zuma** (p83), though more affordable fare is available at **Gallery Mess** (p86). The **City** remains relatively poor for evening and weekend eats, but **Clerkenwell**, next door, is a culinary hotspot: from the **Modern Pantry** (p137) to the Eagle, St John and **Moro** (p137), most London restaurant trends have been kicked off here. Shoreditch, just north-east of the City, is still the place for a top night out – but it's less about clubbing than cocktails now, and the edgy bars have been joined by ever-more upmarket restaurants.

Liberty

WHAT'S BEST
Shopping

In its celebration of both tradition and cutting-edge style, **Liberty** (p119) captures just what's great about London's shopping scene. Meanwhile, **Selfridges** (p95) makes new strides with its mix of upmarket designer labels and teen-friendly high street stuff with a huge denim department and promised £300m facelift. For each fashion-forward new opening – like east London's **House of Hackney** (p149), say – you'll find a classic independent that's still going strong after centuries in operation (like umbrella specialists **James Smith & Sons**, p127).

The city has even learned to love the shopping centre: at least when it combines good eating, quirky events and a mix of chains and higher-end fashion, as at **Westfield Stratford City** (Great Eastern Road, E20, 8221 7300, www.westfield.com), gateway to the Olympic Park and Europe's largest urban mall. But we can't help hoping **Brixton Village** in south London (corner of Coldharbour Lane and Brixton Station Road, SW9 8PR, 7274 2990, http://spacemakers.org. uk) might be more indicative of the future. This largely forgotten arcade was revived a few years ago by means of a benevolent rent regime that rapidly repopulated it with funky food stores and boutiques.

Meanwhile, pop-up shops, packed with limited-edition products, appear and disappear each month; high-street outlets stock young design talent at budget prices; and department stores are refreshed and renewed.

Style city

London's design strength has long been young upstarts: recent graduates firmly entrenched in the youth scene they create for. Most cheerfully mix vintage with high street, shopping in chain stores full of high-profile design collaborations at rock-bottom prices: (Japanese chain **Uniqlo**, p99; the indefatigable **Topshop**, p95; wear-and-discard clothes at **Primark**, 3 Tottenham Court Road, W1D 1AU, www.primark.co.uk). For the vintage side of the equation, Shoreditch still does the math, with the likes of **Blitz** (p159), **Vintage Emporium** (p162) and, in Dalston, **Beyond Retro** (92-100 Stoke Newington Road, N16 7XB, 7613 3636, www.beyondretro.com).

Find out about sample sales, pop-up shops and events in the Shopping & Style section of *Time Out* magazine (available free every Tuesday), or indulge Londoners' obsession with the concept store – Mayfair's hallowed **Dover Street Market** (p98) is the city's most revered example, although the **Shop at Bluebird** (p87) runs it close.

Don't neglect the well-established department stores. Selfridges and Liberty are our long-term favourites, but even **Harrods** (p84) and **Harvey Nichols** (p82) are no longer bywords among locals for 'more money than sense'.

Mount Street (p98), the historic pink-brick Mayfair road, had leapt ahead of the deluxe pack over the last few years, with a gunsmith and butcher joined by goth-rock designer Rick Owens and a five-floor Lanvin flagship, but there are signs Sloane Street might be fighting back: the **Tom Ford** shop (p84) is every bit as handsome as its founder. And **Regent Street** has got livelier with new openings from well-known brands **Karl Lagerfeld** (nos.145-147, 7439 8454, www.karl.com/stores/london) and **J Crew** (no.165, 0800 562 0258, www.jcrew.com), and a

SHORTLIST

Best new
- Celestine Eleven (p49)
- House of Hackney (p149)
- Karl Lagerfeld (left)

Best shopping streets
- Broadway Market (p159)
- Carnaby Street (p117)
- Lamb's Conduit Street (p106)
- Redchurch Street (p161)

Best department stores
- Harrods (p84)
- Liberty (p119)
- Selfridges (p95)

Best books & music
- Fopp (p127)
- Foyles (p119)
- London Review Bookshop (p106)
- Rough Trade East (p162)

Best vintage
- Blitz (p159)
- Vintage Emporium (p162)

Cutting-edge concepts
- Dover Street Market (p98)
- Duke Street Emporium (p98)

Best markets
- Broadway Market (p62)
- Camden Market (p151)
- Columbia Road Market (p161)
- Portobello Road Market (p166)

Best museum shops
- London Transport Museum (p122)
- Museum of London (p141)
- Victoria & Albert Museum (p80)

Best old-style British
- Burlington Arcade (p98)
- Hope & Greenwood (p127)
- James Smith & Sons (p127)

DON'T MISS

much-praised high-tech **Burberry** (p93) in a historic building.

At the other edge of the cutting blade, **Shoreditch** remains the fashionista's first port of call, with shop-packed **Redchurch Street** (p161) and stores such as the **Goodhood Store** (p147), **Celestine Eleven** (p49) and the print-based lifestyle brand **House of Hackney** – one of the most gorgeous stores to land in London in years. For more shops in Shoreditch and around, see our itinerary, **Top of the Shops** (pp48-50).

Get cultural

In a city bursting with history, the steady closure of London's independent bookshops is sad. Still, you can browse travel literature in the Edwardian conservatory of Daunt Books on **Marylebone High Street** (p93) or the never-ending selection of new titles at

Foyles (see p119). Persephone Books on **Lamb's Conduit Street** (p106) and the **London Review Bookshop** (p106) are new London classics, while **Cecil Court** (p127) is an irrepressible old stager.

Don't neglect the museum stores, either: fine one-off and classily London souvenirs can be found at the **London Transport Museum** (p122), **V&A** (p80), **Museum of London** (p141) and **Southbank Centre** (p65). Even the expanded **Sir John Soane's Museum** (p135) and **Charles Dickens Museum** (p104) have found room for retail.

Record and CD shops have also taken a beating, but second-hand vinyl and CDs linger on **Berwick Street** (p117). Indie temple **Rough Trade East** (p162) now feels like it's been on Brick Lane forever, and **Fopp** (p127) continues to do great work – even as a handmaiden of HMV – selling interesting and keenly priced CDs and DVDs.

Foyles

Markets valued

Neighbourhood markets remain the lifeblood of London shopping, but few are the domain of Cockney costermongers. Instead, you'll find fashion kids flashing new vintage sunglasses over a soy latte. **Borough Market** (p62) is still great fun, even as the connoisseurs venture a little further east to **Maltby Street** (p64). For people-watching as much as purchases, **Broadway Market** (p159) is always worth the trek into Hackney. While you're in Hackney, a visit to the **Columbia Road** flower market (p161) is a classic Sunday morning outing; try to get there before 11am, then follow Brick Lane down to **Old Spitalfields Market** (p161) and the nearby Sunday (Up)Market, great for vintage clobber and crafts.

London's two most famous markets are still going strong: despite major redevelopment, Camden's markets remain a major tourist attraction, and – if you can stomach the crowds – **Portobello Road Market** (p166) is terrific for antiques and bric-a-brac.

Neighbourhood watch

Shopping in London can be exhausting, so limit the territory you cover in each outing, sticking to one or two earmarked areas at a time. **Regent Street** remains home to the flagships of many mid-range high-street clothing ranges. For a taste of retail past, the area around **St James's Street** is full of anachronistic specialists, including London's oldest hatter and the royal shoemaker; **Savile Row** has been given a shake-up in recent years by a handful of tailoring upstarts. **Mayfair** – especially Conduit Street, Bond Streets Old and New, and Mount Street – is the domain of catwalk names.

To the north, it's best to hurry across heaving **Oxford Street** with its department stores and budget fashion. Duck instead into pedestrianised Gees Court and St Christopher's Place – interconnecting alleyways lined with cafés and shops. Curving **Marylebone High Street** has fashion, perfumeries, gourmet shops and chic design.

A couple of London's most celebrated streets have recently been lifted out of chain-dominated doldrums. **Carnaby Street** has been salvaged by an influx of quality youth-clothing brands and Kingly Court; the decline of the **King's Road** has been arrested with some hip new stores, taking cues from the Shop at Bluebird.

Similarly, **Covent Garden** can no longer be written off as a tourist trap. New flagships have opened in the piazza, while, to the north-west, cobbled Floral Street and the offshoots from Seven Dials remain fertile boutique-browsing ground. Don't miss sweet little Neal's Yard, with its wholefood cafés and herbalist. A little further north, **Lamb's Conduit Street** crams in appealing indie shops.

Unless you're working the plastic in the designer salons of **Sloane Street** or plan to marvel at the art nouveau food halls of Harrods, there's little reason to linger in **Knightsbridge**. Instead, for deluxe designer labels without the crush of people, try **Notting Hill**, especially where Westbourne Grove meets Ledbury Road.

On the other side of town, **Brick Lane** (mostly around the Old Truman Brewery and, at its northern end, Redchurch Street) has a dynamic collection of offbeat clothing and homeware shops.

The boutiques of **Islington** are also worth having a nose around, along Upper Street and on former antiques haven Camden Passage.

Studio 338

WHAT'S BEST
Nightlife

Years ago, London's most popular venues were large and several of them surprisingly central. But rocketing rents and aggressive action against noise pollution have seen the closure of many of the capital's historic nightlife venues – the likes of Turnmills and the Cross. Which doesn't mean the end of London nightlife – far from it – but finding the clubs takes a little effort these days. Not least because the merry-go-round of parties sees no need to stick to one venue: the jargon is 'microscenes', the reality is that there is no prevailing taste or mood in the city. You can often stumble across the greatest nights bubbling out of pub-clubs such as Camden's **Lock Tavern** (p152), warehouse spaces such as **XOYO** (p149), or – initially mostly in and around Dalston – makeshift clubs in kebab restaurant

basements, former cosmetics shops and estate social clubs.

Some big clubs have continued to thrive. **Fabric** (p138) is still doing a roaring trade in leftfield electronic wiggery, while the **Ministry of Sound** (p64) has kept right on hauling in big-name DJs for marquee nights... now for over two decades. There's even a new contender: **Studio 338** (338 Boord Street, SE10 0PF, 8293 6669, www. studio338.co.uk) opened in 2014, with a terrace space that the owners promised would bring a bit of Ibiza to the Greenwich Peninsula.

There have been signs over the last year or so of a return of raving as your grandad knew it, with derelict industrial buildings in far-flung bits of London such as Croydon providing the venues – and social media the flyers – for huge illegal

parties. But as drug-related deaths at these parties return to the news, it can't be long before the police are instructed to crackdown on such activities.

Clubbing

If recession forced some promoters out of business, it made the survivors get creative: hence the birth of Dalston (easily accessible on the new Overground) as London's centre of edgy nights out, a land where surreal bars used to open every week under Turkish cafés. Even here licensing and opening hours have begun to become more formalised. A hit ever since it opened, the **Dalston Superstore** (p157) is already a clubbing reference point in the area, but this is also where you'll find the **Shacklewell Arms** (p157) and **Dance Tunnel** (p157). Keeping the scene from ossifying there are still plenty of short-lived dive bars and one-offs: check out the audiophile bar and Japanese restaurant **Brilliant Corners** (470 Kingsland Road, E8 4AE, http://brilliantcornerslondon. co.uk), for instance, where you might stumble across a banging all-vinyl disco night or get to chill out to all four sides of Hendrix's *Electric Ladyland* at Classic Album Sundays (http://classicalbumsundays.com). Go on social media to find the latest places, but for a round-up of our settled favourites, see box p157.

It's many years since Shoreditch was the watchword for clubbing cool (when the hens and stags roll in, it's time to head out), but there has been a revival of sorts. Venues such as the **Book Club** (p149) continue to make a virtue of diverse programming, but XOYO is a bit more like the glory days: great music in an old-fashioned loft setting. One of the few remaining fixtures from way back when, **Plastic People** (p149) continues to rock the block.

S H O R T L I S T

Best for bands
- Borderline (p119)
- 100 Club (p103)
- Koko (p152)

Best for full-scale raving
- Fabric (p138)
- Oval Space (p30)
- Studio 338 (p27)

Best stadium gigs
- O2 Arena (p166)

Rockin' pub-clubs
- Lock Tavern (p152)
- Shacklewell Arms (p157)

Best basement dives
- Dalston (see box p157)

Best leftfield dance action
- Plastic People (p149)
- XOYO (p149)

Best for jazz & folk
- Cecil Sharp House (p30)
- Ronnie Scott's (p120)
- Vortex Jazz Club (p162)

For the outer limits
- Café Oto (p162)

Best comedy
- Comedy Store (p119)
- Invisible Dot (p110)
- Soho Theatre (p122)

Best gay clubbing
- Dalston Superstore (p157)
- Horse Meat Disco (p30)

Best cabaret
- Bethnal Green Working Men's Club (p162)
- RVT (p30)
- Soho Theatre (p122)

DON'T MISS

Again flexibility and a willingness to set up in relatively distant parts of the city are becoming key factors in London nightlife: there are great nights, for instance, at Peckham's superb post-industrial **Bussey Building** (133 Rye Lane, SE15 4ST, www.clfartcafe.org), home to Zonk Disco and South London Soul Train, and an extraordinary range of events at Bethnal Green's massive **Oval Space** (29-32 The Oval, E2 9DT, www.ovalspace.co.uk), a hangar-style space at the bottom of a disused gasworks.

Gay clubbing

Despite the influx of straight ravers to some club nights, 'Vauxhall Village' remains the hub for all folks gay and out who want to party hard: **Fire** (South Lambeth Road, SW8 1RT, 3242 0040, www.firelondon.net) is the all-out rave destination. **RVT** (372 Kennington Lane, SE11 5HY, 7820 1222, www.rvt.org.uk), however, is the cultural must-see, a friendly, historic gay tavern that hosts comedy nights, arty performance parties and discos, and **Horse Meat Disco** has been a pioneer of open-minded, hedonistic, disco-inflected partying at the Eagle (349 Kennington Lane, SE11 5QY, 7793 0903, www.eaglelondon.com) each Sunday for more than a decade.

The closure of numerous West End venues has encouraged plenty of club nights to up sticks to Shoreditch and Dalston, creating a third gay scene to add to Vauxhall and, of course, the now rather grown-up Soho. **Dalston Superstore** is the stand-out for the new breed of young, gay hipster.

Gigs

London's music scene is defined by rampant diversity. On any night, you'll find death metal, folk whimsy and plangent griots on one or other of the city's many stages.

At the top of the tree, and London's most popular concert venue year after year (selling approaching 2m tickets a year), is the **O2 Arena** (p166). This enormodome has pretty much cornered the market for classic rock and retro gigs (from Led Zeppelin to Duran Duran), as well as booking pop stars (Britney to Barry Manilow).

Although club/gig mash-ups have taken up some of the slack, London's mid-size venues have suffered carnage over the last several years: **Koko** (p152) and the **Scala** (p110) are the pick of the survivors. On a much smaller scale, Oxford Street's redoubtable **100 Club** (p103) has managed to stay afloat in the West End by dint of sponsorship deal.

Meanwhile, the roster at upmarket jazz classic **Ronnie Scott's** (p120) has stayed safe but appealing, leaving plenty of space for the far more inventive **Vortex Jazz Club** (p162) to thrive. In fact, Dalston shines bright on the cutting edge of live music: **Café Oto** (p162) has a ridiculously diverse programme. For something explicitly traditional, head to Camden: **Cecil Sharp House** (2 Regent's Park Road, NW1 7AY, 7485 2206, www.efdss. org) is the guardian of all folk traditions, which is *much* more fun than it sounds.

Cabaret

Burlesque continues to bring out the kitsch and feathers, with many a regular club nights adding a stripper, twisted magic or some surreal cabaret. The best alternative nights are at **RVT** and the **Bethnal Green Working Men's Club** (p162), while the basement at the **Leicester Square Theatre** (p119) offers more mainstream fare and **Soho Theatre** (p122) attracts a young, hip crowd to the theatre/comedy/cabaret crossover scene.

Invisible Dot

Comedy

Stand-up comedy has gone stadium-sized: Louis CK, Miranda Hart and Micky Flanagan have all played the O2 Arena, as did the reformed Monty Pythons in 2014. It's not all supernova shows, though: on an extremely boisterous scene, check out 1980s pioneer the **Comedy Store** (p119), the Soho Theatre – for interesting solo shows from breaking comics rather than another three-on-a-bill stand-up fest at the local boozer – and, for the current cutting edge, the **Invisible Dot** (p110).

While London's nightlife is lively all year, anyone who's come here to see some comedy in late July or August is likely to be disappointed. Most of the city's performers head to Scotland for the Edinburgh Festival and consequently many venues are dark. Come in June or October instead: comedians are either trying out fresh shows or touring their Edinburgh triumph.

Making the most of it

Whatever you're doing, check the transport before you go: festivals, repairs and engineering tinkerage throw spanners in the works all year, notably on public holidays, but also many weekends. Regularly updated information can be found at **www.tfl.gov.uk**. Public transport isn't as daunting as you might think. The tube is self-evident, even to newcomers, but it doesn't run much after midnight (New Year's Eve is the exception). Black cabs are pricey and hard to find at night, but safe. There are also licensed minicabs; on no account take an illegal minicab, even though they're touted outside every club. Far better to research the slow but comprehensive **night bus** system (p184) before leaving your hotel (see www.tfl.gov.uk's Journey Planner) or download the life-saving free app **City Mapper** (https://citymapper.com), which is simple enough to use even after you've been on the shandies all night.

You'll also kick yourself if you came all this way to see an event, only to arrive the one weekend it isn't on – or to find dates have changed. We've done our best to ensure the information in this guide is correct, but things change with little warning: www.timeout.com has the latest details or, if you're already here, pick up a free *Time Out* magazine on Tuesday. Record shops are invaluable for flyers and advice – try the friendly folk at **Rough Trade East** (p162) for starters.

If the dates won't quite work out, don't despair. There's something going on here, no matter the day, no matter the hour. Even established Londoners fall across brand new happenings just by taking the wrong turning, and the best way to get a taste of 'real London' – instead of the city every postcard-collecting tourist sees – is to go with the flow. Someone tells you about a party? Check it out. Read about a new band? Get a ticket. Sure, you've some 'essentials' in mind, but if you miss them this time… hell, come back next year.

National Theatre

Arts & Leisure

London isn't just the political hub of Britain. It's the country's cultural and sporting capital too. Classical music of all types is studied and performed here, ambitious and inventive actors, directors and dancers learn their chops, and films are premièred and shot. The city has three of the nation's top six football teams, national stadiums for football and rugby, and international centres of tennis and cricket, as well as the still functioning 2012 **Olympic Stadium** (p164).

Theatre & musicals

London's theatreland is looking oddly healthy. It seems economic hard times have sent people to the theatre in search of distraction, rather than chasing them away. It's also a time of significant change among key theatre personnel: in 2013 Vicky Featherstone took over at the **Royal Court** (p87) and Rupert Goold at the **Almeida** (p152), while Michael Grandage had already been succeeded by Josie Rourke at the **Donmar** (p129) in 2012. Next, in 2015, after each spending a successful decade as artistic director, both Nicholas Hytner at the **National Theatre** (p65) and Kevin Spacey at the **Old Vic** (p65) will depart; Rufus Norris takes over at the National, Matthew Warchus at the Old Vic.

Producers are perhaps becoming bolder. You can expect the usual crop of celebrity-led revivals and musicals piggy-backed on nostalgia for hit movies, but there is also significant theatre. Among the musicals, the excellent *Billy Elliot* (**Victoria Palace Theatre**, p72)

DON'T MISS

Best of the West End
- *The Book of Mormon* (p122)
- *The Curious Incident of the Dog in the Night-time* (p120)
- *Matilda the Musical* (p129)
- *War Horse* (p130)

Best classical venues
- Kings Place (p110)
- Royal Opera House (p130)
- Wigmore Hall (p95)

Best cinemas
- BFI Southbank (p64)
- Curzon Soho (p120)

Best for plays
- Donmar Warehouse (p129)
- National Theatre (p65)
- Royal Court Theatre (p87)
- Candlelit performances in the Wanamaker Theatre at Shakespeare's Globe (p56)

Best contemporary dance
- Sadlers Wells (p152)

Most innovative work
- Café Oto (p162)
- Kings Place (p110)

Best arts festivals
- City of London Festival (see p42)
- Greenwich & Docklands International Festival (p42)
- London Film Festival (p37)
- The Proms (p42)

Best bargains
- Half-price West End shows from tkts (p122)
- Prince Charles Cinema (p120)
- 'Groundling' (standing) tickets at Shakespeare's Globe (p56)
- £10 Monday at the Royal Court Theatre (p87)
- £15 Travelex tickets at the National Theatre (p65)

continues, and while the blockbuster musical's dominance is under no immediate threat – the 25th anniversary of *Les Misérables* (**Queen's Theatre**, p122) a few years back saw three versions play simultaneously in London, and West End impresario Cameron Mackintosh chose to revive *Miss Saigon* in 2014 (see p123) – grand productions such as the Sam Mendes-directed *Charlie & the Chocolate Factory* (**Theatre Royal Drury Lane**, p130) and quirky joys such as the Royal Shakespeare Company's *Matilda the Musical* (**Cambridge Theatre**, p129) or scabrous import *The Book of Mormon* (**Prince of Wales Theatre**, p122) seem likely to prevent the return to the West End of wall-to-wall Lloyd Webber shows.

Despite decreasing subsidies, the National Theatre has had a terrific few years as it passed its 50th anniversary. It currently has three major plays running in the West End: both *War Horse* (**New London Theatre**, p130) and the relocated

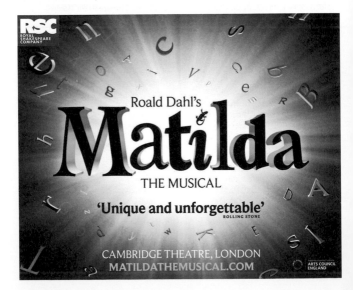

Curious Incident of the Dog in the Night-time (**Gielgud Theatre**, p120) could run and run. At the National itself, the Cottesloe theatre is closed until late 2014, when it will reopen as the enlarged Dorfman. While it's closed, the National's most inventive work was staged in the Shed, a brightly painted, Thameside pop-up theatre; the temporary structure was such a success the National sought and received planning permission to make it permanent – although it will have to change its name.

The Donmar Warehouse continues to show resourcefulness beyond its shoebox size (in addition to bringing real star power to its tiny space – Nicole Kidman, Ewan McGregor), but the massive success of *Chimerica* at the Almeida suggests it may have a competitor.

Shakespeare's Globe (p56) makes a wonderfully authentic setting for works by the Bard, both in a classic 'wooden O' that's largely open to the elements, and in the new wood-clad, candlelit, Jacobean-style Sam Wanamaker Theatre alongside it. Shakespeareans should also check out the annual London season of the **Royal Shakespeare Company** (www.rsc.org.uk), often held at the **Roundhouse** (p152).

Some of the more acrobatic theatre groups show off their skills at the popular annual **Greenwich & Docklands International Festival** (p42) and **LIFT** (p42).

Classical music & opera

The completion of office block-cum-auditorium **Kings Place** (p110), at the heart of the thriving King's Cross Central development, has been the biggest news in classical music over the last several years. It provides headquarters for the very different Orchestra of the Age of Enlightenment (www.oae.co.uk) and London Sinfonietta

(www.londonsinfonietta.org.uk), as well as sculpture galleries and two concert halls with extremely good acoustics.

At the **Barbican** (p146), the London Symphony Orchestra (http://lso.co.uk) continues to play 90 concerts a year, mixing high-brow classical extravaganzas (Scriabin, Britten) with family-friendly concert days. The associated Guildhall School of Music & Drama has opened a new concert hall, Milton Court, near the Barbican's main entrance.

The Royal Festival Hall at the **Southbank Centre** (p65) regularly hosts Esa-Pekka Salonen's Philharmonia Orchestra (www.philharmonia.co.uk), whose roster runs from compelling modernist monstrosities to indefatigable crowd-pleasers such as Elgar. The Southbank's smaller venues – the Purcell Room and Queen Elizabeth Hall – are still in desperate need of refurbishment, but the apparently permanent shelving of the bold, and controversial, 'Festival Wing' plan in 2014 makes this seem a remote possibility.

London also has a pair of fine opera houses: Covent Garden's **Royal Opera House** (p130) combines assured seat-fillers – *Swan Lake*, *Le nozze di Figaro* – with a developing penchant for rarities: none more so than 2011's *Anna Nicole*, an opera about Playmate and celebrity widow Anna Nicole Smith. At the **Coliseum** (p129), the English National Opera performs classics (always in English), but also more experimental projects, such as a site-specific production in 2014 of *Powder Her Face* by Thomas Adès. We applaud the ENO's effort to widen access with cheap tickets (www.eno.org/undress), even though a heavy cut in its subsidy suggests the funding body sees the need for more work on expanding and diversifying audiences.

Much of the city's classical music action happens in superb venues on an intimate scale. The exemplary **Wigmore Hall** (p95), **Cadogan Hall** (p87) and **LSO St Luke's** (p146) are all atmospheric places, and a number of churches host fine concerts.

Film

In the death-struggle against sophisticated home entertainment systems, many London cinemas try to make film-going an event: in with the luxury seats, auditorium alcohol licences and film-watching as an immersive event, an approach pioneered by **Secret Cinema** (www.secretcinema.org) – which arranges screenings in strange locations, with dressing up and lots of collateral entertainment.

Although new cinemas have opened (among them the Hackney Picturehouse, the Curzon Victoria and two replacement screens at the Barbican), mainstream titles have crept on to the bills of even arthouse cinemas, as the likes of the **Curzon Soho** (p120) struggle to keep audiences. Smaller films are finding it hard to breathe in the capital these days: the only major cinema committed to foreign and alternative films is the **BFI Southbank** (p64). However, there are signs of new life, such as **Hollywood Spring** (6 Well Street, E9 7PX, www.hollywood spring.com), which opened in a former Hackney factory in 2014 expressly to host unusual cinema events, as well as some wonderful survivors: East Finchley's Phoenix (52 High Road, N2 9PJ, 8444 6789, www.phoenixcinema.co.uk), in operation since 1910.

Even as the multiplexes stuff their screens with bloated blockbusters, smaller, less formal venues have picked up the slack, and major attractions such as **Tate Modern** (p59) and **St Paul's Cathedral** (p141) include film screenings on their events rosters. Keep an eye on *Time Out* magazine or www.time out.com for these various venues, and for details of the city's frequent film festivals and many unusual screenings, often by film clubs.

Dance

Two companies provide the full blocks-and-tutus experience. The **English National Ballet** (at the Coliseum) and the **Royal Ballet** (at the Royal Opera House) usually oblige with a *Swan Lake* or *Nutcracker* over Christmas. The Royal Ballet's programme includes classics, but increasingly throws in more adventurous fare, not least new – often explosive – commissions from resident choreographer Wayne McGregor. But London offers an unmatched range of performers and styles, going way beyond the usual binary choice of classical or contemporary, and – apart from the quieter summer months – there's something worth seeing every night. **Sadler's Wells** (p152) offers a packed programme of top-quality work and hosts must-see festivals. Autumn sees **Dance Umbrella** (p38) unfold with cutting-edge work from around the world. Keep an eye also on the **Barbican**, **Roundhouse** and **Southbank Centre**, all of which host fine dance-theatre hybrids.

What's on

We've included long-running musicals and plays we think are likely to be long-runners. However, a new crop will inevitably open through the year. *Time Out* magazine is available – for free – throughout London on Tuesdays, giving our selection of that week's best events, while www.timeout.com has even more listings.

Calendar

Somerset House series p42

This is our pick of the best annual events in London. Get the free weekly *Time Out* magazine or visit www.timeout.com/london for updates and one-off events, and be sure to confirm any dates before making plans. Public holidays are given in **bold**.

Autumn

Sept **Totally Thames**
Westminster Bridge to Tower Bridge
http://totallythames.org
A month of arts, cultural and river events presented along 42 miles of river by the Thames Festival Trust.

early Sept **Tour of Britain**
Westminster & Tower Hill
http://thetour.co.uk/tourofbritain
The most-prestigious cycling race in the UK usually finishes with a road circuit in the centre of London.

mid Sept **Kings Place Festival**
Kings Place, p110
www.kingsplace.co.uk/festival
More than 100 events over three days – classical, jazz and experimental music.

mid Sept **London Fashion Week**
Somerset House, p136
www.londonfashionweek.co.uk
The autumn edition of the biannual fashion jamboree.

mid Sept **OnBlackheath**
Blackheath
www.onblackheath.com
This music festival made its debut in 2014, with Massive Attack headlining.

mid Sept **London Design Festival**
www.londondesignfestival.com

mid Sept **Open-House London**
www.open-city.org.uk
For one weekend only, there's access to some 500 amazing buildings that are normally closed to the public.

late Sept **Great River Race**
Thames, Docklands to Richmond
www.greatriverrace.co.uk
With 300 exotic rowing craft.

late Sept **Pearly Kings & Queens Harvest Festival**
Guildhall Yard, the City
www.pearlysociety.co.uk

THE ONLY PLACE TO SEE ALL OF
LONDON IN HIGH DEFINITION.

THE VIEW

FROM THE SHARD

YOU'LL BE WALKING ON AIR AMONGST THE CLOUDS.
BUT, IF THEY SPOIL YOUR VIEW, YOU CAN RETURN FOR FREE.*

THEVIEWFROMTHESHARD.COM   LONDON BRIDGE

*Terms and conditions apply.

Oct **Big Draw**
www.campaignfordrawing.org
A nationwide frenzy of drawing, using anything from pencils to vapour trails.

Oct **Dance Umbrella**
Various venues
www.danceumbrella.co.uk
Innovative celebration of dance covering many styles and choreographers.

Oct **BFI London Film Festival**
BFI Southbank & various venues
www.bfi.org.uk/lff
The most significant of the capital's film festivals: expect red-carpet celebs.

Oct **London Frieze Art Fair**
Regent's Park, p88
http://friezelondon.com
Massive, buzzy contemporary art fair.

Winter

early Nov **London to Brighton Veteran Car Run**
Serpentine Road in Hyde Park, p83
www.veterancarrun.com

5 Nov **Bonfire Night**
Firework displays all over town, marking the arrest of Guy Fawkes, and the thwarting of the attempt to blow up Parliament on 5 November 1604.

early Nov **Lord Mayor's Show**
The City, p131-149
www.lordmayorsshow.org
A grand inauguration procession for the Lord Mayor of the City of London.

early Nov **Remembrance Sunday Ceremony**
Cenotaph, Whitehall
Always held on the Sunday nearest to 11 November, this solemn commemoration honours those who died fighting in the World Wars and later conflicts

Nov **Diwali**
Trafalgar Square, p70
www.london.gov.uk
Hindu, Jain and Sikh Festival of Light.

mid Nov **London Jazz Festival**
www.londonjazzfestival.org.uk

Nov-Dec **Christmas Tree & Lights**
Trafalgar Square, p70
www.london.gov.uk
An impressive Norwegian spruce tree is mounted and lit in the centre of the city, with carol-singing.

Diwali

mid Dec **Spitalfields Festival**
www.spitalfieldsfestival.org.uk
Biannual festival of classical music;
returns in June.

25 Dec **Christmas Day**

26 Dec **Boxing Day**

31 Dec **New Year's Eve
Celebrations**
Several years ago, public celebrations
moved from overcrowded Trafalgar
Square to the full-on fireworks display
launched from the London Eye (p56)
and barges on the Thames.

1 Jan **New Year's Day**
www.londonparade.co.uk
If your hangover isn't too bad, you can
join the annual, costumed New Year's
Day Parade.

Jan **London International
Mime Festival**
www.mimefest.co.uk

Jan-Feb **Chinese New Year Festival**
Chinatown, north of Leicester
Square
www.lccauk.com
Launch the Years of the Sheep (19 Feb
2015) and Monkey (8 Feb 2016) in style.

Feb **London Fashion Week**
See above Sept.

late Mar **BFI Flare: London LGBT
Film Festival**
BFI Southbank, p64
www.llgff.org.uk

Spring

early Mar-May **Kew Spring Festivals**
Kew Gardens, p154
Five million flowers carpet the grounds
in spring.

mid Mar **St Patrick's Day Parade
& Festival**
Trafalgar Square, p70

Parade followed by toe-tapping tunes
in Trafalgar Square, on the Sunday
closest to 17 March.

Apr **Oxford & Cambridge Boat Race**
On the Thames, Putney to Mortlake
www.theboatrace.org
Elite rowers from Oxford and
Cambridge universities battle it out.

mid Apr **London Marathon**
Greenwich Park to the Mall
www.virginlondonmarathon.com

mid May **FA Cup Final**
Wembley Stadium
The final of this historic knockout
tournament – the oldest in the world
– is a highlight for many football fans.

late Apr **Sundance London**
O2 Arena, p166
www.sundance-london.com
Robert Redford's indie film festival.

early May **Breakin' Convention**
Sadler's Wells, p152
www.breakinconvention.com
Jonzi D's street dance festival provides
spectacular entertainment.

mid May **Covent Garden May Fayre
& Puppet Festival**
St Paul's Covent Garden, p124
*www.punchandjudy.com/
coventgarden.htm*
All-day puppet mayhem devoted to Mr
Punch at the site of his first recorded
sighting in England in 1662.

May **State Opening of Parliament**
Houses of Parliament, p69
www.parliament.uk
The Queen reopens Parliament after
its recess, arriving and departing in the
golden State Coach, accompanied by
Household Cavalry troopers.

Apr-mid June **Spring Loaded**
The Place
www.theplace.org.uk
Contemporary dance festival.

late May **Chelsea Flower Show**
Royal Hospital Chelsea
www.rhs.org.uk
Admire perfect blooms, or get ideas for
your own plot, with entire gardens laid
out for the show.

Summer

June **London Festival of
Architecture**
www.londonfestivalofarchitecture.org
Talks, discussions, walks, screenings
and other events.

early June **Beating the Retreat**
Horse Guards Parade, Whitehall
www.army.mod.uk
See box p14.

June-Aug **Opera Holland Park**
www.operahollandpark.com
A canopied outdoor theatre hosts a
season of opera.

Sat in June **Trooping the Colour**
Buckingham Palace, p72
www.royal.gov.uk
See box p14.

mid June **Open Garden Squares
Weekend**
www.opensquares.org
For one weekend, private gardens are
open to the public.

June **Spitalfields Summer Festival**
www.spitalfieldsfestival.org.uk
A series of mainly classical concerts
in June, based at Christ Church
Spitalfields, with performances also
taking place at other local venues. The
festival returns in December each year.

mid June **Meltdown**
Southbank Centre, p65
www.southbankcentre.co.uk
Music and culture festival, curated by a
different musician every year.

late June-July **Wimbledon Lawn
Tennis Championships**

Man with the bowler hat

The City of London Festival has a new director.

Since 1962, **City of London
Festival** (p42) has quietly been
programming music, art, tours
and talks, taking advantage of
the Square Mile's atmospheric
venues and its keenness on
corporate sponsorship. Recent
years saw the festival loosen its
collar a bit – the half-century in
2012 was celebrated with 50
gold street pianos – but, in 2014,
it went a bit further. The catalyst
was new director Paul Gudgin,
who previously spent eight years
as director of the Edinburgh
Fringe, doubling ticket sales
to 1.6m in his last year there.

Gudgin was running the Fringe
when pop-up cow-shaped
comedy venue the Udderbelly
was birthed, and has not let his
experience with silly inflatable
venues go to waste: CoLF 2014
featured a 30ft-tall blow-up
bowler hat, within which there
was stand-up comedy and kids
theatre. Less flamboyant, but
perhaps more interesting, he put
on some Duke Ellington concerts
in a secret masonic temple in
the Andaz hotel – Ellington was
himself a freemason. And the
stunning centrepiece of the
festival was a stern rebuke to
anyone who might mistake
Gudgin for a populist: the London
Symphony Orchestra played
Bruckner's huge 9th Symphony
in St Paul's (p141) – a sublime
pairing that bore out his ambition
'to create a unique energy in the
Square Mile… each summer'.

All England Lawn Tennis Club,
Wimbledon
www.wimbledon.org

June LIFT (London International Festival of Theatre)
www.liftfest.org.uk

late June-mid July
City of London Festival
The City, pp131-149
www.colf.org
A terrific series of mostly free music
and art, usually in historic City venues,
increasingly with installations and
other outdoor events. See box p39.

late June Greenwich & Docklands International Festival
www.festival.org
Outdoor theatricals held in dramatic
settings, usually on an impressively
large scale.

late June Pride London
Various venues
http://londoncommunitypride.org
A week-long celebration of the LGBT
community, with the Pride parade held
on the Saturday.

July Somerset House Series
Somerset House, p136
www.somersethouse.org.uk/music
A dozen concerts in the fountain court.

July Wireless Festival
Finsbury Park
www.wirelessfestival.co.uk
Three nights of rock and dance acts.

mid July Camden Lock Live
Camden
www.camdenlockmarket.com
Free 'urban boutique' festival.

mid July Lovebox
Victoria Park, Hackney
www.lovebox.net
Top-quality weekend music festival,
which has headlined everyone from Sly
Stone and Blondie to MIA.

mid July-mid Sept The Proms (BBC Sir Henry Wood Promenade Concerts)
Royal Albert Hall, p82
www.bbc.co.uk/proms
London's best classical music festival,
packed with top-class performers –
tickets are at bargain prices if you're
happy to stand.

late July-late Aug Watch This Space
www.nationaltheatre.org.uk
This long-term fixture on the Thames
bank outside the National Theatre
(p65) now takes its free, alfresco shows
to a variety of local venues.

early Aug RideLondon
www.prudentialridelondon.com
Around 50,000 people don branded
fluorescent vests and ride a ten-mile
traffic-free route between Festival Zones
in the City. There are professional
races, a cycling show at ExCeL and
other entertainments too.

mid Aug Great British Beer Festival
Olympia, London
www.gbbf.org.uk

late Aug Notting Hill Carnival
Notting Hill, p166
www.thenottinghillcarnival.com
Europe's biggest street party brings
the Caribbean to Notting Hill with a
costume parade and mobile sound
systems. Held on the late August bank
holiday weekend.

late Aug South West Four
Clapham Common
www.southwestfour.com
Dance music festival – covering every
genre from trance to house – over the
Bank Holiday weekend.

late Aug London Mela
Gunnersbury Park, Ealing
www.londonmela.org
A huge celebration involving South
Asian music and street arts.

Itineraries

Millennium Bridge and St Paul's Cathedral

The Sights in a Trice

Got a couple of free days? Fancy ticking off the major sights in double-quick time? This two-day itinerary is mostly on foot, but uses some public transport, so slip on comfy trainers, grab your Oyster card (p182) and get set... go!

Day 1

The **Tower of London** (p143) gets mobbed as the day progresses, so it's a good place to start. Get there for 9am (10am Mon, Sun) and take the travelator past the Crown Jewels before the queue builds up. Then join one of the Yeoman Warder ('Beefeater') tours for an entertaining overview of the place, before checking out the armaments and garderobes in the White Tower and the prisoner graffiti in Beauchamp Tower.

Next, take in the brilliant views as you stroll across **Tower Bridge**; www.towerbridge.org.uk gives

bridge lift times. Turn right, down to the Queen's Walk, and head west along the South Bank, passing the sloped black helmet of **City Hall** and **HMS Belfast** (p53). Have a gourmet refuel at **Borough Market** (p62): perhaps a pastry from Flour Station, some Ibérico Bellota ham or manchego cheese from Brindisa, or a Kappacasein toasted cheese sandwich. Then pep yourself up for the next stint with a latte from Monmouth Coffee.

Continue along the Thames until you hit **Tate Modern** (p59), the world's most-visited modern art gallery. The displayed works are superb, of course, but so is the river vista from the Espresso Bar or the Tate Modern Restaurant.

Cross the Millennium Bridge and walk up the broad, snaking staircase to **St Paul's Cathedral** (p141), Wren's masterwork. Then take a nostalgic ride on a classic red double-decker bus to Aldwych. The post-war Routemaster has been phased out of ordinary use, but a few lovingly restored old buses – complete with redundant bell pulls to request stops – continue to run on a single route: Heritage Route 15. (Mayor Boris Johnson's handsome but costly New Bus for London, nicknamed the 'New Routemaster', came into service in 2012 and is now running routes all over town.) Board at Stop SJ, outside St Paul's, for a ride west along Fleet Street, past the Royal Courts of Justice (look right after the wyvern statue in the middle of the road) and along the Strand.

Get off at Savoy Street (Stop U) for the deco entranceway to the **Savoy Hotel** (p176), then nip across the busy road into Covent Garden for supper (there are plenty of options on pp124-126) – before checking out the buzz and buskers of Covent Garden Market (p122).

Day 2

Grab a coffee perk-me-up and sandwiches for lunch at Green Park tube (ubiquitous but decent chain Pret A Manger has a branch here), then walk across the lawns to **Buckingham Palace** (p72). The crisp, red-jacketed choreography of the Changing of the Guard happens here at 11.30am daily from May to July (alternate days August to April), lasting half an hour. The Royal Mews, the palace stables and limo garage can be visited, and in summer, when the royal family is on holiday, you can tour the State Rooms of the palace itself.

When you're done with royalty, either head into lovely **St James's Park** (p72) for your picnic or take the second left at the Queen Victoria Memorial roundabout on to Spur Road. Follow Birdcage Walk to see Westminster's finest structures. Admire the twin towers and flying

buttresses of **Westminster Abbey** (p70), pop into the **Houses of Parliament** (p69) to watch a peppery debate, or just listen to the familiar tune of the tallest four-faced chiming clock in the world – the clock tower of **'Big Ben'** (p66).

Wander north up Whitehall, with its war memorials and blank-faced government buildings. On your left, you pass **Downing Street** – home of the Prime Minister (at no.10) and his Chancellor (at no.11), but with no public access – and, at Horse Guards, sword-bearing cavalrymen in sentryboxes. **Trafalgar Square** (p70) opens out at the end of Whitehall. Before you enter the square, behind the black statue of a mounted Charles I, a plaque marks the **official centre of London**. You'll also see the **Fourth Plinth** – a site for contemporary sculpture commissions: in early 2015 Hans Haacke's skeletal *Gift Horse* will replace Katharina Fritsch's ultramarine blue *Hahn/Cock*, to be replaced in its turn by summer 2016 by David Shrigley's giant thumb's-up *Really Good*. Now climb the steps on to the square's pedestrianised northern side.

You're in front of the **National Gallery** (p69), one of the world's greatest repositories for art. Admission is free, as are ace guided tours that might steer you to masterpieces by Raphael, Rembrandt or Monet. For dinner, the gallery has two options: the **National Dining Rooms** (p71), with a bakery-café (open to 5.30pm, or 8.30pm on Fridays) and rather more expensive restaurant, and the darkly handsome **National Café**, open until 11pm (6pm on Sunday).

Finally, head due north. There's no call to linger in **Leicester Square** (p110), despite recent improvements. Instead push past Chinatown and into Soho – for great pubs, restaurants and hip bars.

ITINERARIES

Three Mills Island

Urban Exploring

An odd development in London over the last several years has been the growing interest of its citizens in urban nature: beekeepers on the roofs of West End department stores, birdwatchers training binoculars on peregrine falcons swooping from the brick cliff of **Tate Modern** (p59), even crowds on Tower Bridge to watch a pod of harbour porpoises. The mood was caught in the subtitle of Lucy Scott and Tina Smith's charming *Lost in London* in 2013: 'Adventures in the city's wild outdoors'. This isn't the unsullied wild of Romantic poets – it's the edgeland, the ruderal habitat, the curious intertwining of rural and urban that characterises a surprising amount of modern London.

To begin our quest, get out at **Bromley-by-Bow underground station** (it's on the District line, with good connections to central London at Victoria, Embankment and Bank/

Monument). Outside the station, walk through the underpass under the roaring A12 and head left along the far side of the road. This bit of the walk is more urban than rural, but better things await straight after a right turn at the Tesco superstore. You're now on Three Mill Lane, the grey cobbles of which lead to **Three Mills Island**.

This surprisingly quiet island between tributaries of the River Lea takes its name from the three mills that ground flour and gunpowder here. The House Mill (8980 4626, www.housemill.org.uk), built in 1776, is the oldest and largest tidal mill in Britain and opens to the public on Sunday afternoons (May-Oct; £3, free-£1.50 reductions). There are willows on the bank between the Lea and Channelsea rivers – that way you can walk all the way to the Thames at Limehouse, via a splendidly steep modern bridge over locks, but we're

and redevelopments. Turn off the river, right on to Marshgate Lane.

Follow Marshgate Lane, keeping right, until – beyond Pudding Mill Lane DLR station – you can zigzag up a bank to fluorescent lime-green shipping containers. These have been reconditioned into the **View Tube**, and have a fine café: Moka East (open 9am-5pm daily). The floor-to-ceiling windows give an excellent view of the **Olympic Park** (p163), with Anish Kapoor's 376ft-tall curly-wurly red ArcelorMittal Orbit (www.arcelormittalorbit.com; free-£15 to visit) and the stadium right ahead.

Keep north along the signposted Greenway, before heading down beside the Lea and under a bridge. You'll soon find yourself climbing on a little bridge to beguiling **Old Ford Lock**, at the junction of the River Lea proper and the die-straight Lee Navigation. Keep up the riverbank of the Lee Navigation, where coots nest from spring through summer, and you'll often see herons fishing. On the far bank is Forman's salmon smokery (the big pink building), and the Counter Café (Stour Space, 7 Roach Road, www.thecountercafe. co.uk), which has a pontoon terrace for when the sun shines.

You could follow the Lee Navigation up through Hackney Marshes, passing several nature reserves along the way. But we're going to head up the steep cobbled slope to the bridge just after the point where the Hertford Union Canal joins the Lee Navigation at a right angle. Turn left across the bridge over the Lee, and on your right (down some steps) is the **Crate Brewery** (White Building, Unit 7, Queens Yard, www. cratebrewery.com) – for fine beer and pizza. And you're a short walk from **Hackney Wick Overground station**, which rejoins the Tube network eastbound at Stratford, or westbound at Highbury & Islington.

heading the other way, through the courtyard between mills, part of which is now a production studio.

Turn left up the Three Mills Wall river, where narrowboats are often docked. In summer you might the insects irritating, but they bring the swifts down to glide across the river's surface, wingtips almost touching the water. The extraordinary, Byzantine **Abbey Mills Pumping Station** – by Victorian sewer engineer Sir Joseph Bazalgette – can be seen not far away to your right.

Keeping heading north up the bank, crossing the narrow pedestrian bridge over the Prescott Channel, and continue, to exit at the road bridge, which carries the A118 (Stratford High Street) over the river. Cross the busy thoroughfare, on to Blaker Road. You can see the Olympic Stadium beyond the end of the road – currently being repurposed for West Ham FC – but turn left away from it, keeping beside the water. This is another tributary of the Lea – the Bow Back River – and you're in the midst of light industrial buildings

Celestine Eleven

Top of the Shops

As the focus of London's creative energy shifted eastwards over the last decade, there's been a proliferation of small, independent and distinctive shops in the area: fashion boutiques, lifestyle stores, places selling homewares and accessories – all refreshingly different from the high-street norm. For this itinerary, we take you on a shopping trip to discover some outstanding merchandise in some of the city's most interesting shops.

Where else to start but Shoreditch? It's no longer the heart of London clubbing, nor a gallery nexus, but this chunk of London directly north-east of the centre is a retail must-see. Take the Overground to Shoreditch High Street (or go to Liverpool Street station and walk ten minutes north up Bishopsgate). From the station, first cross Shoreditch High Street and enter Holywell Lane opposite. **Celestine**

Eleven (4 Holywell Lane, www. celestineeleven.com) is a lifestyle boutique that showcases talented London designers like JW Anderson and Atalanta Weller alongside amazing new finds, like bags from label-of-the-future Niels Peeraer. There are holistic treatments on site too. After rifling through the exclusive merch, head back to the high street and turn left, then take the first right down Redchurch Street. This has been a key shopping street for several years. At nos.41-43 you'll find **Hostem** (www.hostem. co.uk), a dark-edged and moody-looking cult menswear store (it does have some women's pieces too), stocking unusual labels such as Rik Owens, Ann Demeulemeester and S.N.S. Herning, plus a bespoke service. Further along the road is a shop with a design ethos that's very different but every bit as strong. **Labour & Wait** (no.85, www.labourandwait.co.uk) is a well-established neighbourhood pioneer that made its name with lo-fi home accessories like galvanised steel buckets, enamel dishes and Welsh wool rugs – all simple, functional and very desirable.

Avoid the fairly grim stretch of Shoreditch High Street heading north from here by taking Boundary Street north. Turn left on to Calvert Avenue and you'll emerge on to Shoreditch High Street, a short distance (turn right from the end of Calvert Avenue) from **House of Hackney** (at no.131, p149), a lifestyle brand whose headline-grabbing palm and leopard-skin prints are the antithesis of minimalism. HOH started as an interiors label, but with founders (and couple) Frieda Gormley and Javvy M Royle both hailing from fashion backgrounds, it was only natural that their prints made their way first on to clothing and accessories, and more recently washbags, notepads and crockery. The glorious store is bedecked in the deliberately over-the-top juxtapositions of print-on-print-on-print that have made the brand's name.

Head back to the corner of Calvert Avenue, and then a little further south. Here is **Present** (140 Shoreditch High Street, www.present-london.com), a mini-department store for (hip) men, stocking rare brands, heritage labels and clever, in-house staples.

Next, cross the road into Rivington Street, to **Start London**, which has three shops (40, 42 & 59 Rivington Street, www.start-london.com) selling hot designer pieces for men and women. At no.42, ladies can ogle glitzy clutches from Philippe Audibert, try on Sophia Webster heels, strut in Kenzo printed trousers or nab something from Isabel Marant's Étoile.

Follow Rivington Street to its end, where you'll come to a busy crossing at Old Street. Cross over into Pitfield Street. At nos.31-35 is the luxurious **Pitfield London** (www.pitfield london.com) – a maximalist mix of fabrics, colours and textures; of vintage and new; and of shopping and, in the adjacent café, dining.

Just off Pitfield Street is Coronet Street, home to the **Goodhood Store** (no.41, p147), a fashion favourite for edgy mens- and womenswear with a sense of humour. Well-known Brit classics

ITINERARIES

House of Hackney

like Paul Smith and YMC share space with other upbeat labels from further afield: Cast of Vices from LA, perhaps, or Neighbourhood, the Japanese brand responsible for porcelain incense burners shaped like skulls and guns.

By now you'll be thirsty, and maybe hungry. The **Cycle Lab & Juice Bar** at 18A Pitfield Street (www. cyclelab.co.uk) combines bike repairs with a café serving crêpes alongside coffees and juices. If you'd like a more substantial lunch, there's a British menu at **Master & Servant** (8-9 Hoxton Square, www.masterand servant.co.uk), which is run by alumnae of St John (the key restaurant for new Brit cooking). Weekend brunches are served until 1pm, and there's a prix-fixe lunch.

Refreshed and restored, it's time for part two of our tour. For some truly original pieces, old and new, we're now going to head south. If you're tired of walking, hop on a bus back down Shoreditch High Street to Bishopsgate. We're going to explore another fashion micro-hub: the area around Brick Lane. Brick Lane's name has been synonymous with immigrant life since the arrival of Huguenot refugees from the early 17th century, followed by East European Jews in the 19th century. It is these days characterised by arrivals from Bangladesh, who settled here from the 1970s, establishing a plethora of curry-houses that now serve so-so food – and sell it hard.

Most recently, gentrification to the west of Brick Lane has seen a fashion takeover of the area between Brick Lane and Bishopsgate: Spitalfields. All traces of fruit and veg wholesaling have been exiled to the distant east, although the lovely market building remains with a variety of stalls through the week, and the vicinity of the market is now home to small retailers.

Head from Bishopsgate along the north side of the market, where at 17 Lamb Street you'll find the **Mercantile London** (www. themercantilelondon.com), home to wearable, easygoing fashion and accessories from little-known European labels.

Continue across Commercial Street into Hanbury Street. Walking along the street, you'll cross over **Brick Lane**. Carry on; we'll come back here shortly, but there's a shop not to be missed at 55-59 Hanbury Street: vintage emporium **Blitz** (www.blitzlondon.co.uk). Blitz towers over the many other vintage shops in the area. A veritable department store of second-hand wonders, it takes up all floors of an old furniture factory. After you've rummaged, and possibly unearthed something wonderful, turn back and on to Brick Lane, then turn right to find the Old Truman Brewery at no.91. Among the retailers in this creative centre is **Rough Trade East** (www.roughtrade.com), another amazing emporium, this one with an expertly curated collection of vinyl, CDs and books; it also hosts early evening in-store gigs (pre-order the band's CD to get a wristband).

Then, for a final fashion fix, continue north to reach **Bernstock Speirs** at no.234 (www.bernstock speirs.com). Hat-making duo Paul Bernstock and Thelma Speirs have been creating outrageous and playful headgear since 1982. You can buy many of the best designs from their archives here, including the beanie with a veil, a baseball cap with bunny ears and a visor covered in mohair.

Time to relax with a cocktail. The basement bar at **Hawksmoor Spitalfields** (157 Commercial Street, www.thehawksmoor.com) is an architectural jewel in east London's bar scene. Perch at the copper bar to witness some cocktail craftsmen at work.

London by Area

London Eye p56

The South Bank

Tourists have been coming to the South Bank for centuries, but the entertainments have changed a little. Shakespeare's Globe has risen again, but for the associated prostitutes, gamblers and bear-baiting you'd need a time machine. Instead, enjoy a revitalised cultural hub – the Southbank Centre, BFI Southbank cinema complex and Hayward gallery – or join the multitude strolling the broad riverside walkway between Tower Bridge (p141) and Westminster Bridge. This strings together fine views and must-see attractions such as the Shard, Tate Modern, and the London Eye.

Sights & museums

East of Tower Bridge, the **Design Museum** (Shad Thames, SE1 2YD, 7403 6933, www.designmuseum.org, admission £11) will continue its fine programme of temporary exhibitions until it moves to a grand new Kensington location in 2016 (see box p81).

Garden Museum
Lambeth Palace Road, SE1 7LB (7401 8865, www.gardenmuseum. org.uk). Lambeth North tube or Waterloo tube/rail. **Open** 10.30am-5pm Mon-Fri; 10.30am-4pm Sat. **Admission** £7.50; free-£6.50 reductions. **Map** p54 A4 **1**
The world's first horticulture museum fits neatly into the old church of St Mary's. A 'belvedere' gallery, built out of eco-friendly wood sheeting, contains the permanent collection of art, antique tools and horticultural memorabilia, while the ground floor hosts temporary exhibitions. In the small back garden, a replica 17th-century knot garden was created in honour of John Tradescant, intrepid plant-hunter and gardener to Charles I; Tradescant is buried here.

Hayward Gallery

Southbank Centre, Belvedere Road, SE1 8XX (0844 875 0073, www.southbank centre.co.uk). Waterloo tube/rail or Embankment tube. **Open** noon-6pm Mon-Wed, Sat, Sun; 10am-8pm Thur, Fri. **Admission** varies. **Map** p54 A2 ❷

This versatile gallery continues its fine programme of contemporary art, often with a strong interactive element – from illuminated installations to a room full of balloons. Casual visitors can hang out in the industrial-look café-bar, Concrete.

HMS Belfast

Morgan's Lane, Tooley Street, SE1 2JH (7940 6300, www.iwm.org.uk). London Bridge tube/rail. **Open** *Mar-Oct* 10am-6pm daily. *Nov-Feb* 10am-5pm daily. **Admission** £15.50; free-£12.40 reductions. **Map** p55 F2 ❸

This 11,500-ton light cruiser is the last surviving big gun World War II warship in Europe. Built in 1938, the *Belfast* escorted Arctic convoys to Russia, and supported the Normandy landings. It now makes an unlikely playground for kids, who tear round its guns, bridge and engine room. An interactive display in the Operations Room has a radar simulation.

Imperial War Museum

Lambeth Road, SE1 6HZ (7416 5000, www.iwm.org.uk). Lambeth North tube or Elephant & Castle tube/rail. **Open** 10am-6pm daily. **Admission** free. *Special exhibitions* prices vary. **Map** p54 B4 ❹

IWM London, which covers the history of 20th- and 21st-century conflict, reopened in summer 2014 to commemorate the outbreak of the Great War with brand-new World War I galleries. The Central Hall, redesigned by Fosters + Partners with terraced spaces, remains the attention-grabbing repository of major artefacts: guns, tanks and aircraft hung from the ceiling (including a Harrier GR9 that saw action in Afghanistan). Permanent exhibitions include A Family in Wartime, chronicling the World War II experiences of a London family, Secret War, on espionage, and the Holocaust Exhibition, which uses objects, film, photographs and survivors' testimony to bear witness to Nazi atrocities (not recommended for under-14s).

London Bridge Experience

2-4 Tooley Street, SE1 2SY (0800 043 4666, www.thelondonbridgeexperience. com). London Bridge tube/rail. **Open** 10am-5pm Mon-Fri, Sun; 10am-6pm Sat. **Admission** £23; free-£21 reductions; £74 family. **Map** p55 E2 ❺

Old London Bridge, finished in 1209, was the first Thames crossing made of stone – and London's only Thames bridge until Westminster Bridge was finished in 1750. This kitsch, family-focused exhibition is a costumed tour of the crossing's past, as well as a scary adventure into the haunted foundations: pestilential catacombs peopled by animatronic torture victims (suitable for over-11s only).

London Dungeon

County Hall, Westminster Bridge Road, SE1 7PB (0871 423 2240, www.the dungeons.com). Westminster tube or Waterloo tube/rail. **Open** *Term-time* 10am-5pm Mon-Wed, Fri; 11am-5pm Thur; 10am-6pm Sat, Sun. *School holidays* 10am-7pm Mon-Wed, Sat, Sun; 11am-7pm Thur, Fri. **Admission** £18.50-£25.20; £16.95-£19.80 reductions. **Map** p54 A3 ❻

The Dungeon moved its gore and black comedy from Tooley Street in spring 2013 to reopen here in a bigger and more high-tech form. A jokey celebration of torture, death and disease, the attraction sends visitors on a journey back in time to London's plague-ridden streets (rotting corpses, rats, vile boils and projectile vomiting come as standard) to meet unsavoury characters, from Guy Fawkes to demon barber Sweeney Todd. The 'blood'-splattered actors are joined by 'virtual' guests, such as Brian Blessed as Henry

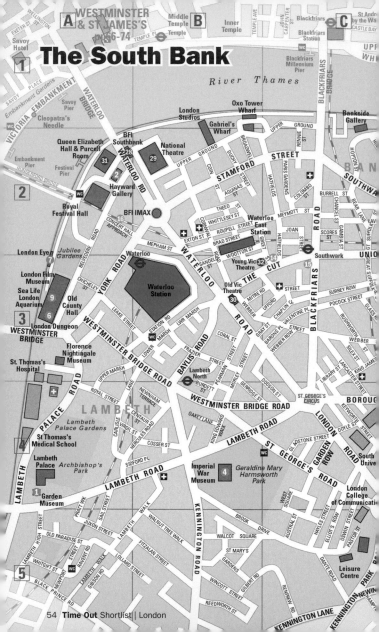

The South Bank

WESTMINSTER & ST JAMES'S pp66-74 **A**

Middle Temple **B**

Inner Temple

Temple

Blackfriars **C**

Blackfriars Station

St Andrew by the Wardrobe

Castle Bay

1

Savoy Hotel

WELLINGTON

EXETER ST

SAVOY PLACE

Savoy Gardens

Embankment Gardens

Savoy Pier

Cleopatra's Needle

VICTORIA EMBANKMENT

Embankment Pier

Festival Pier

WATERLOO BRIDGE

HUNGERFORD BRIDGE

River Thames

London Studios

Oxo Tower Wharf

Gabriel's Wharf

Blackfriars Millennium Pier

Bankside Gallery

B A N

BLACKFRIARS BRIDGE

UPPER WHI

2

BFI Southbank **28**

Queen Elizabeth Hall & Purcell Room **31**

National Theatre **29**

Hayward Gallery **2**

Royal Festival Hall

BFI IMAX **16**

UPPER GROUND

STAMFORD STREET

SOUTHWARK

WC

Embankment Pier

CONCERT HALL APPROACH

UPPER GROUND

DUCHY ST

COIN ST

BROADWALL

HATFIELDS

UPPER GROUND

PARIS GARDENS

RENNIE ST

HOPTON ST

COLOMBO

BURRELL

CHANCEL ST

BEAR LANE

SCORES ST

SOUTHWA

LAVI

GAMBIA ST

3

London Eye

Jubilee Gardens

London Film Museum

Sea Life London Aquarium **9**

Old County Hall **6**

London Dungeon

WESTMINSTER BRIDGE

Florence Nightingale Museum

St Thomas's Hospital

YORK ROAD

BELVEDERE ROAD

CHICHELEY ST

Waterloo **→**

Waterloo Station

WESTMINSTER BRIDGE ROAD

LEAKE STREET

STATION RD

LOWER MARSH

LWR. MARSH

LEAKE ST

WC

AQUINAS ST

THEED ST

CORNWALL RD

WHITTLESEY ST

EXTON ST

ROUPELL ST

BRAD STREET

MEPHAM ST

WOOTTON ST

Waterloo East Station **→**

Young Vic Theatre **32**

Old Vic Theatre **30**

THE CUT

JOAN

MEYMOTT ST

Southwark **→**

HATFIELDS GREET

SANDELL ST

MITRE RD

WEBBER

UFFORD

CHAPLIN CL

GRAY ST

VALENTINE PL

BLACKFRIARS ROAD

UNION

15

SURREY ROW

POCOCK STREET

RUSHWORTH STREET

KING JAMES

LIBRARY ST

LANCASTER STREET

WEBBER

SILEX ST

GLASS

4

LAMBETH

Lambeth Palace Gardens

St Thomas's Medical School

UPPER MARSH

ROYAL STREET

CENTAUR ST

NEWNHAM TERRACE

CARLISLE LANE

VIRGIL ST

HERCULES RD

COSSER ST

LAMBETH NORTH **→**

BAYLIS ROAD

LOWER MARSH

FRAZIER STREET

PEARMAN STREET

MORLEY STREET

CORAL ST

BARONS PL

DODSON ST

GERRIDGE ST

WESTMINSTER BRIDGE ROAD

ST. GEORGE'S CIRCUS

KEWORTH ST

BOROUG

LONDON ROAD

BOROUG

5

PALACE ROAD

Lambeth Palace

Garden Museum **1**

Archbishop's Park

LAMBETH HIGH ST

OLD PARADISE ST

WHITGIFT ST

BLACK PRINCE RD

NEWPORT ST

LAMBETH ROAD

PRATT WK

SAIL STREET

JUXON STREET

LAMBETH WALK

REGENT ST

GIBSON RD

SIDFORD PL

FITZALAN STREET

LOLLARD STREET

WALNUT TREE WALK

WC

Imperial War Museum **4**

Geraldine Mary Harmsworth Park

LAMBETH ROAD

ST GEORGE'S ROAD

KENNINGTON ROAD

GARDEN ROW

BROOK DRIVE

WEST SQUARE

AUSTRAL ST

HAYES PLACE

ELLIOT'S ROW

OSWIN ST

PASTOR ST

DOYLE ST

STONE STREET

GARDEN ROW

South Unive

London College of Communicati

Leisure Centre

WALCOT SQUARE

ST MARY'S GARDENS

SULLIVAN RD

GILBERT RD

WINCOTT ST

REEDWORTH ST

KENNINGTON LANE

DANTE RD

RENFREW RD

PARK D

KENNINGTON NEWIN

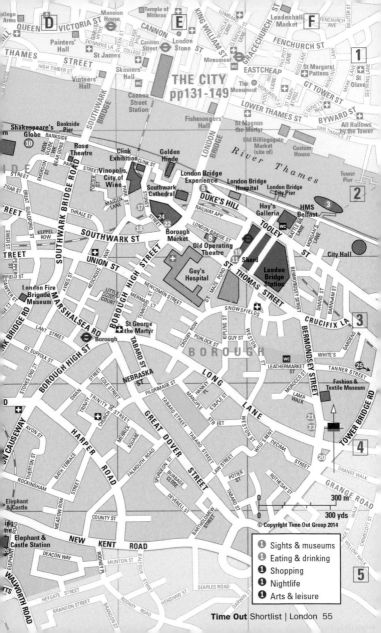

THE CITY
pp131-149

Time Out Shortlist | London 55

VIII. There are 18 different shows and 'surprises' – get chased by the Ripper or lost in Victorian sewers. There are also two rides: a turbulent boat trip down the Thames towards execution, and a dark plunge three storeys in the pitch-black. Unsuitable for young or easily scared children.

London Eye

Jubilee Gardens, SE1 7PB (0870 500 0600, www.londoneye.com). Waterloo tube/rail or Westminster tube. **Open** varies through the year; check website. **Admission** £19.95; free-£17.96 reductions. **Map** p54 A3 **❼**

It's hard to believe this giant wheel was only meant to turn for five years: it has proved so popular that no one wants it to come down, and refurbishment to fit it for another two decades was completed in 2012 – just in time for it to take on key rival, the Shard (p59). A 'flight' takes half an hour, allowing plenty of time to get your snaps of the landmarks. Some people book in advance (taking a gamble with the weather), but you can turn up and queue for a ticket on the day.

Old Operating Theatre, Museum & Herb Garret

9A St Thomas's Street, SE1 9RY (7188 2679, www.thegarret.org.uk). London Bridge tube/rail. **Open** 10.30am-5pm daily. **Admission** £6.50; free-£5 reductions. No credit cards. **Map** p55 E2 **❽**

The atmospheric tower that houses this salutary reminder of antique surgical practice used to be part of the chapel of St Thomas's Hospital. Visitors enter by a vertiginous wooden spiral staircase to view an operating theatre dating from 1822 (before the advent of anaesthetics), with tiered viewing seats for students. As fascinatingly gruesome are the operating tools, which look like torture implements.

Sea Life London Aquarium

County Hall, Westminster Bridge Road, SE1 7PB (0871 663 1678, tours 7967
8007 www.sealife.co.uk). Westminster tube or Waterloo tube/rail. **Open** *Term time* 10am-7pm daily. *School holidays* 10am-8pm. **Admission** £21.60; free-£15.90 reductions. **Map** p54 A3 **❾**

This is one of Europe's largest aquariums and a hit with kids. Inhabitants are grouped by geographical origin, beginning with the Atlantic, where blacktail bream swim alongside the Thames Embankment. There are poison arrow frogs, crocodiles and piranha in the 'Rainforests of the World' exhibit. The Ray Lagoon is still popular, though touching the friendly flatfish is no longer allowed (it's bad for their health). Starfish, crabs and anemones can be handled in special open rock pools instead, and the clown fish still draw crowds. There's a mesmerising Seahorse Temple, a tank full of turtles and enchanting Gentoo penguins. The centrepieces, though, are the two massive Pacific and Indian Ocean tanks, with menacing sharks quietly circling fallen Easter Island statues and dinosaur bones. Book online to keep the entry price down.

Shakespeare's Globe

21 New Globe Walk, SE1 9DT (7401 9919, www.shakespearesglobe.com). Southwark tube, or Blackfriars or London Bridge tube/rail. **Open** *Exhibition* Feb-Oct 9am-5.30pm daily; Nov-Jan 10am-5.30pm daily. *Tours* Globe Theatre & Rose Theatre Mar-Oct daily; check website for details. **Admission** £13.50; free-£12 reductions. **Map** p55 D2 **❿**

The original Globe Theatre, co-owned by Shakespeare and where many of his plays were first staged, burned down in 1613. Nearly 400 years later (it celebrated its 15th birthday in 2012), the Globe was rebuilt not far from its original site, using construction methods and materials as close to the originals as possible. It's a fully operational theatre, with historically authentic performances mixed with brand-new plays in a season running

Clockwise from top left:
Shakespeare's Globe;
Sea Life London Aquarium;
Tate Modern p59

Seen London Lately?

from June through to autumn. Year-round performances can also be seen in the new on-site indoor theatre the Sam Wanamaker Playhouse. A rich, dark space embellished with gold, with a beautiful ornate ceiling, it's built to feel even smaller than its 340-seat capacity. There's an exhibition on the reconstruction and Renaissance London in the UnderGlobe, and guided tours (lasting an hour and a half) run all year, visiting the nearby site of the Rose Theatre during Globe matinées. **Event highlights** 'Groundling' tickets (standing in the unsheltered centre of the theatre) for a performance are a one-off experience – and cheap too.

Shard

32 London Bridge Street, SE1 9SS (0844 499 7111, www.theviewfrom theshard.com). London Bridge tube/rail. **Open** 10am-8.30pm daily. **Admission** £24.95; free-£18.95 reductions. **Map** p55 E3 ⓫
The View from the Shard offers 360° views across the capital and beyond (up to 40 miles on a clear day) from 800ft up – almost twice the height of any other viewpoint in London. The attraction is a two-level deck (the first enclosed, the second open to the elements above head-height) on floors 68 to 72 of the skyscraper, to which visitors are whisked in two stages in super-smooth, high-speed lifts, taking just 30 seconds. Digital 'Tell:scopes' update the traditional coin-in-the-slot binoculars – touchscreens allow you to call up additional information on the buildings you're looking at. Note: there are no toilets or refreshments on the viewing levels.

Tate Modern

Bankside, SE1 9TG (7887 8888, www. tate.org.uk). Southwark tube or London Bridge tube/rail. **Open** 10am-6pm Mon-Thur, Sun; 10am-10pm Fri, Sat. *Tour* 11am, noon, 2pm, 3pm daily. **Admission** free. *Special exhibitions* prices vary. **Map** p55 D2 ⓬

Thanks to its industrial architecture, this powerhouse of modern art is awe-inspiring even before you enter. It ceased operating as Bankside Power Station in 1981, then opened as a spectacularly popular museum in 2000. The gallery now attracts five million visitors a year to a building intended for half that number. To accommodate them, the gallery has undertaken the immensely ambitious, £215m TM2 extension, the first fruits from which opened in 2012: the Tanks, so-called because they occupy vast former oil tanks, stage performance and film art. As for the rest of the extension, a huge new origami-like structure, designed by Herzog & de Meuron, is gradually taking shape, but the work won't interrupt normal service in the main galleries. Work is also in progress linking the old and the new parts of Tate Modern with the building of a bridge across the top of the Turbine Hall. The permanent collection draws from the Tate's magnificent collection of international modern art to display the likes of Matisse, Rothko, Picasso and Beuys. The Tate-to-Tate boat service (£6.50 adult) – polka-dot decor by Damien Hirst, bar on board – links with the London Eye (p56) and Tate Britain (p70) every 40 minutes.

Eating & drinking

Borough Market (p62) and newcomer **Maltby Street** (p64) are great for gourmet snackers, while superior chain eateries cluster around the Royal Festival Hall.

Albion Neo Bankside

Pavilion B, Holland Street, SE1 9FU (7827 4343, www.albioncafes.com). Southwark tube. **Open** 8am-11pm Mon-Sat; 9am-10.30pm Sun. **££**. **British. Map** p55 D2 ⓭
This glass-walled eatery just behind Tate Modern is the second of Terence Conran's poshed-up British cafés. A secluded outdoor terrace overlooks

A bridge too far?

Thomas Heatherwick's latest headline-grabbing design.

It's hard to imagine now, but for most of the city's history, London had but a single bridge – the one that still bears its name. Built by the Romans in around 50 AD, London Bridge had no companions this side of Putney before Westminster Bridge was completed in 1750. Now, despite there already being a dozen bridges spanning the Thames in central London alone, planning has been sought for an ambitious 'Garden Bridge', to run between the South Bank and Temple. With backing from Mayor Boris Johnson and central government (each to the tune of £30m), the smart money is on it being complete for 2018.

TV star Joanna Lumley's support got the idea moving, but the recruitment of designer Thomas Heatherwick has been key to the idea gaining traction. The architect's renderings (above) look amazing, with the notion being to create an infrastructure link so beautiful people choose to linger.

Heatherwick has some serious credentials – and there are several examples of his work in London. He was behind Boris's New Bus for London, which can now be seen trundling through much of the city. He also designed the quirky Rolling Bridge in Paddington Basin, which curls up on itself like a snail every Friday at noon, and the lovely 2012 Olympic Cauldron (due to go on permanent display in July 2014 at Museum of London, p141). *www.heatherwick.com*

a beautifully landscaped garden of mature silver birches – although the front tables get a view of the gallery extension works. Breakfast runs from toast and Marmite to a full English or kedgeree. Later on, the menu expands to include fish and chips, pies, bread and butter pudding and afternoon teas.

Anchor & Hope

36 The Cut, SE1 8LP (7928 9898). Southwark or Waterloo tube/rail. **Open** 5-11pm Mon; 11am-11pm Tue-Sat; 12.30-5pm Sun. **££ Gastropub**. Map p54 C2 ⓮
The most common complaint about this relaxed Waterloo gastropub is the no-booking policy. Those who end up having to wait at the bar can salivate over the seasonal British menu on the blackboard: thinly sliced ox tongue with lentils, green sauce and mustard fruits, say, or braised suckling kid with bacon, fennel, chickpeas and aïoli.

Baltic

74 Blackfriars Road, SE1 8HA (7928 1111, www.balticrestaurant.co.uk). Southwark tube. **Open** 5.30-11.15pm Mon; noon-3pm, 5.30-11.15pm Tue-Sat; noon-4.30pm, 5.30-10pm Sun. **£££**. **Eastern European**. Map p54 C3 ⓯
This stylish spot (in the high-ceiling restaurant, a stunning chandelier is made of hundreds of amber shards) remains London's brightest star for east European food. The menu gives the best of eastern Europe – from Georgian-style lamb with aubergine to Romanian soured cream *mamaliga* (polenta). Great cocktails, many vodkas and friendly service add to the appeal.

Bar Topolski

150-152 Hungerford Arches, Concert Hall Approach, SE1 8XU (7620 0627, www.bartopolski.co.uk). Waterloo tube/rail. **Open** 11am-11pm Mon-Wed; 11am-midnight Thur; 11am-1am Fri, Sat. **££**. **Bar**. Map p54 A2 ⓰
The former Topolski Century, an extensive mural by Polish-born artist Feliks Topolski depicting an extraordinary

procession of 20th-century events and faces, has been turned into a bar-café. Occupying two capacious brick arches beneath Hungerford Bridge (some of Topolski's artworks are incorporated into the design), it serves cured meat, fish and cheese and other snacks, both savoury and sweet. There are assorted musical entertainments too.

Elliot's

12 Stoney Street, SE1 9AD (7403 7436, www.elliotscafe.com). London Bridge tube/rail. **Open** 8am-10pm Mon-Sat. **£££**. **Brasserie**. Map p55 E2 ⓱
Light and airy, with stripped brick walls and a contemporary feel, Elliot's is a busy little spot. Sit out front and watch the world go by, perch at the bar or take a seat in the bright back area. The seasonal menu is small but innovative, and carefully sourced. Smaller plates such as crab on toast or buffalo mozzarella and polenta are listed alongside larger plates such as lemon sole, wild garlic and fino. Drinks include a selection of natural wines (orange wines are listed alongside the expected white, red and rosé).

Gelateria 3bis

4 Park Street, SE1 9AB (7378 1977 www.gelateria3bis.it). London Bridge tube/rail. **Open** *Summer* 8am-10pm Mon-Sat; 10am-6pm Sun. *Winter* 8am-8pm Mon-Sat; 11am-6pm Sun. **£**. **Ice-cream**. Map p55 E2 ⓲
Step inside and watch gelato machines churning out new flavours. There's an emphasis on creamy, milky ones, from *fior di panna* ('cream' ice-cream) to panna cotta. While the classics (such as chocolate or pistachio) are not neglected, the team likes to experiment – gooseberry gelato was a big hit.

Hutong

Level 33, The Shard, 31 St Thomas Street, SE1 9RY (7478 0540, www. hutong.co.uk). London Bridge tube/rail. **Open** noon-3pm, 6-11pm daily. **££££**. **Chinese**. Map p55 E3 ⓳

The original Hutong in Hong Kong is a glitzy restaurant with magnificent views. This branch, halfway up the Shard, is exactly the same. The same Sichuanese and northern Chinese menu, the same mix of plate glass and ersatz Old Beijing decor. Prices are high: but then this is the Shard, not Chinatown. It's a great place to impress a date. For the Shard's bars, which are even higher, see box p145.

M Manze

87 Tower Bridge Road, SE1 4TW (7407 2985, www.manze.co.uk). Bus 1, 42, 188. **Open** 11am-2pm Mon; 10.30am-2pm Tue-Thur; 10am-2.30pm Fri; 10am-2.45pm Sat. **£**. No credit cards. **Pie & mash. Map** p55 F4 ⑳

The finest remaining purveyor of the dirt-cheap traditional food of London's working classes. This Manze is not only the city's oldest pie shop, established in 1902, but also in its functional way the most beautiful, with marble-top tables and spick-and-span tiles. Expect scoops of mash, beef pies and liquor (a thin parsley sauce).

Pizarro

194 Bermondsey Street, SE1 3TQ (7378 9455, www.pizarrorestaurant.com). Borough tube or London Bridge tube/rail. **Open** noon-3pm, 6-11pm Mon-Fri; noon-11pm Sat; 10am-10pm Sun. **£££**. **Tapas. Map** p55 F4 ㉑

Chef José Pizarro's reputation was built at the Brindisa tapas bars (below), but this place showcases his classier side. The interior is polished rustic, and the kitchen takes classic Spanish dishes and moves them upmarket: velvety ham croquetas, razor clams with chorizo, rosemary-scented lamb on puy lentils. There's a strong selection of sherry and Iberian wines, and staff are knowledgeable and charming.

Tapas Brindisa

18-20 Southwark Street, SE1 1TJ (7357 8880, www.brindisa.com). London Bridge tube/rail. **Open** 10am-11.30pm Mon-Fri; 9am-11.30pm Sat; 11am-10pm Sun. **£££**. **Tapas**. **Map** p55 E2 ㉒

Top-quality ingredients have always been the key at Brindisa, but its genius lies in the ability to assemble them into delicious and deceptively simple tapas. The set-up here is as basic as the food: there's a bar area dotted with high tables, and a close-packed, concrete-floored dining room at the other end. Both are generally thronged.

Zucca

184 Bermondsey Street, SE1 3TQ (7378 6809, www.zuccalondon.com). London Bridge tube/rail or Bermondsey tube. **Open** noon-3pm, 6-10pm Tue-Fri; noon-3.30pm, 6-10pm Sat; noon-4pm Sun. **££**. **Italian**. **Map** p55 F4 ㉓

The formula here is simple and impeccably executed: modern Italian food based on top-notch ingredients at competitive prices, served by clued-up staff in contemporary surroundings. Wrap-around windows offer great people-watching opportunities, as does the open kitchen running half the length of the room. A forte is the fresh pasta: for example, intensely golden-yellow taglierini with fresh peas, lemon and ricotta.

Shopping

Borough Market

Southwark Street, SE1 1TL (7407 1002, www.boroughmarket.org.uk). London Bridge tube/rail. **Open** 10am-5pm Wed, Thur; 10am-6pm Fri; 8am-5pm Sat. No credit cards. **Map** p55 E2 ㉔

Demolition works to make way for a rail viaduct overhead have left Borough – London's busiest foodie market – with a swanky new frontage, the striking glass Market Hall, which belies the market's origins in the 13th century. Traders satisfy a seemingly insatiable appetite for artisan cheeses and ham from acorn-fed pigs, beautifully displayed organic fruit and veg, cakes, bread, olive oil, fish, meat and booze. Leave home hungry to take

advantage of the numerous free samples. The market is now open every day except Sunday: lunch stalls until Wednesday, then fully open for the rest of the week – Saturday is monstrously busy. Seasonal tasting days run all year, and opening hours are extended in the run-up to Christmas.

Maltby Street

Maltby Street, Druid Street, Dockley Road & around, SE1, SE16 (www.spaterminus.co.uk). London Bridge tube/rail. **Map** p55 F3 **25**

Maltby Street is an unlikely place to find food retailers, but there's been a buzz about the Saturday openings since they began in 2010. It was emphatically not a street market – merely rented railway arches where Borough Market stalwarts had set up storage. When the traders – including Monmouth Coffee Company and Neal's Yard Dairy, along with smaller enterprises – decided to experiment with public opening, London's foodies had a new destination. It has since then expanded into a proper market on neighbouring Ropewalk (also open Sundays) and Spa Terminus. Most producers are open on Saturday mornings (9am-2pm), some on Sundays too; the increasing number of permanent venues now include the likes of St John, who added a Bakery Room café (Arch 42, Ropewalk) to their bakery in 2014. The website has a useful map showing locations and opening hours.

Nightlife

As well as classical music and dance, the **Southbank Centre** (p65) stages terrific rock and global gigs.

Corsica Studios

4-5 Elephant Road, SE17 1LB (7703 4760, www.corsicastudios.com). Elephant & Castle tube/rail. No credit cards. **Map** p55 D5 **26**

This flexible performance space is increasingly used as one of London's more adventurous live music venues and clubs, supplementing the bands and DJs with sundry poets, live painters and wigged-out projectionists. Its club nights are second to none, running from cranium-caving dubstep to soulful house via world-class techno.

Ministry of Sound

103 Gaunt Street, SE1 6DP (7740 8600, www.ministryofsound.com). Elephant & Castle tube/rail. **Map** p55 D4 **27**

This refurbished clubbing powerhouse left the most important aspect of its success intact: the killer sound system. It's still one of London's iconic venues after more than two decades, and punters flock to the club's five rooms for the experience as much as the big-name DJs. While weeklies like Saturday Sessions and Friday's the Gallery serve up the best electro and trance, Ava Word's recent spots on Sunday have been unmissable – featuring the likes of deep house god Osunlade.

Arts & leisure

There are also regular performances at **Shakespeare's Globe** (p56) – where work by the Bard and contemporary plays are performed to partially unsheltered audiences – and in the neighbouring, indoor Sam Wanamaker Theatre, where largely Jacobean plays are atmospherically and authentically lit by candles.

BFI Southbank

South Bank, SE1 8XT (7928 3535, 7928 3232 tickets, www.bfi.org.uk). Embankment tube or Waterloo tube/rail. **Map** p54 A2 **28**

An esteemed London institution, with an unrivalled programme of retrospective seasons and previews, as well as regular director and actor Q&As. The riverside seating outside the main café is hugely popular, but there's also a handsome cocktail bar/

restaurant inside near the terrific Mediatheque (a free archive-viewing room). A short walk away, the BFI IMAX (1 Charlie Chaplin Walk, 0870 787 2525) shows made-for-IMAX kiddie pics and wow-factor documentaries on the biggest screen in the country, as well as ace all-night screenings of film trilogies.

Event highlights London Film Festival (Oct).

National Theatre

South Bank, SE1 9PX (7452 3400 information, 7452 3000 tickets, www. nationaltheatre.org.uk). Embankment or Southwark tube, or Waterloo tube/rail. **Map** p54 B2 ㉙

This concrete monster is the flagship venue of British theatre, with three auditoriums allowing for different kinds of performance: in-the-round, promenade, even classic proscenium arch. They are soon to be joined by the new Dorfman Theatre, currently under construction in the space occupied by the now-closed Cottesloe. The Shed, the temporary theatre that was the Cottesloe's replacement – described as looking like an upside-down cow and supposed to be open for a year – is now going to remain until at least 2017, under a yet- to-be-decided new name. There has also been a change in leadership, with successful outgoing director Nicholas Hytner being replaced by Rufus Norris. The Travelex season ensures a widening audience by offering seats for £15 (they get snapped up fast), £25 and £35, and there are usually free outdoor performances by the riverbank in summer.

Old Vic

The Cut, SE1 8NB (0844 871 7628, www.oldvictheatre.com). Southwark tube or Waterloo tube/rail. **Map** p54 B3 ㉚

Oscar-winner Kevin Spacey has been artistic director here since 2003, bringing commercial success, especially when he or one of his Hollywood chums take to the stage. His replacement,

Matthew Warchus, takes over in autumn 2015. Warchus has directed a number of productions at the Old Vic, including 2008's *Speed-the-Plow* with Spacey and Jeff Goldblum. He inherits a beautiful venue, with programming that runs from grown-up Christmas pantomimes to serious drama.

Southbank Centre

Belvedere Road, SE1 8XX (7960 4200 information, 0844 875 0073 tickets, www.southbankcentre.co.uk). Embankment tube or Waterloo tube/rail. **Map** p54 A2 ㉛

In addition to the Hayward (p53), there are three main venues here: the Royal Festival Hall, a 3,000-seat venue with the Orchestra of the Age of Enlightenment and the Philharmonia as residents; the 900-seat Queen Elizabeth Hall; and, for recitals, the 365-capacity Purcell Room. A £90m renovation a few years back improved the RFH, externally and acoustically, and since Jude Kelly took over as artistic director, the programming has been rich in variety, with music and performance of all types, often appealingly themed into festivals. Her controversial plan for a new Festival Wing was shelved due to mayor Boris Johnson's obection to removing the well-known skate park from the Undercroft. The foyer stage hosts hundreds of free concerts, and the river terrace is thronged in good weather.

Young Vic

66 The Cut, SE1 8LZ (7922 2922, www.youngvic.org). Southwark tube or Waterloo tube/rail. **Map** p54 B3 ㉜

As the name suggests, this Vic (actually now in its forties) has more youthful bravura than its older sister up the road, and draws a younger crowd, who pack out the balcony at its popular restaurant and bar at weekends. They come to see European classics with a modern edge, new writing with an international flavour and collaborations with leading companies.

LONDON BY AREA

Trafalgar Square

Westminster & St James's

For many the heart of London – if not Britain – Westminster is more formal than inviting. It is home to the **Houses of Parliament**, the seat of government power for 1,000 years; its **'Big Ben'** clock tower has starred in many holiday snaps. Britain's very first Parliament met in nearby **Westminster Abbey**, site of almost every British coronation. Here too are more photo opportunities in the shape of **Nelson's Column** and **Trafalgar Square**.

Sights & museums

Banqueting House

Whitehall, SW1A 2ER (0844 482 7777, www.hrp.org.uk). Westminster tube or Charing Cross tube/rail. **Open** 10am-5pm Mon-Sat. **Admission** £6; free-£5 reductions. **Map** p67 C2 ❶
This Italianate mansion was built in 1620 and is the sole surviving part of the Tudor and Stuart kings' Whitehall Palace. It has a lavish ceiling by Rubens that glorifies James I, 'the wisest fool in Christendom', and a small new exhibit that commemorates the building's key contribution to history: the execution outside of Charles I on 30 January 1649.

'Big Ben'

Bridge Street, SW1A 2PW. Westminster tube. **Map** p67 C3 ❷
'Big Ben' – which, as precocious schoolchildren will love to tell you, is the name of the clock tower's 13-ton bell, not the clock tower itself – is now (in honour of the Queen's Diamond Jubilee of 2012) officially called the Elizabeth Tower. You can climb it only if you're a UK resident and apply in writing, far in advance, to your MP. But it's a favourite photo-op, most often from across the road at the statue of marauding Iceni queen Boudicca.

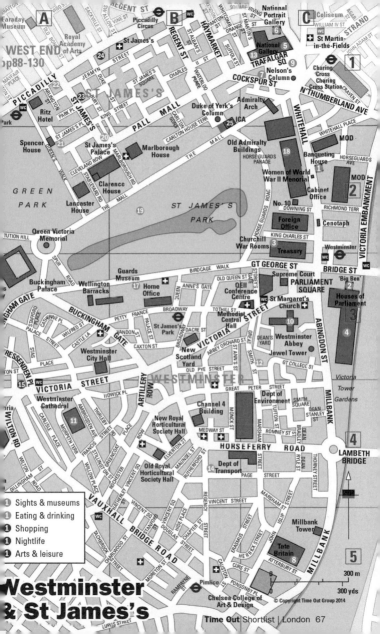

Faraday Museum

A

WEST END
pp88-130

PICCADILLY
Ritz Hotel
Spencer House
Royal Academy of Arts

ST JAMES'S
St James's Palace
Marlborough House
Clarence House
Lancaster House

B

Piccadilly Circus
REGENT ST
HAYMARKET
PALL MALL
THE MALL
Duke of York's Column

GREEN PARK

Queen Victoria Memorial
TUITION HILL

Buckingham Palace
Wellington Barracks
Guards Museum
Home Office

BUCKINGHAM GATE

Westminster City Hall
New Scotland Yard
St James's Park
Methodist Central Hall

VICTORIA STREET

Westminster Cathedral

New Royal Horticultural Society Hall
Old Royal Horticultural Society Hall

VAUXHALL BRIDGE ROAD

1 Sights & museums
1 Eating & drinking
1 Shopping
1 Nightlife
1 Arts & leisure

Westminster & St James's

C

National Portrait Gallery
Coliseum
STRAND
St Martin-in-the-Fields
National Gallery
TRAFALGAR
Nelson's Column
Charing Cross
Charing Cross Station
COCKSPUR ST
Admiralty Arch
ICA
Old Admiralty Buildings
HORSE GUARDS PARADE
Women of World War II Memorial
Banqueting House
WHITEHALL
MOD
MOD
Cabinet Office
No. 10 Downing Office
Foreign Office
Cenotaph
Churchill War Rooms
Treasury
Westminster
VICTORIA EMBANKMENT

GT GEORGE ST
BRIDGE ST
Supreme Court
PARLIAMENT SQUARE
'Big Ben'
Houses of Parliament
QEII Conference Centre
St Margaret's Church
Westminster Abbey
Jewel Tower
ABINGDON ST

WESTMINSTER

Dept of Environment
Channel 4 Building
MILLBANK
Victoria Tower Gardens

HORSEFERRY ROAD
LAMBETH BRIDGE

Dept of Transport

Millbank Tower
Tate Britain
Pimlico
Chelsea College of Art & Design

300 m
300 yds
© Copyright Time Out Group 2014

Time Out Shortlist | London 67

Top: Houses of Parliament;
bottom: National Gallery

Churchill War Rooms

Clive Steps, King Charles Street, SW1A 2AQ (7930 6961, www.iwm.org.uk). St James's Park or Westminster tube. **Open** 9.30am-6pm daily. **Admission** £17.50; free-£14 reductions. **Map** p67 C3 ❸

Beneath Whitehall, the cramped and spartan bunker where Sir Winston Churchill planned the Allied victory in World War II remains exactly as he left it on 16 August 1945. The sense of wartime hardship is reinforced by wailing sirens and the great man's wartime speeches on the free audio guide.

Houses of Parliament

Parliament Square, SW1A 0AA (Commons information 7219 4272, Lords information 7219 3107, www. parliament.uk). Westminster tube. **Open** (when in session) *House of Commons Visitors' Gallery* 2.30-10.30pm Mon; 11.30am-7.30pm Tue, Wed; 9.30am-5.30pm Thur; 9.30am-3pm Fri. *House of Lords Visitors' Gallery* 2.30-10.30pm Mon, Tue; 3-10pm Wed; 11am-7.30pm Thur; from 10am Fri. *Tours* 9.15am-4.30pm Sat & summer recess; check website for details. **Admission** *Visitors' Galleries* free **Tours** £16.50; £7-£14 reductions; free under-15s with adult. **Map** p67 C3 ❹

Visitors are welcome to observe the debates at both the House of Lords and House of Commons – at noon on Wednesday Prime Minister's Question Time is peppery – but tickets must be arranged in advance through your MP or embassy. In any case, the best way to truly absorb the history of the Palace of Westminster is to take one of the 75-minute guided tours (book ahead). The tours head through both Houses – and end in Westminster Hall, where Charles I and Guy Fawkes were tried, one of the few remaining parts of the original fabric of Parliament. Most of the original buildings burned down in 1834, and were replaced by the current neo-Gothic extravaganza in 1860.

National Gallery

Trafalgar Square, WC2N 5DN (7747 2885, www.nationalgallery.org.uk). Leicester Square tube or Charing Cross tube/rail. **Open** 10am-6pm Mon-Thur, Sat, Sun; 10am-9pm Fri. *Tours* 11.30am, 2.30pm Mon-Thur, Sat, Sun; 11.30am, 2.30pm, 7pm Fri. *Gallery A* 10am-6pm Wed, 1st Sun of the mth. **Admission** free. *Special exhibitions* prices vary. **Map** p67 C1 ❺

The National Gallery is one of the world's great repositories for art, with masterpieces from virtually every European school. One of the most important works, Titian's *Diana and Actaeon*, was secured for the Gallery (in a share with the Scottish National Gallery) by outgoing director, Nicholas Penny, who leaves in 2015 having also led the gallery to record attendance figures in 2013.

The modern Sainsbury Wing extension contains the gallery's earliest works: Italian paintings by the likes of Giotto and Piero della Francesca, as well as the Wilton Diptych, the finest medieval English picture in the collection. In the West Wing are Italian Renaissance masterpieces by Correggio, Titian and Raphael, while the North Wing is home to 17th-century Dutch, Flemish, Italian and Spanish Old Masters, as well as works by Turner and landscape artists Claude and Poussin. In the East Wing are works by the French Impressionists and Post-Impressionists, with Monet's *Water-Lilies*, one of Van Gogh's *Sunflowers* and Renoir's *Les Parapluies*. In 2014, the scruffily endearing 'secret' Gallery A – previously open only on Wednesday afternoons – reopened after a two-year refurb in a much better lit and curated state, showing a mix of barely known artists and lost works of masters.

You can't see everything in one visit, but free guided tours, audio guides and the superb Art Start planning computer help you to make the best of your time.

National Portrait Gallery

St Martin's Place, WC2H 0HE (7306 0055, www.npg.org.uk). Leicester Square tube or Charing Cross tube/ rail. **Open** 10am-6pm Mon-Wed, Sat, Sun; 10am-9pm Thur, Fri. **Admission** free. *Special exhibitions* prices vary. **Map** p67 C1 **6**

Portraits don't have to be stuffy – and Sandy Nairne, who steps down as director of the Portrait Gallery in 2015, has done a great deal to get that message across, increasing visitor numbers by a third over his decade here. The NPG has everything from oil paintings of stiff-backed royals to photos of soccer stars and gloriously unflattering political caricatures. The portraits of musicians, scientists, artists, philanthropists and celebrities are arranged in chronological order from the top to the bottom of the building, and include the Chandos portrait of Shakespeare.

Routemaster buses

Cockspur Street, Stops B & (opposite) S. **Map** p67 C1 **7**

London's iconic red double-decker was withdrawn from service in 2005, but refurbished Routemasters – in classic London Transport livery – run on Route 15 (Stop S) every 15mins, 9.30am-6.30pm. Buses head east via St Paul's (p141) to Tower Hill.

Tate Britain

Millbank, SW1P 4RG (7887 8888, www.tate.org.uk). Pimlico tube. **Open** 10am-6pm daily; 10am-10pm 1st Fri of mth. *Tours* 11am, noon, 2pm, 3pm Mon-Fri; noon, 3pm Sat, Sun. **Admission** free. *Special exhibitions* prices vary. **Map** p67 C5 **8**

Tate Modern (p59) gets all the attention, but the original Tate Gallery has a broader and more inclusive brief. Housed in a stately Portland stone building on the riverside, it's second only to the National Gallery (p69) for British art in London. An improvement programme is conserving the building's original features, upgrading the galleries and opening new spaces. First, a superb major rehang of the collections was revealed. Covering British art from Holbein in the 1540s up to the present, including works by Hogarth, Gainsborough, Reynolds and Constable, the collection is now shown largely in chronological order. A few key artists are given more substantial treatment: the Turners remain in their own galleries, and works by Henry Moore and William Blake are grouped rather than being separated by date. In addition, architects Caruso St John have improved the building's fabric. Sturdier floors mean more sculpture has been displayed, and the amount of natural light has been increased. Other additions include a stained-glass window at the Millbank entrance by Turner Prize-winner Richard Wright, and a fine spiral staircase. The Tate-to-Tate boat (7887 8888; £6.50 adult single) zips east along the Thames every 40mins.

Trafalgar Square

Leicester Square tube or Charing Cross tube/rail. **Map** p67 C1 **9**

Trafalgar Square was conceived in the 1820s as a homage to Britain's naval power. Always a natural gathering point – semi-pedestrianisation in 2003 made it more so – the square now regularly hosts celebrations and festivals, and even some protests. The focus is Nelson's Column, a Corinthian pillar topped by a statue of the naval hero, supported by four lions, but the changing contemporary sculpture on the Fourth Plinth bring fresh colour – with a horse skeleton by Hans Haacke and David Shrigley's elongated thumbs-up featuring in 2015 and 2016.

Westminster Abbey

20 Dean's Yard, SW1P 3PA (7222 5152, 7654 4834 tours,

www.westminster-abbey.org).
St James's Park or Westminster
tube. **Open** *May-Aug* 9.30am-3.30pm
Mon, Tue, Thur, Sat; 9.30am-6pm Wed;
9.30-1pm Fri. *Sept-Apr* 9.30am-3.30pm
Mon, Tue, Thur, Fri; 9.30am-6pm Wed;
930am-1.30pm Sat. *Abbey Museum,*
Chapter House & College Gardens Times
vary; phone for details. **Admission** £18;
free-£15 reductions. *Abbey Museum* free.
Tours £3. **Map** p67 C3 ⑩

The cultural significance of the
Abbey is hard to overstate. Edward
the Confessor commissioned it,
but it was only consecrated on 28
December 1065, eight days before
he died. William the Conqueror had
himself crowned here on Christmas
Day 1066, followed by every British
king and queen since – bar two. This
is also where, in 2011, HRH Prince
William married Kate Middleton. In
addition, many notables are interred
in the abbey – Poets' Corner is
always a draw. The Abbey Museum
occupies one of the oldest parts of the
Abbey: you'll find effigies of British
monarchs, among them Edward II and
Henry VII, wearing the actual robes
they wore in life.

Westminster Cathedral

42 Francis Street, SW1P 1QW (7798
9055, www.westminstercathedral.org.
uk). Victoria tube/rail. **Open** 7am-7pm
Mon-Fri; 8am-8pm Sat, Sun. *Exhibition*
10am-5pm Mon-Fri; 10am-6pm Sat,
Sun. *Bell tower* 9.30am-4.30pm daily.
Admission free; donations appreciated.
Exhibition £5; free-£2.50 reductions;
£11 family. *Tower & exhibition* £8;
free-£4 reductions; £17.50 family.
Map p67 A4 ⑪

With domes, arches and a soaring
tower, the architecture of England's
most important Catholic church
(built 1895-1903) has a Byzantine look
heavily influenced by Hagia Sophia. A
brooding, dark ceiling sets off mosaics
and marble columns with Eric Gill's
savage *Stations of the Cross* at their
head. A lift runs up the 273ft bell tower,

for great views, and an exhibition
shows off holy relics, a Tudor chalice
and the architect's original model.

Eating & drinking

Cinnamon Club

Old Westminster Library, 30-32 Great
Smith Street, SW1P 3BU (7222 2555,
www.cinnamonclub.com). St James's Park
or Westminster tube. **Open** 7.30-10am,
noon-2.45pm, 6-10.45pm Mon-Fri; noon-
2.45pm, 6-10.45pm Sat. **££££. Indian.**
Map p67 C3 ⑫

Aiming to create a complete Indian
fine-dining experience, Cinnamon
Club provides cocktails, fine wines,
tasting menus, breakfasts (Indian,
Anglo-Indian, British), as well as
private dining-rooms and all attendant
flummery in an impressive, wood-
panelled space. Executive chef Vivek
Singh devises innovative dishes,
including a well-priced set meal.

National Dining Rooms

Sainsbury Wing, National Gallery,
Trafalgar Square, WC2N 5DN
(7747 2525, www.peytonandbyrne.
co.uk). Charing Cross tube/rail. **Open**
Bakery 10am-5pm Mon-Thur, Sun;
10am-8pm Fri; 10am-7.30pm Sat.
Restaurant noon-3pm Mon-Thur,
Sat; Sun; noon 3pm, 5-7.30pm Fri.
Bakery £. Restaurant **£££. British.**
Map p67 C1 ⑬

Oliver Peyton's restaurant in the
National Gallery (p69) offers far
better food than the usual museum
fare, albeit at a price: oak-smoked
Cornish duck, pea shoots with
quince jelly and aval fries, perhaps,
followed by wild wood pigeon with
currant and beetroot glaze. The few
window seats have prized views over
Trafalgar Square, and the bakery
ably fulfils the cakes-and-cuppa role
of a traditional museum café.

Regency Café

17-19 Regency Street, SW1P 4BY (7821
6596). St James's Park tube or Victoria

tube/rail. **Open** 7am-2.30pm, 4-7.15pm Mon-Fri; 7am-noon Sat. **Café**. Map p67 B4 ⑭

Behind its blacked-tiled art deco exterior, this classic caff has been here since 1946. Customers sit on brown plastic chairs at Formica-topped tables, watched over by muscular boxers and Spurs stars of yore, whose photos hang on the tiled walls. Lasagne, omelettes, salads and every conceivable cooked breakfast are joined by stodgetastic own-made specials like steak pie.

Arts & leisure

Victoria Palace Theatre
Victoria Street, SW1E 5EA (0844 248 5000, www.victoriapalacetheatre.co.uk). Victoria tube/rail. **Map** p67 A4 ⑮

Billy Elliot, scored by Elton John, is set during the 1984 coal miners' strike. A working-class lad loves ballet – to the consternation of his salt-of-the-earth dad. Production subject to change.

St James's

Traditional, quiet and exclusive, St James's is where **Buckingham Palace** presides over lovely **St James's Park**. Everything is dignified and unhurried, whether you're shopping at **Fortnum's** or entertaining at the **Wolseley**.

Sights & museums

Buckingham Palace & Royal Mews
The Mall, SW1A 1AA (7766 7300 Palace, 7766 7301 Queen's Gallery, 7766 7302 Royal Mews, www.royal collection.org.uk). Green Park tube or Victoria tube/rail. **Admission** check website for details. **Map** p67 A3 ⑯

The London home of the Queen is open to the public each year while the family are away on their summer hols; you'll be able to see the State Apartments, which are still used to entertain guests of state. At other times of year, visit the Queen's Gallery to see the Queen's personal collection of treasures, including paintings by Rembrandt, Sèvres porcelain and the Diamond Diadem crown. Further along Buckingham Palace Road, the Royal Mews is home to the royal Rolls-Royces, the splendid royal carriages and the horses that pull them.

Event highlights The Changing of the Guard (except in rain: 11.30am alternate days, daily Apr-July).

Guards Museum
Wellington Barracks, Birdcage Walk, SW1E 6HQ (7414 3428, www.the guardsmuseum.com). St James's Park tube. **Open** 10am-4pm daily. **Admission** £5; free-£2.50 reductions. **Map** p67 B3 ⑰

This small museum tells the 350-year story of the Foot Guards, using flamboyant uniforms, medals, period paintings and intriguing memorabilia, such as the stuffed body of Jacob the Goose, the Guards' Victorian mascot.

Household Cavalry Museum
Horse Guards, Whitehall, SW1A 2AX (7930 3070, www.householdcavalry museum.co.uk). Westminster tube or Charing Cross tube/rail. **Open** Mar-Sept 10am-6pm daily. Oct-Feb 10am-5pm daily. **Admission** £7; free-£5 reductions; £15 family. **Map** p67 C2 ⑱

Members of the Household Cavalry, the Queen's official guard, tell their stories through video diaries at this diverting little museum. Separated from the stables by a mere pane of glass, you'll also get a peek – and sniff – of the huge horses that parade outside.

Event highlights Changing of the Guard (except in rain: 11am Mon-Fri; 10am Sat).

St James's Park
St James's Park or Westminster tube. **Map** p67 B2 ⑲

Tate Britain p70

Many Londoners consider St James's their most beautiful park. The central lake is home to numerous species of wildfowl, including pelicans that are fed at 2.30pm daily, and the bridge gives glimpses west to the palace.

Eating & drinking

The lakeside café-restaurant in St James's Park, **Inn the Park** (7451 9999, www.innthepark.com) is wonderfully located, even if the food quality is uneven.

Boulestin

5 St James's Street, SW1A 1EF (7930 2030, www.boulestin.com). Green Park tube. **Open** 7am-3pm, 5-11pm Mon-Wed; 7am-3pm, 5-11.30pm Thur, Fri; 11.30am-4pm, 5-11.30pm Sat. £££.
French. **Map** p67 A2 ❷⓪
Named after Marcel Boulestin – a pioneer of pre-war London cooking – this new Boulestin is no relation, though it does pay homage to the era of the great chef. Classic French cooking at its best shines in dishes like daube of beef and boudin noir. A few dishes seem almost daringly modern, with their rocket and preserved lemons; but for the most part, this menu is as classic, French and retro as the grand setting.

Dukes Bar

35 St James's Place, SW1A 1NY (7491 4840, www.campbellgrayhotels.co.uk). Green Park tube. **Open** 2-11pm Mon-Sat; 4-10.30pm Sun. **Cocktail bar**. **Map** p67 A2 ❷❶
This titchy bar looks like an upper-class Georgian sitting room. Dukes' dry martinis are flamboyantly made at your table – you pay for the privilege, but this is drinking at its most elegant.

Wolseley

160 Piccadilly, W1J 9EB (7499 6996, www.thewolseley.com). Green Park tube. **Open** 7am-midnight Mon-Fri; 8am-midnight Sat, Sun. ££££.
Brasserie. **Map** p67 A1 ❷❷

In a gorgeous room, the Wolseley shimmers with 1920s glamour, its dining room filled with lively social energy and battalions of waiters. It's a sought-after venue at all times of day: breakfast, brunch, lunch, tea or dinner.

Shopping

DR Harris

29 St James's Street, SW1A 1HB (7930 3915, www.drharris.co.uk). Green Park or Piccadilly Circus tube. **Open** 8.30am-6pm Mon-Fri; 10am-5pm Sat. **Map** p67 A1 ❷❸
Founded in 1790, this venerable chemist has a royal warrant. Wood-and-glass cabinets are full of bottles, jars and old-fashioned shaving brushes. It was getting a refurb at the time of writing, and is due to re-open in mid 2015.

Fortnum & Mason

181 Piccadilly, W1A 1ER (7734 8040, www.fortnumandmason.co.uk). Green Park or Piccadilly Circus tube. **Open** 10am-8pm Mon-Sat; noon-6pm Sun. **Map** p67 A1 ❷❹
In business for over 300 years, F&M is a stunning department store: a spiral staircase sweeps through the four-storey building, light flooding down from a central glass dome. The classic eau de nil blue and gold colour scheme with flashes of rose pink is everywhere, both as decor and on the packaging of the fabulous ground-floor treats – chocolates, preserves and, of course, tea.

Arts & leisure

ICA

The Mall, SW1Y 5AH (7930 0493, 7930 3647 box office, www.ica.org.uk). Piccadilly Circus tube or Charing Cross tube/rail. **Open** *Galleries* 11am-6pm Tue, Wed, Fri-Sun; 11am-9pm Thur. **Admission** free. **Map** p67 B1 ❷❺
Founded in 1947 by an arts collective, the Institute of Contemporary Arts hosts arthouse cinema, discussions, exhibitions and edgy club nights.

Harrods p84

South Kensington & Chelsea

South Kensington

This area is home to the **Natural History Museum**, **Science Museum** and **V&A**; such is the wealth of exhibits in each you'd be foolish to try to 'do' more than one in any single day. The grandiose **Royal Albert Hall** and overblown **Albert Memorial** also pay homage to the man behind it all, with **Kensington Gardens** a refreshing green backdrop. The Gardens are also the location of Zaha Hadid's latest work: the **Serpentine Sackler** art gallery.

Sights & museums

Albert Memorial

Kensington Gardens, SW7 (7936 2568). South Kensington tube. **Map** p76 B1 ❶
An extraordinary memorial, with a 180ft spire, unveiled 15 years after Prince Albert's death. Created by Sir George Gilbert Scott, it centres on a gilded, seated Albert holding a catalogue of the 1851 Great Exhibition, guarded on four corners by Africa, America, Asia and Europe. A 45min tour points out the highlights (2pm, 3pm June-Sept 1st Sun of mth; £6, £5 reductions).

Design Museum

Kensington High Street, W8 6NQ (020 7403 6933, http://designmuseum. org). High Street Kensington tube. **Map** p76 A2 ❷
See box p81.

Kensington Palace & Kensington Gardens

Kensington Gardens, W8 4PX (0844 482 7777, 0844 482 7799 reservations, www.hrp.org.uk). High Street Kensington or Queensway tube. **Open** *Palace* Mar-Oct 10am-6pm daily. Nov-Feb 10am-5pm daily. **Admission** £16.50; free-£13.75 reductions. **Map** p76 A1 ❸

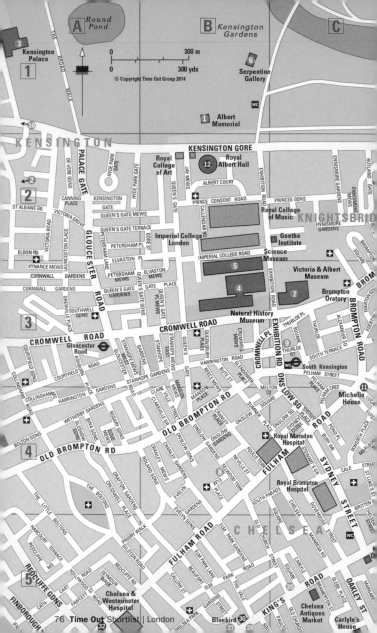

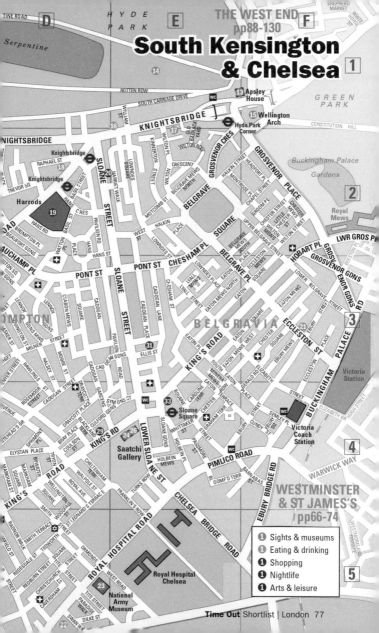

South Kensington & Chelsea

THE WEST END pp88-130
SHEPHERD MARKET
HYDE PARK
Serpentine
GREEN PARK
PINE ROAD
ROTTEN ROW
SOUTH CARRIAGE DRIVE
WILLIAM
KNIGHTSBRIDGE
Apsley House
Wellington Arch
Hyde Park Corner
CONSTITUTION HILL
Buckingham Palace Gardens
KNIGHTSBRIDGE
Knightsbridge
RAPHAEL ST
Knightsbridge
TREVOR SQ
Harrods
SLOANE STREET
LOWNDES SQUARE
WILTON PL
KINNERTON STREET
CRESCENT
BELGRAVE MEWS NORTH
GROSVENOR CRES
HALKIN STREET
HEADFORT PL
MONTROSE PL
GROSVENOR PLACE
Royal Mews
BEAUCHAMP PL
BROMPTON RD
HANS RD
C CRES
PAVILION RD
HANS ST
WEST
HALKIN
PLACE
MOTCOMB ST
LOWNDES ST
BELGRAVE SQUARE
UPPER BELGRAVE STREET
CHAPEL STREET
CHESTER STREET
LITTLE CHESTER ST
WILTON ST
WILTON MEWS
HOBART PL
GROSVENOR GDNS
LWR GROS PL
LWR GROS PL
PONT ST
CHESHAM PL
BELGRAVE PL
ECCLESTON
BELGRAVE MEWS SOUTH
EATON MEWS NORTH
LOWER BELGRAVE STREET
BROMPTON
SLOANE STREET
PONT ST
LOWNDES PLACE
EATON
BELGRAVIA
EATON SQUARE
CHESTER SQUARE
ECCLESTON STREET
ECCLESTON ST
GROSVENOR GDNS
PALACE
LENNOX
CADOGAN
PAVILION
ROAD
ELLIS ST
KING'S ROAD
EATON MEWS WEST
EATON TERRACE
MINERA MEWS
GERALD ELIZABETH
EBURY MEWS
EBURY ST
BUCKINGHAM
Victoria Station
MILNER
CADOGAN GARDENS
DRAYCOTT TERRACE
SYMONS CT
BOURNE
CAROLINE
EATON TERRACE
EBURY
SEMLEY PL
Victoria Coach Station
ROSEMOOR STREET
DRAYCOTT PLACE
Sloane Square
WHITTAKER ST
GRAHAM TERR
CUNDY STREET
King's Rd
BLACKLAND
COULSON ST
CULFORD GDNS
HOLBEIN PL
PASSMORE
PIMLICO ROAD
WARWICK WAY
ELYSTAN PLACE
BYWATER
MARKHAM SQUARE
Saatchi Gallery
HOLBEIN MEWS
CHELTENHAM TERR
WALPOLE ST
ROYAL AVE
OOMFD TERR
BARNABAS ST
EBURY BRIDGE RD
WESTMINSTER & ST JAMES'S pp66-74
KING'S ROAD
WELLINGTON SQUARE
SMITH
TEDWORTH SQUARE
WOODFALL ST
ST LEONARD'S TERRACE
TURKS ROW
FRANKLIN'S ROW
LOWER SLOANE ST
CHELSEA BRIDGE ROAD
ROYAL HOSPITAL ROAD
RADNOR WALK
REDESDALE STREET
REDBURN STREET
CHRISTCHURCH
CAVERSHAM
SMITH TERRACE
ORMONDE
TITE STREET
WEST ROAD
Royal Hospital Chelsea
National Army Museum
PARADISE WALK
DILKE ST
SWAN W

- ① Sights & museums
- ① Eating & drinking
- ① Shopping
- ① Nightlife
- ① Arts & leisure

Top: Natural History Museum;
bottom: Victoria & Albert
Museum p80

The Palace – parts of which are still occupied by royalty: William and Kate have a flat here – reopened to the public after a £12m refurbishment in 2012, with a fine new garden providing improved access from the park. It was in 1689 that William III – averse to the dank air of Whitehall Palace – relocated here, sectioning off a corner of Hyde Park for his residence. Nowadays, Kensington Gardens is delineated from Hyde Park (p83) only by the line of the Serpentine and the Long Water. It's lovelier than its easterly neighbour, with gorgeous trees, a bronze Peter Pan statue, the paddling-friendly Diana, Princess of Wales Memorial Fountain (near the Serpentine Gallery, p80) and the Diana, Princess of Wales Memorial Playground, with its massive wooden pirate ship in a vast sandpit.

The Palace itself was radically altered first by Wren and again under George I, when intricate trompe l'oeil ceilings and staircases were added. Visitors follow a whimsical trail focused on four 'stories' of former residents – Diana; William and Mary, and Mary's sister Queen Anne; Georges I and II; Queen Victoria – unearthing the facts through handily placed 'newspapers'. Artefacts include paintings by the likes of Tintoretto, contemporary art and fashion installations, and even Victoria's (tiny) wedding dress.

Natural History Museum

Cromwell Road, SW7 5BD (7942 5000, www.nhm.ac.uk). South Kensington tube. **Open** 10am-5.50pm daily. **Admission** free. *Special exhibitions prices vary.* **Map** p76 B3 ❹

The NHM opened in a magnificent, purpose-built, Romanesque palazzo in 1881. Now, the vast entrance hall is taken up by a cast of a *Diplodocus* skeleton, and to the left, the Blue Zone has a 90ft model of a blue whale and often queues as long to see the animatronic *T Rex* – get there early to minimise the wait. The Green Zone displays a

cross-section through a giant sequoia tree, as well as an amazing array of stuffed birds, among which you can compare the fingernail-sized egg of a hummingbird with an elephant bird egg as big as a football. Here too, 'Treasures' shows prime objects from the botany, entomology, mineralogy, zoology- and palaeontology collections, with a 147m-year-old fossil *Archaeopteryx* at centre-stage. Beyond is the Red Zone, where 'Earth's Treasury' is full of precious metals, gems and crystals, and 'From the Beginning' attempts to give the expanse of geological time a human perspective.

Another 22 million insect and plant specimens are housed in the Darwin Centre's white, eight-storey Cocoon, where you can watch the museum's myriad research scientists at work.

Science Museum

Exhibition Road, SW7 2DD (7942 4000, 0870 870 4868 information, www.sciencemuseum.org.uk). South Kensington tube. **Open** 10am-6pm daily. **Admission** free. *Special exhibitions* prices vary. **Map** p76 B3 ❺

Only marginally less popular with the kids than its natural historical neighbour, the Science Museum celebrates technology in the service of daily life: from Puffing Billy, the world's oldest steam locomotive (built in 1815), via classic cars, to the Apollo 10 command module, all dramatically displayed in the main hall. Upstairs in the main body of the museum, the second floor holds displays on computing, marine engineering and mathematics. Much of the third floor is dedicated to flight: stunning new flight simulators (for which you pay extra) and a terrific gallery of aviation, plus the Launchpad gallery – which features levers, pulleys, explosions and all manner of experiments for kids (an early appearance here will get you markedly more tranquil playing time). The three floors of the Wellcome wing are where the museum makes sure it stays on the cutting edge of science, with Antenna, a web-savvy look at breaking science stories, and the Who Am I? gallery, which explores genetics, brain science and psychology. There's also a new media space on the second floor, for exhibitions drawn from the museum's impressive photographic archive.

Event highlights Science Museum Lates (adult events throughout the year).

Serpentine & Serpentine Sackler Galleries

Kensington Gardens, nr Albert Memorial, W2 3XA (7402 6075, www. serpentinegallery.org). Lancaster Gate or South Kensington tube. **Open** 10am-6pm daily. **Admission** free; donations appreciated. **Map** p76 B1 ⑥

Housed in a small 1930s tea house, the Serpentine is an attractive destination for contemporary-art lovers. The rolling two-monthly programme of exhibitions features a mix of up-to-the-minute artists and edgy career retrospectives.

In 2013 the gallery underwent a massive expansion – opening a second location, the Serpentine Sackler, just north across the bridge. Devoted to emerging art in all forms, the Sackler is a Grade-II listed, Palladian former gunpowder store, over the restaurant area of which starchitect Zaha Hadid has cast a billowing white cape of roof.

Event highlights Serpentine Pavilion (June-Sept): built by an internationally renowned architect each summer to host cultural events.

Victoria & Albert Museum

Cromwell Road, SW7 2RL (7942 2000, www.vam.ac.uk). South Kensington tube. **Open** 10am-5.45pm Mon-Thur, Sat, Sun; 10am-10pm Fri. *Tours* 10.30am, 12.30pm, 1.30pm, 3.30pm daily. **Admission** free. *Special exhibitions* prices vary. **Map** p76 C3 ⑦

The V&A is a superb showcase for applied arts from around the world, and its brilliant FuturePlan programme has revealed some stunning new galleries – not least the wonderfully visual Medieval & Renaissance Galleries a few years back. The latest grand opening, set for December 2014, is the ambitious Europe 1600-1800 galleries, with seven new galleries taking both a chronological and a thematic approach to European clothes, furnishings and other artefacts. Pieces created for Louis XIV and Marie Antoinette in France and Catherine the Great in Russia will be exhibited, as well as recreated interiors and court rooms. Meanwhile, the magnificent double-height Cast Courts are being restored to their Victorian splendour: 46a has reopened; 46b will follow. They contain full-scale casts of Classical monuments (among them Trajan's Column) and European sculpture, including an 18ft cast of Michelangelo's *David*.

Among the unmissable highlights of the collections are the seven Raphael Cartoons (painted in 1515 as Sistine Chapel tapestry designs), the Great Bed of Ware and the splendid Ardabil carpet, the world's oldest floor covering. On the first floor are the Theatre and Performance Galleries, the William & Judith Bollinger Gallery of European jewellery (including diamonds that belonged to Catherine the Great) and the Gilbert Collection of gold snuffboxes and urns. There are also some superb architectural models.

Eating & drinking

The trio of tea rooms at the **V&A** are just a chandelier or two different from how they were in the 19th century – oh, and self-service these days. The Lido café in **Hyde Park** (p83) is also good.

Anglesea Arms

15 Selwood Terrace, SW7 3QG (7373 7960, www.capitalpub company.com). South Kensington tube.

A new Design

Conran's museum moves to a building that is itself a classic.

Throughout his career, Terence Conran has been a pioneer of great a century ago, that London must have a Design Museum. The museum (p52) opened in 1989, in one of the warehouses of Shad Thames that had been left dilapidated when major shipping left the Pool of London. The premises were soon unrecognisable, as a clean-lined white building emerged from the fabric of a 1940s banana warehouse.

Now, Sir Terence is helping the Design Museum move to a new phase – with a £17.5m donation towards new premises in the former Commonwealth Institute in Kensington High Street.

It was the arrival of new director Deyan Sudjic, in 2006, that sharpened the focus on ambitious expansion plans: for one thing, there had never been enough room to show off the museum's own design collection. It was under Sudjic's auspices that eyes turned to the disused Commonwealth Institute, closed since 2002. The Grade II*-listed building is a distinctive sight, built to look like a tent, with a remarkable hyperbolic paraboloid roof (made of 25 tonnes of copper mined in what is now Zimbabwe). The museum bought the Institute in 2010, and the Shad Thames building has since been sold to Zaha Hadid Architects. (Hadid has history with the museum, which hosted her first UK solo show in 2007.)

The new museum (p75) has been designed by John Pawson, at a cost of £80m, and is scheduled to open at the end of 2015. As well as bringing a classic modernist building back into use – appropriate for a design museum – the conversion will create three times as much gallery space than at Shad Thames, and the museum hopes to increase visitor numbers from 200,000 to 500,000 per year. And access to part of the collection will be free. You can watch work in progress on newdesignmuseumtumblr.com.

Open 11am-11pm Mon-Sat; 11am-10.30pm Sun. **Pub**. Map p76 B4 ❽

Formerly the local of both Charles Dickens and DH Lawrence, this old boozer is packed tight on summer evenings, the front terrace and main bar filled with professional blokes chugging ale, and their female equivalents putting bottles of Sancerre on expenses. But it has more aura than the average South Ken hostelry: perhaps it's the link with the Great Train Robbery, which was reputedly planned here.

Daquise

20 Thurloe Street, SW7 2LT (7589 6117, www.daquise.co.uk). South Kensington tube. **Open** noon-11pm daily. **££**. **Polish**. Map p76 C3 ❾

This much-loved grande dame of Polish restaurants (established in 1947) was saved from closure by staff and previous owners. In the shabby chic, light and airy interior, robust, flavourful, traditional dishes are served with great charm. Classic cold starters of tender herring with cream apple, onion and flax oil, or beetroot with subtly warming horseradish, are ladled directly from spacious earthenware bowls, while mains are assembled directly at table from well-worn saucepans.

Yashin

1A Argyll Road, W8 7DB (7938 1536, www.yashinsushi.com). High Street Kensington tube. **Open** noon-2.15pm, 6-10pm daily. **££**. **Sushi**. Map p76 A1 ❿

In a discreet location just off Kensington High Street, Yashin has a modern eclectic look and superior sushi. Behind the green-tiled sushi counter, a neon sign states 'without soy sauce – if you want to', a reference to the fact that the chefs disapprove of the salty sauce masking their sushi. Instead, the industrious throng of *itamae* (sushi chefs) finish their nigiri with a drizzle of truffle oil, a quick

blast from a blowtorch or some other carefully considered garnish.

Shopping

Conran Shop

Michelin House, 81 Fulham Road, SW3 6RD (7589 7401, www.conranshop.co.uk). South Kensington tube. **Open** 10am-6pm Mon, Tue, Fri; 10am-7pm Wed, Thur; 10am-6.30pm Sat; noon-6pm Sun. Map p76 C4 ⓫

Sir Terence Conran's flagship store in this lovely 1909 building showcases furniture and design for every room in the house, and the garden. Portable accessories, gadgets, books, stationery and toiletries make great gifts.

Arts & leisure

Royal Albert Hall

Kensington Gore, SW7 2AP (7589 3203, 0845 401 5045 box office, www.royalalberthall.com). South Kensington tube or bus 9, 10, 52, 452. Map p76 B2 ⓬

In constant use since 1871, with boxing matches, motorshows and Allen Ginsberg's 1965 International Poetry Incarnation among the headline events, the Royal Albert Hall continues to host a very broad programme. The classical side is dominated by the superb Proms, which sees a huge array of ensembles battling the difficult acoustics. It's well worth catching a concert that features the thunderous Grand Organ.

Event highlights The BBC Proms (mid July-mid Sept).

Knightsbridge

Knightsbridge is about designer shops, many of them along Sloane Street, which leads down to Sloane Square, as well as a pair of landmark department stores, **Harrods** (p84) and **Harvey Nichols** (109-125 Knightsbridge, SW1X 7RJ, 7235 5000, www.harveynichols.com).

Sights & museums

Apsley House

149 Piccadilly, W1J 7NT (7499 5676, www.english-heritage.org.uk). Hyde Park Corner tube. **Open** *Nov-Mar* 10am-4pm Sat, Sun. *Apr-Oct* 11am-5pm Wed-Sun. **Admission** £6.90; £5.30-£6.20 reductions. **Map** p77 E1 ⑬

Called No.1 London because it was the first London building encountered on the road to the City from Kensington village, Apsley House was the Duke of Wellington's residence for 35 years. His descendants still live here, but several rooms are open to the public and give a superb feel for the man and his era. **Event highlights** Twilight tours show off the chandeliers to great effect.

Hyde Park

7298 2000, www.royalparks.gov.uk. Hyde Park Corner, Lancaster Gate or Marble Arch tube. **Map** p77 E1 ⑭

One of the largest Royal Parks, Hyde Park is 1.5 miles long and a mile wide. It was a hotspot for demonstrations in the 19th century and remains so – a 2003 march against the Iraq War that ended in the park was the largest in British history. The legalisation of public assembly here led to the creation of Speakers' Corner in 1872 (near Marble Arch tube), where political and religious ranters still have the floor on Sunday afternoons, and Marx, Orwell and the Pankhursts once spoke; it was given a spruce up in 2014. Rowing boats can be hired on the Serpentine – but adjoining Kensington Gardens (p75) is really much prettier.

Wellington Arch

Hyde Park Corner, W1J 7JZ (7930 2726, www.english-heritage.org.uk). Hyde Park Corner tube. **Open** *Apr-Oct* 10am-5pm daily. *Nov-Mar* 10am-4pm daily. **Admission** £4.20; free-£3.80 reductions. **Map** p77 F1 ⑮

Built in the 1820s as a triumphal arch to mark Britain's victory over Napoleonic France and initially topped by a vast statue of Wellington; since 1912 the bronze *Peace Descending* has finished the Arch with a flourish. Inside, there's a new exhibition on the first floor about the arch's history, and an additional exhibition space, the Quadriga Gallery, hosting temporary exhibitions exploring diverse aspects of the history and heritage of England. There's also an English Heritage shop on site.

Eating & drinking

Bar Boulud

Mandarin Oriental Hyde Park, 66 Knightsbridge, SW1X 7LA (7201 3899, http://danielnyc.com/restaurants). Knightsbridge tube. **Open** noon-11pm Mon-Sat; noon-10pm Sun. **£££**. **Brasserie**. **Map** p77 E1 ⑯

It's within the luxe Mandarin Oriental Hotel, but you don't have to be minted to eat at this superb bistro. A winning informality prevails over a room that is always busy. The burgers are among the best in town: try the trademark 'BB', where the patty is topped by a layer of short-ribs (braised in red wine), a slice of foie gras and a truffle garnish.

Blue Bar

The Berkeley, Wilton Place, SW1X 7RL (7235 6000, www.the-berkeley.co.uk). Hyde Park Corner tube. **Open** 4pm-1am Mon-Sat; 4-11pm Sun. **Cocktail bar**. **Map** p77 E2 ⑰

This David Collins-designed bar lives up to its name: sky-blue bespoke armchairs, deep-blue ornate plasterwork and navy-blue leather-bound menus combine with discreet lighting to striking effect. It's more a see and be seen place than somewhere to kick back, but don't let the celeb-heavy reputation put you off: the staff treat all customers like royalty and the cocktail-making is a masterclass.

Zuma

5 Raphael Street, SW7 1DL (7584 1010, www.zumarestaurant.com).

Knightsbridge tube. **Open** *Restaurant*
noon-2.45pm, 6-10.45pm Mon-Fri; 12.30-
3.15pm, 6-10.45m Sat, Sun. *Bar* noon-
11pm Mon-Fri; 12.30-11pm Sat, Sun.
££££. Japanese fusion/bar.
Map p77 D2 ⓲
There's been no recession at this ultra-
chic destination, where the bar and
dining room buzz with well-heeled
diners. The interior design is earthy,
with stone flooring and cedar-wood
furniture. Sushi and sashimi are of
Premier League quality, the raw tuna
belly and sea urchin being notable
gems. An impressively diverse saké list
tops it off.

Shopping

Harrods
*87-135 Brompton Road, SW1X 7XL
(7730 1234, www.harrods.com).
Knightsbridge tube.* **Open** 10am-
8pm Mon-Sat; noon-6pm Sun.
Map p77 D2 ⓳
All the glitz and marble can be a bit
much, but this is a store that boasts
of selling everything – so a browse is
always entertaining. The food halls
are legendary, but it's on the fashion
floors that Harrods comes into its
own, with well-edited collections from
the heavyweight designers – and an
impressive shoe department.

Tom Ford
*201-202 Sloane Street, SW1X 9QX
(3141 7800, www.tomford.com).
Knightsbridge tube.* **Open** 10am-6pm
Mon-Sat; noon-6pm Sun. **Map** p75 D2 ⓴
Just when Sloane Street's reputation
for boutiques that are expensive
but hardly classy seemed secure, up
rocks the coolest man in fashion. No
one who knows Ford's suave tailoring
will be surprised that his first stand-
alone store in Britain is stunning,
with an eye-catchingly sci-fi spiral
staircase the centrepiece. Expect
big labels for gents, hip-hugging
skirts and dresses for ladies – and
consummate good taste.

Belgravia & Pimlico

This area is characterised by a host
of embassies and the fact that many
of the people living here are very
rich. Enjoy strolling through tiny
mews, then settle into some plush
dining, drinking or shopping.

Eating & drinking

Boisdale
*13-15 Eccleston Street, SW1W 9LX
(7730 6922, www.boisdale.co.uk).
Victoria tube/rail.* **Open** noon-1am Mon-
Fri; 6pm-1am Sat. **Admission** free
before 10pm, then £12. **Whisky bar**.
Map p77 F3 ㉑
From the labyrinthine bar and
restaurant spaces and heated cigar
terrace to overstated tartan accents,
Boisdale is a brilliantly preposterous
spot. After all, it's hard not to love a
posh, Scottish-themed enterprise that
specialises in single-malt whiskies.
Live jazz six nights a week is another
of its attractions.

Chelsea

It's been five decades since *Time*
magazine declared that London
– by which it meant the **King's
Road** – was 'swinging'. These
days you're more likely to find
suburban swingers wondering
where it went than the next Jean
Shrimpton, but there are some
good shops and attractions.

Sights & museums

Chelsea Physic Garden
*66 Royal Hospital Road, SW3 4HS
(7352 5646, www.chelseaphysicgarden.
co.uk). Sloane Square tube or bus 11,
19, 22.* **Open** *Apr-June, Oct* 11am-6pm
Tue-Fri, Sun. *July, Aug* 11am-6pm Mon,
Tue, Thur, Fri, Sun; 11am-10pm Wed.
Tours times vary; phone to check.
Admission £9.90; free-£6.60
reductions. **Map** p77 D5 ㉒

Chelsea Physic Garden

The capacious grounds of this gorgeous, historic botanic garden are filled with healing herbs and vegetables, rare trees and dye plants. The garden was founded in 1673 by Sir Hans Sloane with the purpose of cultivating and studying plants for medical purposes. The new medicinal garden area gives fascinating information on medicinal plants, some of which have been used for thousands of years – various poisonous ones are helpfully marked with a skull – but don't miss the ancient glasshouse with filmy ferns.

National Army Museum

Royal Hospital Road, SW3 4HT (7730 0717, www.national-army-museum.ac.uk). Sloane Square tube or bus 11, 137, 170. **Open** 10am-5.30pm daily. **Admission** free. **Map** p77 D5 ㉓

More entertaining than its dull exterior suggests, this museum of the history of the British Army tells the story of the individual soldier's life. The Redcoats gallery covers the Army's formative years under leaders such as Cromwell and the Duke of Cumberland, known as the 'Butcher of Culloden'. Among the exhibits is the pencil-written scrap of paper that launched the Charge of the Light Brigade in 1854.

Saatchi Gallery

Duke of York's HQ, King's Road, SW3 4RY (7811 3070, www.saatchi-gallery.co.uk). Sloane Square tube. **Open** 10am-6pm daily. **Admission** free. **Map** p77 E4 ㉔

Charles Saatchi's gallery has three floors, providing more than 50,000sq ft of space for temporary exhibitions that generally show Saatchi's taste is broader than his reputation as a champion of Brit Art suggests. Still, some of his famous British acquisitions – notably Richard Wilson's brilliant sump-oil installation *20:50* – remain.

Eating & drinking

The art deco **Bluebird** (350 King's Road, SW3 5UU, 7559 1000, www.bluebird-restaurant.co.uk) has a modern European eatery, as well as the lovely **Shop** (p87).

Cadogan Arms

298 King's Road, SW3 5UG (7352 6500, www.thecadoganarmschelsea.com). Sloane Square tube then bus 19, 22, 319. **Open** 11am-11pm Mon-Sat; 11am-10.30pm Sun. **Gastropub**. **Map** p76 C5 ㉕

This renovated 19th-century pub has a countrified look, complete with stuffed animals and fly-fishing displays. It remains a proper boozer, with top-quality real ales, notwithstanding the snug and smoothly run dining area, where great food is on offer.

Gallery Mess

Saatchi Gallery, Duke of York's HQ, King's Road, SW3 4LY (7730 8135, www.saatchigallery.com/gallerymess). Sloane Square tube. **Open** 10am-11.30pm Mon-Sat; 10am-7pm Sun. **££. Brasserie. Map** p77 E4 ㉖

The Saatchi Gallery (p86) is home to a great brasserie. There's a simple breakfast menu (pastries, eggs, fry-ups) to 11.30am, then lunch and dinner take over, with salads, pastas and burgers joined by daily specials: perhaps steamed salmon served in a yellow 'curry' broth, or saddle of lamb drizzled with yoghurt. You can sit inside surrounded by modern art, or head to the portable tables (until 6pm in fair weather) outside.

Medlar

438 King's Road, SW10 0LJ (7349 1900, www.medlarrestaurant.co.uk). Fulham Broadway tube or bus 11, 22. **Open** noon-3pm, 6.30-10.30pm daily. **££. Modern European**. **Map** p76 B5 ㉗

Medlar's seasonal menu and wine list are close to perfection. Roast hake with summer bean ragoût and palourde clams followed by raspberry and frangipane tart are typical of the dishes relished by Chelsea's lunching ladies. Staff are exemplary and the experience is very civilised.

Mona Lisa

417 King's Road, SW10 0LR (7378 5447). Fulham Broadway tube or bus 11,22. **Open** *6.30am-11pm Mon-Sat; 8.30am-5.30pm Sun.* **£. Italian/café.** **Map** p76 B5 ㉓
Not much to look at, Mona Lisa is hidden away at the 'wrong' end of the King's Road, just beyond World's End. But its bonhomie is infectious, and if you order the right thing, such as the meltingly tender calf's liver *alla salvia* (with butter and sage) served with old-school potatoes and veg, and you won't care about the homely decor. The menu ranges across breakfasts, sandwiches, burgers, omelettes, jacket potatoes and pastas to three course blow-outs.

Shopping

John Sandoe

10 Blacklands Terrace, SW3 2SR (7589 9473, www.johnsandoe.com). Sloane Square tube. **Open** *9.30am-6.30pm Mon-Sat; 11am-5pm Sun.* **Map** p77 D4 ㉙
Tucked away on a Chelsea side street, this 50-year-old independent looks just as a bookshop should. The stock is literally packed to the rafters, and of the 25,000 books here, 24,000 are a single copy – so there's serious breadth.

Shop at Bluebird

350 King's Road, SW3 5UU (7351 3873, www.theshopatbluebird.com). Sloane Square tube. **Open** *10am-7pm Mon-Sat; noon-6pm Sun.* **Map** p76 B5 ㉚
Part lifestyle boutique and part design gallery, the Shop at Bluebird offers a shifting showcase of clothing for men, women and children (Emma Cook, Peter Jensen, Marc Jacobs), accessories, furniture and gadgets. The place has a bit of a retro feel, all vintage furniture, reupholstered seats and hand-printed fabrics.

Arts & leisure

Cadogan Hall

5 Sloane Terrace, SW1X 9DQ (7730 4500, www.cadoganhall.com). Sloane Square tube. **Map** p77 E3 ㉛
Built as a Christian Science church, this austere building is now a light, airy auditorium. Programming at the 900-capacity venue is mainly classical (the Royal Philharmonic is resident), and the acoustics are excellent.

Chelsea Football Club

Stamford Bridge, Fulham Road, SW6 1HS (0871 984 1905, www. chelseafc.com). Fulham Broadway tube. **Map** p76 A5 ㉜
Having won the 2011/12 Champions League and 2012/13 Europa League, but subsided a little in domestic competition, Chelsea were pleased to welcome back their most successful manager, Jose Mourinho – who didn't quite steer them back to first place in 2013/14. You're unlikely to get tickets to see any league action, but you can visit the excellent museum or check online for tickets to European matches or cup ties against lower league opposition. And the Under the Bridge nightclub beneath the stadium hosts some outstanding gigs.

Royal Court Theatre

Sloane Square, SW1W 8AS (7565 5000, www.royalcourttheatre.com). Sloane Square tube. **Map** p77 E4 ㉝
From John Osborne's *Look Back in Anger*, staged in the theatre's opening year of 1956, to its many recent discoveries (Sarah Kane, Joe Penhall, Polly Stenham), the emphasis at the Royal Court has always been on new voices in British theatre. Vicky Featherstone, who took over as artistic director in 2013, has continued the tradition, with a play by Abi Morgan among her early productions.

LONDON BY AREA

Piccadilly Circus p95

The West End

Oxford Street & north

There is relentless trade on Oxford Street, home to hip **Selfridges**, doughty **John Lewis** and chain flagships for **Uniqlo** and **Topshop**, but few locals esteem the historic thoroughfare. Despite the Shibuya-style diagonal crossing at Oxford Circus, perhaps an inkling of future improvements, clogged pavements make for unpleasant shopping. Escape the crowds among the pretty boutiques on **Marylebone High Street** to the north. Among the sights, the **Wallace** is too often overlooked, and **Regent's Park** is one of London's finest green spaces.

Sights & museums

Madame Tussauds

Marylebone Road, NW1 5LR (0870 400 3000, www.madametussauds.com/london). Baker Street tube. **Open** times vary; check website for details.

Admission £30; free-£25.80 reductions; £108 family. **Map** p89 A1 ❶

Madame Tussaud brought her show to London in 1802, 32 years after it was founded in Paris, and it's been here since 1884. There are 300 figures in the collection now, under various themes: 'A-list Party' (Brad, Keira, Kate Moss), 'Première Night' (Monroe, Chaplin, Arnie), 'By Royal Appointment' and so on. In the Chamber of Horrors in 'Scream', only teens claim to enjoy the floor drops and scary special effects; they're similarly keen on the Iron Man, Spiderman and an 18ft Hulk in Marvel Super Heroes 4D. Get here before 10am to avoid huge queues, and book ahead online to make prices more palatable.

Regent's Park

Baker Street or Regent's Park tube. **Open** 5am-dusk daily. **Map** p89 B1 ❷

Regent's Park is one of London's most popular open spaces. Attractions run from the animal noises and odours of London Zoo (p150) to enchanting Open

Marylebone & Mayfair

Sights & museums
Eating & drinking
Shopping
Nightlife
Arts & leisure

Numbered locations refer to the Marylebone and Mayfair sections on pp88-99.

Regent's Park p88

Air Theatre versions of *A Midsummer Night's Dream* that are an integral part of a London summer. Hire a rowing boat on the lake or take a stroll through the rose garden.

Wallace Collection

Hertford House, Manchester Square, W1U 3BN (7935 0687, www.wallace collection.org). Bond Street tube. **Open** 10am-5pm daily. **Admission** free. **Map** p89 A2 ❸

This handsome house, built in 1776 and being steadily returned to its original state after 'improvements' in previous generations, has an exceptional collection of 18th-century French paintings and objets d'art, as well as armour and weapons. Rooms contain Louis XIV and XV furnishings and Sèvres porcelain, but the real highlight is the Great Gallery – due to reopen after major refurbishment in late September 2014 – which is hung with such masterpieces as Franz Hals's *Laughing Cavalier*, Rubens' *Rainbow Landscape*, Poussin's *Dance to the Music of Time* and Velazquez's *Lady with a Fan*. You'll also find work by Titian, Gainsborough and Fragonard.

Eating & drinking

Busaba Eathai

8-13 Bird Street, W1U 1BU (7518 8080, www.busaba.com). Bond Street tube. **Open** noon-11pm Mon-Thur; noon-11.30pm Fri, Sat; noon-10pm Sun. **££.Thai. Map** p89 B3 ❹

All the branches of this handsome Thai canteen are excellent and busy, but this one is superbly located for Oxford Street shoppers. Interiors in all branches combine shared tables and bench seats with a touch of dark-toned oriental mystique, and the dishes are always intriguing and well executed.

Chiltern Firehouse

NEW *1 Chiltern Street, W1U 7PA (7073 7676, www.chilternfirehouse. com). Bond Street or Baker Street tube.*
Open 5-11pm Mon-Fri; 11am-3pm, 6-11pm Sat, Sun. **££££. Modern European. Map** p89 A2 ❺

Becoming the latest place to see and be seen soon after opening, the Chiltern Firehouse produces brilliant food in tune with international trends under the auspices of chef Nuno Mendes. The kitchen can do fiddly and pretty, exemplified by stunning appetisers. But good flavour combinations and modern cooking techniques are also to the fore in dishes like monkfish cooked in a sealed pan using hot charcoal and fresh pine, with the pine aroma infusing the flesh. The best seats are at the kitchen counter, where you can watch the chefs at work in their lavishly appointed open kitchen.

Fischer's

NEW *50 Marylebone High Street, W1U 5HN (020 7466 5501, www.fischers. co.uk). Bond Street tube.* **Open** 8am-11pm Mon-Sat; 8am-10.30pm Sun. **£££. Austrian. Map** p89 B1 ❻

The pair behind this venture, Chris Corbin and Jeremy King, previously opened the Wolseley (p74), the Delaunay (p124), and – way back in 1990 – the legendary Ivy (now no longer theirs). The interior is another permutation of the European Grand Café that they have made their signature, but with some 20th-century modern-art touches that evoke a sense of place. Classic Viennese dishes are present and correct: a bismarck herring starter with preserved vegetables; wiener schnitzel, and würstchen (sausages) with proper sauerkraut and caramelised onions.

La Fromagerie

2-6 Moxon Street, W1U 4EW (7935 0341, www.lafromagerie.co.uk). Baker Street or Bond Street tube. **Open** 8am-7.30pm Mon-Fri; 9am-7pm Sat; 10am-6pm Sun. **££. Café. Map** p89 A2 ❼

Famed with foodies for its dedicated cheese room, Patricia Michelson's high-end deli also dishes out freshly cooked, stylish café food. Its communal tables are often packed with devotees.

LONDON BY AREA

Golden Hind

73 Marylebone Lane, W1U 2PN (7486 3644). Bond Street tube. **Open** noon-3pm, 6-10pm Mon-Fri; 6-10pm Sat. **£.**
Fish & chips. Map p89 B2 **8**

The pastel-hued art deco fryer at this chip shop is only used to store menus these days (the cooking's done in a back kitchen), but the Golden Hind still oozes local character. Big portions hit the spot, and the staff really make a fuss of customers.

Purl

50 Blandford Street, W1U 7HX (7935 0835, www.purl-london.com). Bond Street tube. **Open** 5-11.30pm Mon-Thur; 5pm-midnight Fri, Sat. **Bar. Map** p89 A2 **9**

The four young chaps behind this speakeasy-style cocktail bar claim inspiration from the golden age of bartending. Accordingly, a lot of effort goes into each drink: for Mr Hyde's Fixer Upper, a hand-held food smoker pipes applewood smoke into a flask of rum, cola reduction and orange bitters. The flask is then sealed with candlewax before being served with a goblet. Booking advisable.

Roti Chai

3-4 Portman Mews South, W1H 6HS (7408 0101, www.rotichai.com). Marble Arch tube. **Open** noon-10.30pm Mon-Sat; 12.30-9pm Sun. **£. Indian. Map** p89 A3 **10**

Roti Chai ('bread, tea') is dedicated to serving inexpensive, café-style Indian food. It does so with panache. The menu offers street snacks from across India: from crisp bhel pooris to steamed dokhla (a savoury sponge with coconut chutney), from a punchy railway lamb curry to a pungent Bengali fish curry.

Shopping

The major department stores still hold sway over Oxford Street, but only one of the mammoth West End music stores remains: **HMV** (363 Oxford Street, W1C 2LA, 0843 221 0200, www.hmv.com), now back in its original 1921 location.

Burberry

121 Regent Street, W1B 4TB (7806 8904, http://uk.burberry.com). Oxford Circus tube. **Open** 10am-8pm Mon-Sat; noon-6pm Sun. **Map** p89 C4 **11**

Burberry's has transformed an 1820 property into an all-mod-conned 'brand experience', where 500 speakers and 100 screens, plus interactive mirrors and digital signage, regale customers with sights, sounds and information as they 'experience' the store. The full range of menswear, womenswear, accessories, footwear and beauty is here as well as exclusive lines and a bespoke trench coat service.

John Lewis

300 Oxford Street, W1CA 1DX (7629 7711, www.johnlewis.co.uk). Bond Street or Oxford Circus tube. **Open** 9.30am-8pm Mon-Wed, Fri; 9.30am-9pm Thur; 9.30am-7pm Sat; noon-6pm Sun. **Map** p89 B3 **12**

Renowned for solid reliability, the courtesy of its staff and its 'never knowingly undersold' policy, John Lewis also deserves a medal for breadth of stock. The store is also a destination for those in search of fabrics and haberdashery. To celebrate its 150th anniversary in 2014, a new roof garden was opened.

Marylebone High Street

Bond Street or Baker Street tube. **Map** p89 B2 **13**

With tube stations at its top and bottom, this is one of the most accessible shopping streets in town. Browse the likes of handsome Edwardian bookshop Daunt (nos.83-84), the design classics at Skandium (no.86), glorious French cakes at Pâtisserie des Rêves (no.43) and Kabiri's avant-garde jewellery (no.37). Branch off on to Marylebone Lane for 1950s timewarp café Paul Rothe & Son (no.35), via high-fashion artisan shoes at Tracey Neuls (no.29) and the nicely curated designer clothes of KJ's Laundry (no.74).

LONDON BY AREA

THE WALLACE COLLECTION

Take your own Grand Tour

Experience wonderful art from around the world
in one beautiful, central London setting

1st Stop:
Italy

Canaletto, *Venice: the Grand Canal from the Palazzo Foscari to the Carità*, Italy, c. 1740 – 1750, detail

Selfridges

400 Oxford Street, W1A 1AB (0800 123 400, www.selfridges.com). Bond Street or Marble Arch tube. **Open** 9.30am-8pm Mon-Wed, Fri, Sat; 9.30am-9pm Thur; noon-6.15pm Sun. **Map** p89 A3 ⓮

With its plethora of concession boutiques and collections from the hottest brands, Selfridges is as dynamic as a department store could be. While the basement is chock full of hip home accessories and stylish kitchen equipment, it's the fashion floors that really get hearts racing, with a winning combination of new talent, hip and edgy labels, high-street brands and high-end designers. Highlights include the extensive Shoe Galleries, while the 3rd Central contemporary collection is where you'll find the hippest brands of the day. Hits on Level 4 include the new Toy Shop. See also box p97.

Topshop

214 Oxford Street, W1W 8LG (0844 848 7487, www.topshop.com). Oxford Circus tube. **Open** 9am-9pm Mon-Sat; 11.30am-6pm Sun. **Map** p89 C3 ⓯

Topshop's massive, throbbing flagship is a teenage Hades at weekends, but there is absolutely nowhere on the high street that's more on-trend. You'll find a boutique of high-fashion designer capsule ranges, vintage clothes, and even a Hersheson hairstylist and a Metalmorphosis tattoo parlour among cheap and well-cut jeans, and all manner of other temptations. Topman is catching up with its sister, stocking niche labels such as Garbstore, and housing a trainer boutique, a suit section and a new personal shopping suite. Both shops are even more of a hive of activity during Fashion Week (p35, p39), when events are held here.

Arts & leisure

Wigmore Hall

36 Wigmore Street, W1U 2BP (7935 2141, www.wigmore-hall.org.uk). Bond Street tube. **Map** p89 B2 ⓰

Built in 1901 as the display hall for Bechstein Pianos, but now boasting perfect acoustics, art nouveau decor and an excellent basement restaurant, the Wigmore is one of the world's top chamber-music venues.

Mayfair

Mayfair has long meant money, but these days not necessarily stuffy exclusivity, with even the tailors of **Savile Row** loosening their ties.

Sights & museums

Handel House Museum

25 Brook Street (entrance Lancashire Court), W1K 4HB (7399 1953, www.handelhouse.org). Bond Street tube. **Open** 10am-6pm Tue, Wed, Fri, Sat; 10am-8pm Thur; noon-6pm Sun. **Admission** £6.50; free-£5.50 reductions. **Map** p89 B3 ⓱

George Frideric Handel settled in this Mayfair house aged 37, remaining here until his death in 1759. The house has been beautifully restored with original and recreated furnishings, paintings and a welter of the composer's scores (along with photos of Jimi Hendrix, who lived next door – the Hendrix flat is to be restored as another attraction, perhaps to open in autumn 2015). There are recitals every Thursday.

Piccadilly Circus

Map p89 C4 ⓲

Piccadilly Circus has undergone a £14m revamp, with ugly pedestrian-funnelling and cyclist-shredding railings ripped out, but there's really no reason to stop here other than to say you have. Even the famous illuminated advertising panels, technically here since the late 19th century, are these days fired by LEDs rather than neon. Do nip east to look at Albert Gilbert's memorial fountain in honour of child-labour abolitionist Earl Shaftesbury. Erected in 1893, the statue on top represents the Angel of Christian Charity,

LONDON BY AREA

but critics and public alike recognised it as Eros, and the name stuck. It's now encased in a 'snow-globe' each festive period – to stop the damage by drunks.

Royal Academy of Arts

Burlington House, Piccadilly, W1J 0BD (7300 8000, www.royalacademy.org.uk). Green Park or Piccadilly Circus tube. **Open** 10am-6pm Mon-Thur, Sat, Sun; 10am-10pm Fri. **Admission** free. *Special exhibitions* prices vary. **Map** p89 C4 ⑲

Britain's first art school, founded in 1768, moved to the extravagantly Palladian Burlington House a century later, but it's now best known not for education but for exhibitions. You'll have to pay for blockbuster exhibitions in the Sackler Wing or main galleries, but shows in the John Madejski Fine Rooms – from the RA's own impressive holdings, which include the UK's only marble sculpture by Michelangelo – are free. The RA now also has a very grand exhibition space nearby at 6 Burlington Gardens.

Event highlights Summer Exhibition (June-Aug).

Eating & drinking

Bentley's Oyster Bar & Grill

11-15 Swallow Street, W1B 4DG (7734 4756, www.bentleys.org). Piccadilly Circus tube. **Open** *Oyster Bar* noon-midnight Mon-Sat; noon-10pm Sun. *Restaurant* noon-3pm, 5.30-10.45pm Mon-Fri; 5.30-10.45pm Sat. **££££**. **Fish & seafood**. **Map** p89 C4 ⑳

There's something timeless about Richard Corrigan's restoration of this classic oyster house, which first opened its doors in 1916. While the first-floor dining rooms are more sedate and well mannered, the downstairs oyster bar is where the action is.

Burger & Lobster

29 Clarges Street, W1J 7EF (7409 1699, www.burgerandlobster.com). Green Park tube. **Open** noon-10.30pm Mon-Sat; 10am-5.30pm Sun. **££**. **North American**. **Map** p89 B4 ㉑

It isn't hard to decide what to eat at Burger & Lobster: you can have burger, lobster or lobster roll. A pub-style chalkboard at the entrance explains the menu: 'Burger or lobster or lobster roll, all with chips & salad, £20'. Upbeat and enthusiastic service adds to the lively din, and there's a distinct lack of stuffiness – it's hard to be formal when you're all wearing plastic bibs.

Gymkhana

NEW *42 Albemarle Street, W1S 4JH (3011 5900, www.gymkhanalondon. com). Green Park tube.* **Open** noon-2.45pm, 5.30-10.30pm Mon-Sat. **£££**. Indian. **Map** p89 C4 ㉒

Much-lauded Gymkhana looks and feels like an Indian colonial club, with its retro ceiling fans, marble-topped tables and polo and cricket team photos. It serves a splendid spread of modern Indian dishes based on regional masalas and marinades: the likes of Goan pork vindaloo – slow-cooked chunks of suckling pig cheek with a vinegary red chilli and garlic masala, spiced with sweet cinnamon and pounded coriander.

Scott's

20 Mount Street, W1K 2HE (7495 7309, www.scotts-restaurant.com). Bond Street or Green Park tube. **Open** noon-10.30pm Mon-Sat; noon-10pm Sun. **££££**. **Fish & seafood**. **Map** p89 B4 ㉓

Of the capital's celeb hangouts, Scott's is the one that most justifies the hype: from the greeting by the doorman to the look-at-me contemporary British art on the walls and the glossy Rich List crowd. The food – perhaps tiny boar sausages with chilled rock oysters – keeps right on getting better.

Shopping

Despite the arrival of US import Abercrombie & Fitch a few years ago, bespoke tailoring is managing to hold out on **Savile Row** – but there isn't much to see if you're not getting a suit made.

West End winner

Time Out's top store, Selfridges, gets a makeover.

In our recent Top 100 list of London shops, **Selfridges** (p96) came out as no.1. The reason it took the shopping crown is that it really is for everyone – alongside its designer labels and luxurious services it has clip-in hair extensions, cheapo nail bars and a ground floor bursting with fashion that is well within the reach of a teenager's purse.

It even starred in a television series about its genesis – a period drama focusing on founder Harry Gordon Selfridge, whose mantra 'Selfridges is for everyone' seems to have impacted on the store more than ever in recent times. There is always something happening, whether a shoe-tattooing service or the best make-up artist in the world doing free lippy applications.

If you can't find something to buy in Selfridges you simply aren't looking hard enough. In June 2013, it unveiled what is unquestionably the capital's best denim department on the third floor – a vast sweep of jeans that runs the gamut from Primark skinnies at £11 a pair to ludicrous diamond-encrusted Paige bootcuts at £11,000. It's hard to imagine another department store putting aside snobbery

and allowing a raft of Primark products on their shop floor.

Also in 2013, the paltry toy offering was buoyed by a fun new department, complete with a messy Play-Doh station, a car-racing track and a regular programme of events like a bear-fixing-hospital and Makies 3D printing, meaning the place is now as much a children's playground as an adults' one.

If all this talk of egalitarian shopping leaves the luxe customer yearning for a little exclusivity, take heart: Louis Vuitton recently unveiled a three-storey townhouse within the store – a London first.

And things are about to get even better. In June 2014, Selfridges announced a five-year, £300m facelift – apparently the world's biggest ever single retail investment. It will include a fancy new entrance, more space to sell stuff (including an even bigger handbag department) and a tunnel. A tunnel? No, sadly not its own subway from Bond Street station, as proposed by Harry Gordon Selfridge in 1909, but just a link from the shop to some offices. Still, we think Harry would have been down with it.

Browns

*24-27 South Molton Street, W1K 5RD
(7514 0016, www.brownsfashion.com).
Bond Street tube.* **Open** 10am-6.30pm
Mon-Wed, Fri, Sat; 10am-7pm Thur.
Map p89 B3 ㉔

Among the 100-odd designers jostling
for attention in Joan Burstein's five
interconnecting shops (menswear is
at no.23) are Chloé, Christopher Kane
and Balenciaga, with plenty of fashion
exclusives. A classic London boutique.

Burlington Arcade

*Piccadilly, W1 (7355 8317, www.
burlington-arcade.co.uk). Green Park
tube.* **Open** 8am-8pm Mon-Sat;
11am-6pm Sun. **Map** p89 C4 ㉕

The Royal Arcades are a throwback to
shopping past: Burlington is the largest
and, commissioned by Lord Cavendish in
1819, oldest of them. Highlights include
classic watches at David Duggan, iconic
British luxury luggage brand Globe-
Trotter, Sermoneta, which sells Italian
leather gloves in bright colours…and the
top-hatted beadles who keep order.

Dover Street Market

*17-18 Dover Street, W1S 4LT (7518 0680,
www.doverstreetmarket.com). Green Park
tube.* **Open** 11am-6.30pm Mon-Wed;
11am-7pm Thur-Sat. **Map** p89 C4 ㉖

Comme des Garçons designer Rei Kawa-
kubo's six-storey space combines the
edgy energy of London's indoor markets
– concrete floors, Portaloo dressing-
rooms – with rarefied labels. All 14 of
the Comme des Garçons labels are here,
alongside exlusive lines from designers
such as Lanvin and Azzedine Alaïa.

Duke Street Emporium

NEW *55 Duke Street, W1K 5NR (7042
2770, www.dukestreetemporium.com).
Bond Street tube.* **Open** 9.30am-8pm
Mon-Fri; 10am-7pm Sat; noon-6pm Sun.
Map p89 B3 ㉗

The Duke Street Emporium brings
together pieces from mid-range
high street store Jigsaw and lifestyle
boutique the Shop at Bluebird (p87).

But it's more than just a shop: the plan
is that it will also house books, art and
installations, alongside a coffee shop
from Fernandez & Wells.

McQ

*14 Dover Street, W1S 4LW (7318 2220,
www.alexandermcqueen.co.uk/mcq).
Bond tube.* **Open** 11am-7pm Mon-Sat.
Map p89 C4 ㉘

Stepping inside, visitors are faced
with a large white digital dining table
from which you can project catwalk
images and videos of the Alexander
McQueen diffusion brand on to the wall
using small viewing boxes. It's weirdly
addictive. McQ's London home has been
conceived by interior designer David
Collins (the Wolseley, p74; the bar at the
Connaught, p172), but the sleek curves
and high-gloss detailing don't distract
from the clothes, showing the late
designer's trademark sexy futurism.

Mount Street

Bond Street or Green Park tube.
Map p89 B4 ㉙

Mount Street, with its dignified
Victorian terracotta façades, master
butcher Allens (no.117) and cigar shop
Sautter (no.106), has taken on a new,
cutting-edge persona. There are cool
cocktail bars in the Connaught hotel,
American designer Marc Jacobs has
a store at no.24 (his cheaper Marc diffusion line is sold nearby at 56 South
Audley Street), Serbia-born designer
Roksanda Ilincic sells elegant, richly
coloured dresses from no.9, and the
fashion leader Céline is at no.103, not
far from no.108, where Italian shoe
designer Gianvito Rossi displays his
stiletto-heeled ankle boots. Christopher
Kane, Britain's hottest designer, will
join them at no.6 late in 2014.

Paul Smith Sale Shop

*23 Avery Row, W1X 9HB (7493 1287,
www.paulsmith.co.uk). Bond Street tube.*
Open 10.30am-6.30pm Mon-Wed, Fri,
Sat; 10.30am-7pm Thur; noon-6pm Sun.
Map p89 B3 ㉚

Samples and last season's stock can be found at a 30-50% discount. You'll find clothes for men, women and children, as well as a range of accessories.

Postcard Teas

9 Dering Street, W1S 1AG (7629 3654, www.postcardteas.com). Bond Street or Oxford Circus tube. **Open** 10.30am-6.30pm Mon-Sat. **Map** p89 B3 ③
The range in this exquisite little shop isn't huge, but it is selected with care – usually from single estates. There's a central table for those who want to try a pot. Tea-ware and accessories are also sold, and there are tastings on a Saturday morning (10-11am).

Uniqlo

311 Oxford Street, W1C 2HP (7290 7701, www.uniqlo.co.uk). Bond Street or Oxford Circus tube. **Open** 10am-9pm Mon-Sat; noon-6pm Sun. **Map** p89 B3 ③
There are three outposts of Uniqlo, Japan's biggest clothes retailer, on Oxford Street alone – but this one is 25,000sq ft and three storeys of flagship. Not as cheap as Primark but more stylish, Uniqlo sells simple, single-colour staples for men and women.

Fitzrovia

West of Tottenham Court Road and north of Oxford Street, Fitzrovia – once home to radicals, writers and boozers, mostly in reverse order – retains sufficient traces of bohemianism to appeal to the media types that now frequent it. Fine hotels and restaurants cluster at Charlotte Street, but these days the **Draft House** (p103) is a more satisfying place to drink than the Fitzroy Tavern.

Sights & museums

All Saints

7 Margaret Street, W1W 8JG (7636 1788, www.allsaintsmargaretstreet.org.uk). Oxford Circus tube. **Open** 7am-7pm daily. **Admission** free. **Map** p100 B4 ①

This 1850s church was designed by William Butterfield, one of the great Gothic Revivalists. Behind the polychromatic brick façade, the shadowy, lavish interior is one of the capital's ecclesiastical triumphs, with luxurious marble, flamboyant tile work and glittering stones built into its pillars.

BBC Broadcasting House

Portland Place, Upper Regent Street, W1A 1AA (0370 901 1227, www.bbc.co.uk/showsandtours/tours). Oxford Circus tube. **Open** pre-booked tours only. **Admission** £13.50; £9-£11.25 reductions. **Map** p100 A4 ②
There are daily tours of the BBC's HQ. Completed in 1932, this was Britain's first purpose-built broadcast centre; in 2013, it acquired a swanky neighbour, New Broadcasting House. Tours take in the studios, including those used for television and radio news, as well as explaining the history of the original building, with its Eric Gill sculpture of Ariel, and the BBC itself. You'll also be able to read the news and weather on an interactive set.

BT Tower

60 Cleveland Street, W1. Goodge Street tube. **Map** p100 B3 ③
The BT Tower (formerly the Post Office Tower) was designed to provide support for radio, TV and telephone aerials. It was opened in 1964 and its crowning glory was a revolving restaurant, closed to the public in 1971 after a bomb attack by the Angry Brigade, and now used only for corporate functions. The building was Grade II-listed in 2003, but its only public function nowadays is flashing congratulatory LED messages on New Year and the like.

Pollock's Toy Museum

1 Scala Street (entrance Whitfield Street), W1T 2HL (7636 3452, www.pollocks toymuseum.com). Goodge Street tube. **Open** 10am-5pm Mon-Sat. **Admission** £6; free-£5 reductions. **Map** p100 C4 ④

LONDON BY AREA

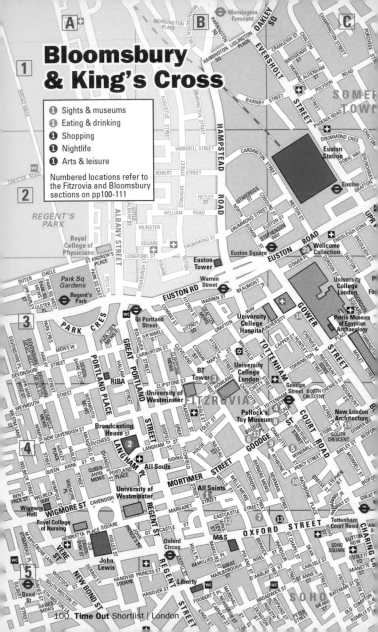

Bloomsbury & King's Cross

1 Sights & museums
1 Eating & drinking
1 Shopping
1 Nightlife
1 Arts & leisure

Numbered locations refer to the Fitzrovia and Bloomsbury sections on pp100-111

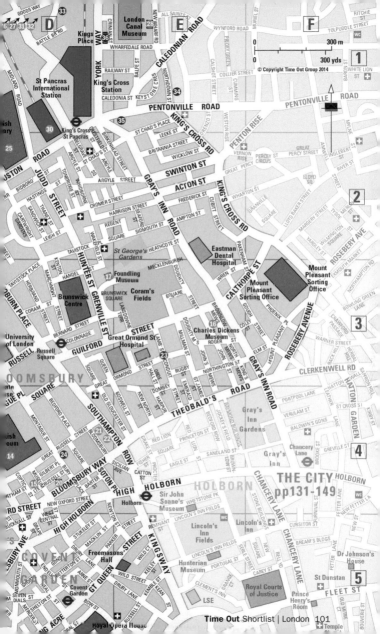

Small plates, big flavours

Ollie Dabbous undergoes a radical change of style.

The hype surrounding the 2012 opening of Ollie Dabbous's eponymous restaurant (39 Whitfield Street, W1T 2SF, 7323 1544, www.dabbous.co.uk) has barely subsided, but his new restaurant, **Barnyard** (right), is such a step-change it's a wonder he didn't fall over. Where the kitchen at Dabbous set a light, contemporary culinary tone concisely expressed in dishes such as 'mixed alliums with chilled pine infusion', the Barnyard menu reads like a motorway service-station caff – cauliflower cheese, sausage roll – until you delve a bit deeper. 'Lard on toast' and 'mince and dumpling' are just that, in small-plates portions – but full-flavoured and beautiful in their simplicity. Unusual flavours, as at Barnyard's high-end sibling, are a signature. . Corn on the cob was rubbed with flowery-scented meadowsweet, which permeated the butter. Hispi cabbage had an unusual taste that turned out to be clover.

Despite the affordable pricing and no-bookings policy, there is haute-cuisine precision in many of the dishes. Ollie doesn't just do hifalutin' cookin', that's clear; he can also do casual and family-friendly. The walls are corrugated iron, the tables planks, plates are enamelled, some seats are oil drums, but service is charming, and the low bill even more agreeable. Just be prepared to queue: the place is tiny.

Housed in a creaky Georgian townhouse, Pollock's is named after one of the last Victorian toy theatre printers. By turns beguiling and creepy, the museum is a nostalgia-fest of old board games, tin trains, porcelain dolls and Robertson's gollies.

Eating & drinking

Barnyard
NEW *18 Charlotte Street, W1T 2LY (7580 3842, www.barnyard-london. com). Goodge Street or Tottenham Court Road tube.* **Open** noon-midnight Mon-Sat; noon-4pm Sun. **££**.
Brasserie. Map p100 C4 **⑤**
Sibling of modernist, haute cuisine Dabbous, Barnyard is a complete change of pace: casual, family-friendly, and affordable, with a simple menu. No bookings are taken. See box left.

Benito's Hat
56 Goodge Street, W1T 4NB (7637 3732, www.benitos-hat.com). Goodge Street tube. **Open** 11.30am-10pm Mon-Wed; 11.30am-11pm Thur-Sat; 11.30am-9pm Sun. **£. Burritos. Map** p100 B4 **⑥**
London's TexMex eateries are ten a peso at the moment, but Benito's Hat is one of the best – no wonder that it has expanded across town, as well as maintaining this original branch. The production line compiles some of the best burritos in town, and a few cocktails and Mexican beer are served.

Berners Tavern
NEW *10 Berners Street, W1T 3NP (7908 7979, www.bernerstavern.com). Oxford Circus or Tottenham Court Road tube.* **Open** *Bar* 11am-11pm daily. *Restaurant* 7-10.30am, noon-2.30pm, 6-10.30pm Mon-Fri; 7-10.30am, 11am-4pm, 6-10.30pm Sat, Sun. **£££. Modern European. Map** p89 C4 **⑦**
The huge lobby bar of the London Edition hotel (p175) looks fabulous, but the vast dining room, with ornate plasterwork ceiling, wall to wall paintings and lively bar area looks even

better. Food is playful and appealing: tender pork belly with capers, golden raisins and apple coleslaw, say, or cod with fennel and cider sauce. Glamtastic.

Draft House

43 Goode Street, W1T 1TA (7323 9361, www.drafthouse.co.uk). Goode Street tube. **Open** noon-11pm Mon-Sat. **Beer café.** Map p100 C4 ⑧

Eclectic beers and pub-style food are clearly a good formula. The mini-chain's fourth branch (followed in 2013 with a fifth at the Tower of London) is smaller than its older siblings – more about supping the excellent pints (or thirds of pints if you want to vary your drinking) than sitting down to a meal. Still, the meaty mix of well-priced US-style fast food and British pub dishes does come with good beer pairings.

Lantana

13 Charlotte Place, W1T 1SN (7637 3347, www.lantanacafe.co.uk). Goode Street tube. **Open** 8-11.30am, noon-3pm Mon-Fri; 9am-3pm Sat, Sun. **£.** **Café.** Map p100 B4 ⑨

The super salads (smoky aubergine or a crunchy sugar snap and red cabbage combo, for example), cakes and sunny breakfasts have drawn throngs of regulars to this Antipodean-style eaterie ever since it opened. The espresso machine is the coffee connoisseur's choice – La Marzocco – and the beans come from the excellent Monmouth.

Lima London

31 Rathbone Place, W1T 1JH (3002 2640, www.limalondon.com). Tottenham Court Road tube. **Open** noon-2.30pm, 5.30-10.30pm Mon-Sat. **££.** **Peruvian.** Map p100 C4 ⑩

The best of a wave of Peruvian restaurants, Lima is understated, but the menu reads like food haiku, with each dish looking like a modernist work of art: artichokes with green lime, fava beans, tree tomato emulsion and molle pink pepper is just one beauty of a dish, as impressive for its bold appearance as for its vibrant flavours. Sweet, sharp and hot are the defining tastes, brilliant counterpoints to the soft blandness of avocado, corn – and, yes, potatoes.

Salt Yard

54 Goode Street, W1DT 4NA (7637 0657, www.saltyard.co.uk). Goode Street tube. **Open** noon-11pm Mon-Sat. **££.** **Spanish-Italian tapas.** Map p100 B4 ⑪

The artful menu of Iberian and Italian tapas standards served at this dark, calm and classy joint is aimed at diners in search of a slow lunch or lightish dinner. Fine selections of charcuterie and cheese front the frequently changing menu, which features the likes of tuna carpaccio with baby broad beans, and ham croquettes with manchego. A top choice for fuss-free tapas.

Yalla Yalla

12 Winsley Street, W1W 8HQ (7637 4748, www.yalla-yalla.co.uk). Oxford Circus tube. **Open** 10am-11.30pm Mon-Fri; 11am-11pm Sat. **£.** **Lebanese.** Map p100 B5 ⑫

Yalla Yalla offers a delectable selection of meze (each wonderfully presented, with slick garnishes of olive oil, herbs and pomegranate seeds where appropriate) and heartier main courses based around the grill. The sticky chicken wings with pomegranate syrup are excellent, as is the grilled halloumi with olives and mint. For dessert, don't miss the honeyed vanilla ice-cream topped with caramelised nuts and dried fruit.

Nightlife

100 Club

100 Oxford Street, W1D 1LL (7636 0933, www.the100club.co.uk). Oxford Circus or Tottenham Court Road tube. Map p100 C5 ⑬

Perhaps the most adaptable venue in London, this wide, 350-capacity basement room has provided a home for trad jazz, pub blues, northern soul and, famously, the early days of punk – the Sex Pistols and the Clash both played here. It even hosts classical nights now.

Bloomsbury

In bookish circles, Bloomsbury is a name to conjure with: it is the HQ of London University and home to the superb **British Museum**. The name was famously attached to a group of early 20th-century artists and intellectuals (Virginia Woolf and John Maynard Keynes among them), and more recently to the (Soho-based) publishing company that gave us Harry Potter. Its green squares are perfect for an afternoon stroll.

Sights & museums

British Museum

Great Russell Street, WC1B 3DG (7323 8299, www.britishmuseum.org). Russell Square or Tottenham Court Road tube. **Open** *Galleries* 10am-5.30pm Mon-Thur, Sat, Sun; 10am-8.30pm Fri. *Great Court* 9am-6pm Mon-Thur, Sat, Sun; 9am-8.30pm Fri. **Admission** free; donations appreciated. *Special exhibitions* prices vary. **Map** p101 D4 ⓮

The British Museum is a neoclassical marvel that was built in 1847, and topped off 153 years later with the magnificent glass-roofed Great Court. The £100m roof, which surrounds the domed Reading Room, where Marx, Lenin, Dickens, Darwin, Hardy and Yeats once worked, has now been joined by the Sainsbury Exhibitions Gallery, which hosts the museum's immensely popular blockbuster shows (mummies, Vikings and the Chinese terracotta warriors have all featured in recent years).

Star exhibits in the astounding permanent collection include ancient Egyptian artefacts – the Rosetta Stone on the ground floor, mummies upstairs – and Greek antiquities that include the stunning marble friezes

from the Parthenon, but the new Sutton Hoo displays (Room 41) are also essential. The King's Library is a calm home to a 5,000-piece collection devoted to the formative period of the museum (a replica Rosetta Stone is here, if the real one's too crowded).

You won't be able to see everything in one day, so buy a guide and pick some showstoppers, or plan several visits. Free eyeOpener tours offer introductions to particular world cultures.

Cartoon Museum

35 Little Russell Street, WC1A 2HH (7580 8155, www.cartoonmuseum.org). Tottenham Court Road tube. **Open** 10.30am-5.30pm Mon-Sat; noon-5.30pm Sun. **Admission** £7; free-£5 reductions. **Map** p101 D4 ⓯

On the ground floor of this former dairy, a brief chronology of British cartoon art is displayed, from Hogarth via Britain's cartooning 'golden age' (1770-1830) to examples of wartime cartoons, ending up with modern satirists such as Ralph Steadman and the *Guardian*'s Steve Bell, alongside fine temporary exhibitions.

Charles Dickens Museum

48 Doughty Street, WC1N 2LX (7405 2127, www.dickensmuseum.com). Chancery Lane or Russell Square tube. **Open** 10am-5pm daily. **Admission** £8; free-£6 reductions. **Map** p101 E3 ⓰

London is scattered with plaques marking addresses where the peripatetic Charles Dickens lived, but this is the only one to have been preserved as a museum. He lived here from 1837 to 1840, during which time he wrote *Nicholas Nickleby* and *Oliver Twist*. Ring the doorbell to gain access to four floors of Dickensiana, collected over the years from various other of his residences. Recent refurbishment has created a pleasant downstairs café.

Foundling Museum

40 Brunswick Square, WC1N 1AZ (7841 3600, www.foundlingmuseum.org.uk).

Russell Square tube. **Open** 10am-5pm Tue-Sat; 11am-5pm Sun. **Admission** £8.25; free-£6 reductions. **Map** p101 D3 ⑰

Returning to England from America in 1720, Captain Thomas Coram was appalled by the number of abandoned children on the streets and persuaded artist William Hogarth and composer GF Handel to become governors of a new hospital for them. Hogarth decreed the hospital should also be Britain's first public art gallery, and work by Gainsborough and Reynolds is shown upstairs. The most heart-rending display is downstairs: a tiny case of mementoes that were all that mothers were allowed to leave the children they abandoned here.

Grant Museum

Rockefeller Building, 21 University Street, WC1E 6DE (3108 2052, www.ud.ac.uk/museums/zoology). Goodge Street tube. **Open** 1-5pm Mon-Sat. **Admission** free. **Map** p100 C3 ⑱

This much-loved collection of animal skeletons, taxidermy specimens and creatures preserved in fluid retains the air of the house of an avid Victorian collector, even though it moved to this Edwardian former library only in 2011. The collection includes remains of many rare and extinct animals, such as a dodo and a zebra-like quagga, as well as bisected heads and a jar full of moles. One recent addition was the Micrarium: a booth walled with illuminated microscope slides.

New London Architecture

26 Store Street, WC1E 7BT (7636 4044, www.newlondonarchitecture.org). Goodge Street tube. **Open** 9.30am-6pm Mon-Fri; 10am-5pm Sat. **Admission** free. **Map** p100 C4 ⑲

NLA stages interesting exhibitions on London's built environment (the Olympic legacy, perhaps, or canals), but its centrepiece is a fascinating 39ft-long scale model of the city on which all major developments that have planning permission are marked

in white. There's also a short film that charts the prodigious growth of London over the centuries.

St George's Bloomsbury/ Museum of Comedy

Bloomsbury Way, WC1A 2HR (7242 1979, www.stgeorgesbloomsbury.org.uk). Holborn or Tottenham Court Road tube. **Open** times vary; phone for details. **Admission** free. **Map** p101 D4 ⑳

Consecrated in 1730, St George's is a grand and typically disturbing work by Nicholas Hawksmoor, with an offset, stepped spire that was inspired by Pliny's account of the Mausoleum at Halicarnassus. Highlights include the mahogany reredos and 10ft-high sculptures of lions and unicorns clawing at the base of the steeple. There are tours and regular concerts.

Britain's first Museum of Comedy (7534 1744, www.museumofcomedy. com; noon-5pm Tue-Sun; £5, £4 reductions) opened in the church's undercroft in June 2014. As well as seeing memorabilia such as Steptoe & Son's stuffed bear and stage clothes worn by the likes of Max Miller, you can even handle props used by Tommy Cooper.

Eating & drinking

All Star Lanes

Victoria House, Bloomsbury Place, WC1B 4DA (7025 2676, www.allstarlanes.co.uk). Holborn tube. **Open** 4-11.30pm Mon-Wed; 4pm-midnight Thur; noon-2am Fri; 11am-2am Sat; 11am-11pm Sun. **Bar & bowling**. **Map** p101 D4 ㉑

Walk past the lanes and smart, diner-style seating, and you'll find yourself in a comfortable, subdued side bar with chilled glasses, classy red furnishings, an unusual mix of bottled lagers and impressive cocktails. There's an American menu and, at weekends, DJs.

Hummus Bros

37-63 Southampton Row, WC1B 4DA (7404 7079, www.hbros.co.uk). Holborn tube. **Open** 11am-9pm Mon-Fri; noon-5pm Sat. £. Café. **Map** p101 D4 ②

The simple and successful formula at this café/takeaway is to serve houmous as a base for a selection of toppings, which you scoop up with excellent pitta bread. The food is nutritious and good value. There's a second branch in Soho (88 Wardour Street, 7734 1311) and a third in the City (128 Cheapside, 7726 8011) – handy for St Paul's (p141).

Shopping

The southern end of **Tottenham Court Road** was known as the city's main street for consumer electronics – but the street is getting a major revamp, and what seems to be emerging is much more varied.

Lamb's Conduit Street

Holborn or Russell Square tube.
Map p101 E3 ②

Tucked among residential back streets, Lamb's Conduit Street is the perfect size for a browse, whether you fancy checking out quality tailoring at Oliver Spencer (no.62), cult menswear and women's knitwear from Folk (no.49), Darkroom's cutting-edge design (no.52) or even a recumbent bicycle at Bikefix (no.48). Head along the main drag to refuel at the traditional Lamb pub (no.94, 7405 0713) or, round the corner, the Espresso Room (31-35 Great Ormond Street, www.theespressoroom.com).

London Review Bookshop

14 Bury Place, WC1A 2JL (7269 9030, www.lrbshop.co.uk). Holborn or Tottenham Court Road tube. **Open** 10am-6.30pm Mon-Sat; noon-6pm Sun. **Map** p101 D4 ②

An inspiring bookshop, from the stimulating presentation to the quality of the selection. Politics, current affairs and history are well represented on the ground floor, while downstairs, audio books lead on to exciting poetry and philosophy sections. There's a good café, and a busy events schedule.

King's Cross

North-east of Bloomsbury, the once-insalubrious area of King's Cross has undergone massive redevelopment around the grand **St Pancras International** station, with its dramatic Victorian glass-and-iron train shed roof, and the now well-established 'new' **British Library**. The gargantuan undertaking is approaching completion, with the refurbishment of **King's Cross** station and transformation (to the tune of £500m) of the former badlands to the north of the station into mixed-use nucleus King's Cross Central pretty much done.

Sights & museums

British Library

96 Euston Road, NW1 2DB (01937 546060, www.bl.uk). Euston or King's Cross St Pancras tube/rail. **Open** 9.30am-6pm Mon, Wed-Fri; 9.30am-8pm Tue; 9.30am-5pm Sat; 11am-5pm Sun. **Admission** free; donations appreciated. **Map** p101 D2 ②

'One of the ugliest buildings in the world,' opined a Parliamentary committee on the opening of the new British Library in 1997. Opinions have changed since then: the interior is a model of cool, spacious functionality, its focal point the King's Library, a six-storey glass-walled tower housing George III's collection in the central atrium. The British Library holds more than 150 million items. In the John Ritblat Gallery, the library's main treasures are displayed: the Magna Carta, the Lindisfarne Gospels, original manuscripts from Chaucer and original Beatles lyrics.

Granary Square

NEW *www.kingscross.co.uk. King's Cross St Pancras tube/rail.* **Map** p101 D1 ②

In 2012, a surprisingly pleasant western concourse opened at King's Cross station, but it was only a taster

top: Granary Square;
bottom: King's Cross station

for the superb redevelopment just to the north. Stroll up King's Boulevard – usually populated by the KERB food stalls (11am-2.30pm Tue-Fri; some Sat in summer) – and you'll find yourself in a terrific new square, with dancing fountains, giant's steps down to the canal, and some good restaurants. It's the apron for the Granary Building, home to the 5,000 staff and students of the University of the Arts London – which, along with its fine restaurants, should ensure the area stays lively. Eye-catching developments continue – a 90m tunnel between St Pancras and King's Cross, complete with LED-lit 'art wall' opened in summer 2014 – but none are likely to top a mooted 'lagoon' for open-air swimming.

House of Illustration

NEW *2 Granary Square, N1C 4BH (3696 2020, www.houseofillustration.org.uk). King's Cross St Pancras tube/rail.* **Open** 10am-6pm Tue-Sun. **Map** p101 D1 ㉗
This new gallery in the revamped Granary Square is dedicated to illustration, and will feature changing exhibitions and regular arty workshops for all ages. It opened in summer 2014 with 'Quentin Blake: Inside Stories', an exhibition featuring the work of one of the country's best-known illustrators.

London Canal Museum

12-13 New Wharf Road, N1 9RT (7713 0836, www.canalmuseum.org.uk). King's Cross St Pancras tube/rail. **Open** 10am-4.30pm Tue-Sun; 10am-7.30pm 1st Thur of the mth. **Admission** £4; free-£3 reductions. No credit cards. **Map** p101 E1 ㉘
The museum is housed in a former 19th-century ice warehouse, used by Carlo Gatti for his ice-cream, and includes an interesting exhibit on the history of the ice trade. The part of the collection looking at the history of the waterways and those who worked on them is rather sparse by comparison.

Wellcome Collection

183 Euston Road, NW1 2BE (7611 2222, www.wellcomecollection.org). Euston Square tube or Euston tube/rail. **Open** 10am-6pm Tue, Wed, Fri, Sat; 10am-10pm Thur; 11am-6pm Sun. **Admission** free. **Map** p100 C2 ㉙
Founder Sir Henry Wellcome, a pioneering 19th-century pharmacist and entrepreneur, amassed a vast, grisly collection of implements and curios – carvings of pregnant women, used guillotine blades, Napoleon's toothbrush – mostly relating to the medical trade. It's now displayed, along with modern art, in this swanky museum, which is undergoing major refurbishment: see box right. Galleries will stay open throughout the process.

Eating & drinking

The new concourse at King's Cross has a good selection of places to eat, including a branch of **Benito's Hat** (p102), but the eating highlights of the area are in **St Pancras** station or around **Granary Square**. The new King's Boulevard provides good street food for weekday lunches.

Booking Office

St Pancras Renaissance London Hotel, NW1 2AR (7841 3566, www.bookingofficerestaurant.com). King's Cross St Pancras tube/rail. **Open** 6.30am-1am Mon-Wed, Sun; 6.30am-3am Thur-Sat. **Bar. Map** p101 D2 ㉚
Superlatives come easily when describing the Booking Office: epic, soaring, magnificent. As part of Sir Gilbert Scott's 1873 Midland Grand Hotel, it was designed to instill in passengers a sense of awe at the power of the railways. These days, it serves as an awe-inspiring bar, and the refit has made the most of the Victorian splendour.

Caravan King's Cross

Granary Building, 1 Granary Square, N1C 4AA (7101 7661, www.caravankingscross.co.uk). King's Cross

St Pancras tube/rail. **Open** 8am-10.30pm Mon-Fri; 10am-3.30pm Sat; 10am-4pm Sun. **££**. **Global**. Map p101 D1 ③

The ethos here is welcoming staff and a menu they call 'well-travelled food'. Most are small plates – deep-fried duck egg with baba ganoush, chorizo oil and cripsy shallots, say, plus a few large plates and a handful of first-class pizzas. The setting, looking out on to Granary Square, is another plus.

Grain Store

Granary Square, at 1-3 Stable Street, N1C 4AB (7324 4466, www.grainstore. com). King's Cross St Pancras tube/ rail. **Open** noon-2.30pm, 6-10.30pm Mon-Fri; 11am-3pm, 6-10.30pm Sat; 11am-4pm Sun. **£££**. **French**. **Map** p101 D1 ②

Grain Store inhabits a corner of the vast Victorian warehouse on Granary Square a little uneasily, but its patron is Bruno Loubet, a superb Bordeaux-born chef, whose cooking is grounded in the classical traditions of south-west France. The menu is a pick 'n' mix of ingredients and cuisines, yet there is a consistency of style and imaginative, successful flavour pairings that is recognisably Loubet. There's a long wait for bookings, but some walk-ins are accommodated – and a wait at the bar is enlivened with excellent Tony Conigliaro cocktails.

Nightlife

EGG

200 York Way, N7 9AX (7871 7111, www.egglondon.net). King's Cross St Pancras tube/rail. **Map** p101 D1 ③

King's Cross was a rave hotspot from the 1990s through to the 2000s, but redevelopment has swept all those clubs away – except for Egg. Having opened a third dancefloor to celebrate its tenth anniversary, and with a new roof terrace to entice smokers, it should be here for many years to come.

Improving on perfect

The excellent Wellcome Collection bigs things up.

It's typical of the **Wellcome Collection** (p108) – one of our favourite London museums ever since it opened in 2007 – that it should put on an imaginative, compelling exhibition as a stop-gap while it undergoes major redevelopment. 'An Idiosyncratic A-Z of the Human Condition' (until Oct 2014) brightened a long, plain hall with a strange abcedarium: 'A for Acts of Faith' illustrates near misses and accidents as inspired by an accompanying selection of ex-voto images; 'P for Philosophy' asks you to take a philosophical fortune cookie to be opened on the way home; 'X for X-rated' has visitors blushing over porcelain fruit showing sexual foreplay.

Why is this self-appointed explorer of 'connections between medicine, life and art in the past, present and future' messing with a winning formula? Success has been its downfall: designed for 100,000 visits a year, it saw 490,000 people through its doors in 2012 alone.

So, by winter 2014/15, the Wellcome will have expanded by 30 per cent, including an entirely new gallery for themed annual exhibitions and a doubling of its public events space. There will be a handsome spiral staircase in the entrance, the Wellcome Library's Reading Room will open to the public for the first time, and an upstairs restaurant has already supplemented the downstairs café and bookshop.

LONDON BY AREA

The Invisible Dot

*2 Northdown Street, N1 9BG (7424 8918,
www.theinvisibledot.com). King's Cross St
Pancras tube/rail.* **Map** p101 E1 **34**

This tiny stand-up comedy venue,
with whitewashed bare-brick walls
and a few rows of chairs, nevertheless
manages to attract big players – you
might find Simon Amstell or Stewart
Lee here, and comic poet Tim Key is
the venue's signature act. New comedy
talent also features, with New Wave
night a regular feature.

Scala

*275 Pentonville Road, N1 9NL (7833 2022,
www.scala-london.co.uk). King's Cross St
Pancras tube/rail.* **Map** p101 E1 **35**

One of London's best-loved gig venues,
this multi-floored monolith is the
frequent destination for one-off super-
parties now that many of London's
superclubs have bitten the dust. Built
as a cinema shortly after World War
I, it is surprisingly capacious and
hosts a laudably broad range of indie,
electronica, avant hip hop and folk. Its
chilly air-conditioning is unrivalled
anywhere else in the city – a definite
boon should the summer get sultry.

Arts & leisure

Kings Place

*90 York Way, N1 9AG (0844 264 0321,
www.kingsplace.co.uk). King's Cross St
Pancras tube/rail.* **Map** p101 D1 **36**

Once a lone pioneer in the revival of
King's Cross, Kings Place suddenly
finds itself part of the King's Cross
Central cultural hub. Beneath seven
office floors and a ground-floor
restaurant-bar (with seats on the canal
basin outside), the 400-seat main hall is
a beauty, dominated by wood carved
from a single, 500-year-old oak tree
and ringed by invisible rubber pads
that kill unwanted noise that might
interfere with the immaculate acoustic.
There's also a versatile second hall.
The programming is tremendous.
It consists of mini-series on diverse,

classical-dominated but wide-ranging
themes, among them year-long series
of concerts of music by a single
composer, chamber music recitals and
experimental classical music.

Event highlights Kings Place Festival:
100 events in three days (Sept).

Soho

Through the 1950s and '60s, Soho
was London at its most game – now
the prostitutes and mackintosh-
wearing perverts have largely
shipped out to leave PRs, shoppers
and tourists to mingle with gays and
sundry party-people. Still, if you
want to drink or eat, you could hardly
find a better part of town in which to
do so. And a wander among the
skinny streets off **Old Compton
Street**, Soho's main artery should
show you a bit of mischief.

Sights & museums

Leicester Square

Leicester Square tube. **Map** p112 C3 **1**

For years locals left the square to
unimaginative tourists and drunk
suburban kids. Then, in 2011, a couple
of high-class hotels arrived, followed
in 2012 by the castle-like red-brick
Hippodrome, reborn as a high-rolling
casino and cabaret venue. Finally,
in 2013, £15.5m renovations were
complete, simplifying the layout of
the square, improving lighting and
ringing the garden (and Shakespeare
statue) with white 'ribbon' seating. Not
all memories of the square's cheerfully
tacky phase have gone: the Swiss
Glockenspiel returned, with its 27 bells
and mechanical mountain farmers.

Photographers' Gallery

*16-18 Ramillies Street, W1F 7LW (0845
262 1618, www.thephotographersgallery.
org.uk). Oxford Circus tube.* **Open**
10am-6pm Mon-Wed, Fri, Sat; 10am-8pm
Thur; 11.30am-6pm Sun. **Admission**
free. **Map** p112 A1 **2**

The new six-storey space for this excellent and long-establised gallery for photography opened in 2012. The UK's first public gallery to be dedicated to the medium, it hosts diverse exhibitions – and has a fine café downstairs that produces an intensely rich hot chocolate.

Ripley's Believe It or Not!

1 Piccadilly Circus, W1J 0DA (3238 0022, www.ripleyslondon.com). Piccadilly Circus tube. **Open** 10am-midnight daily (last entry 10.30pm). **Admission** £26.95; free £24.95 reductions; £87.95 family. **Map** p112 B3 ❸

Over five floors of the Trocadero, this 'odditorium' follows a formula more or less unchanged since Robert Ripley opened his first display in 1933: an assortment of 800 curiosities is displayed, ranging from a two-headed calf to the world's smallest road-safe car.

Soho Square

Tottenham Court Road tube. **Map** p112 C1 ❹

This tree-lined quadrangle, with a weather-beaten Charles II at the centre, beside the Mock Tudor gardeners' hut, fills with smoochy couples and snacking workers on sunny days.

Eating & drinking

Since the 1950s, Gerrard and Lisle Streets have been **Chinatown**, marked by oriental gates, stone lions and telephone boxes topped with pagodas, and still populated by old-style Cantonese diners such as **Mr Kong** (21 Lisle Street, 7437 7341) and **Wong Kei** (41-43 Wardour Street, 7437 8408).

Arbutus

63-64 Frith Street, W1D 3JW (7734 4545, www.arbutusrestaurant.co.uk). Tottenham Court Road tube. **Open** noon-2.30pm, 5-11pm Mon-Thur; noon-2.30pm, 5-11.30pm Fri, Sat; noon-3pm, 5.30-10.30pm Sun. **£££. Modern European. Map** p112 C2 ❺

Providing very fine cooking at very fair prices isn't an easy trick, but this place makes it look easy, producing creative dishes using unusual or less-known ingredients. Although it's not cheap to eat à la carte, the set lunch and dinner are famously good value. It also pioneered offering 250ml carafes for sampling wine from the well-edited list.

Brasserie Zédel/ Bar Américain

20 Sherwood Street, W1F 7ED (7734 4888, www.brasseriezedel.com). Piccadilly Circus tube. **Open** 4.30pm-midnight Mon-Sat; 4.30pm-11am Sun. **Brasserie/ cocktail bar. Map** p112 B3 ❻

There's scant room left on the Prohibition-theme bandwagon, but this is how it should be done. Corbin and King, also behind the Wolseley (p74), Delaunay (p124), Fischer's (p91) and a new hotel (the Beaumont, p168), have taken an art deco setting – the former ballroom of a vast hotel – to create a superb destination bar. A short list of mixed drinks ('classic' and 'house') are faithful to the golden age of cocktails: martini, manhattan, mint julep, sazerac… all at £9.75 – even those with bubbly. The attentive bar service isn't always matched in the ocean-liner-size restaurant room, but the old-school French menu (including very reasonable set meals) is terrific. There are regular cabaret performances as well.

Ceviche

17 Frith Street, W1D 4RG (7297 2040, www.cevicheuk.com). Leicester Square tube. **Open** noon-11.30pm Mon-Sat; noon-10.15pm Sun. **££. Peruvian. Map** p112 C2 ❼

Corn, potatoes and the signature dish of ceviche – raw citrus-marinated fish (or veg), served here in seven versions – are the stars. The restaurant isn't a flawless rendition of Peruvian cuisine, but it's a good-time place with a colourful interior and a buzzing pisco bar at the front: staff mix a mean pisco sour.

LONDON BY AREA

A

B

C

Tottenham
Court Road

MARGARET STREET

GREAT TITCHFIELD STREET

WELLS STREET

EASTCASTLE STREET

BERNERS STREET

NEWMAN ST

RATHBONE PLACE

HANWAY ST

HANWAY ST

55

OXFORD STREET

WINSLEY ST

HILLS PL

RAMILLIES ST

M&S

RAMILLIES PL

2

POLAND STREET

NOEL STREET

BERWICK ST

WARDOUR STREET

GT CHAPEL ST

DEAN STREET

SOHO ST

SOHO
SQUARE

4

SUTTON
ROW

CHARING CROSS RD

GOSLETT
YD

ARGYLL ST

21

Liberty

Great Marlborough Street

26

WC

FOUBERT'S PL

D'ARBLAY STREET

17

BROADWICK ST

CARLISLE ST

32

14

St ANNE'S
CT

41

FRITH STREET

5

28

MANETTE ST

19

24

2

27

23

15

NEWBURGH ST

MARSHALL STREET

CARNABY ST

GANTON STREET

KINGLY STREET

HOPKINS STREET

BERWICK STREET

INGESTRE PL

20

22

25

PETER STREET

BATEMAN ST

MEARD
ST

DEAN STREET

OLD COMPTON ST

GREEK STREET

11

7

33

39

8

9

ROMILLY ST

34

12

SOHO

REGENT STREET

BEAK STREET

WARWICK STREET

HEDDON ST

GOLDEN SQUARE

JAMES ST

BRUCE LANE

LOWER JAMES ST

BREWER STREET

GT PULTENEY STREET

LEXINGTON STREET

GT WINDMILL ST

PETER STREET

BREWER STREET

31

18

ARCHER ST

RUPERT ST

35

SHAFTESBURY AVENUE

GERRARD STREET

GERRARD PLACE

WARDOUR STREET

LISLE

30

37

SAVILE ROW

10

3

SHERWOOD ST

DENMAN ST

6

40

Trocadero

PICCADILLY CIRCUS

COVENTRY STREET

29

39

WC

LEICESTER SQUARE

1

VIGO STREET

GLASSHOUSE STREET

Piccadilly
Circus

WC

OXENDON ST

WHITCOMB ST

PANTON ST

ORANGE

HAYMARKET

CRAN

OLD BURLINGTON STREET

SACKVILLE STREET

SWALLOW ST

VINE ST

REGENT STREET

ST ALBAN'S ST

OLD BOND STREET

BURLINGTON ARCADE

Royal
Academy
of Arts

16

ST JAMES'S STREET

BARNABES

SUFFOLK ST

WHITCOMB ST

St James's

JERMYN STREET

JERMYN STREET

DUKE STREET

BURY STREET

DUKE OF YORK ST

ST JAMES'S
SQUARE

WESTMINSTER
& ST JAMES'S
pp66-74

CHARLES II STREET

PALL MALL

WATERLOO PLACE

COCKS

ARLINGTON STREET

CARLTON GDNS

PALL MALL

CARLTON HOUSE TERR

Duke of York's
Column

ICA

0   200

0   200

5

Soho &
Covent Garden

© Copyright Time Out Group 2014

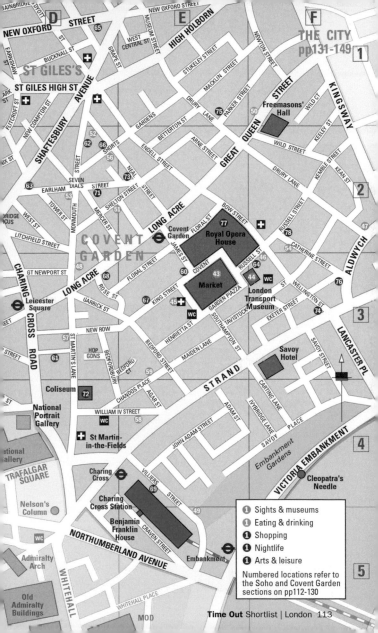

D NEW OXFORD STREET
NEW OXFORD 65
STREET
E HIGH HOLBORN
F THE CITY
pp131-149

1

St GILES'S
St GILES HIGH ST

52
62
56
63
71
73

Freemasons' Hall

2

COVENT GARDEN
LONG ACRE
Covent Garden 77 Royal Opera House
68
60
43 Market
COVENT GARDEN PIAZZA
44
London Transport Museum

3

Leicester Square

Savoy Hotel

4

Coliseum
72
National Portrait Gallery
St Martin-in-the-Fields
Charing Cross
Charing Cross Station
Benjamin Franklin House
69
Embankment
Cleopatra's Needle

TRAFALGAR SQUARE
Nelson's Column
Admiralty Arch
Old Admiralty Buildings

Embankment Gardens

❶ Sights & museums
❶ Eating & drinking
❶ Shopping
❶ Nightlife
❶ Arts & leisure

Numbered locations refer to the Soho and Covent Garden sections on pp112-130

5

top: Herman Ze German;
bottom: French House

French House

49 Dean Street, W1D 5BG (7437 2799, www.frenchhousesoho.com). Leicester Square tube. **Open** noon-11pm Mon-Sat; noon-10.30pm Sun. Pub. **Map** p112 C2 **8**

Titanic post-war drinkers, the Bacons and the Behans, frequented this small but significant boozer, while the venue's French heritage enticed De Gaulle to run his Resistance operation from the upstairs. Little has changed: beer is served in half pints and bottles of Breton cider are plonked on the famed back alcove table.

Herman Ze German

NEW *33 Old Compton Street, W1D 5JU (no phone, www.herman-ze-german. co.uk). Leicester Square tube.* **Open** 11am-11.30pm Mon-Thur; 11am-midnight Fri, Sat; 11am-10.30pm Sun. £. German. **Map** p112 C2 **9**

Herman Ze German is a purveyor of German sausages, with a playfully utilitarian interior. The sausages are imported from the Schwarzwald (Black Forest) and made from high-quality pork, with juicy, springy middles. More bonus points for serving them in chewy baguettes.

Hix/Mark's Bar

66-70 Brewer Street, W1F 9UP (7292 3518, www.marksbar.co.uk). Piccadilly Circus tube. **Open** noon-1am Mon-Sat; noon-midnight Sun. £££. British/cocktail bar. **Map** p112 B3 **10**

In the dimly lit basement under Mark Hix's fine Soho restaurant, the superb Mark's Bar is an homage to New York – albeit with a bar billiards table – from the tin ceiling tiles to the cocktails. The ground-floor dining room is more modern and pared down, apart from crazy mobiles by Damien Hirst and Sarah Lucas. Prices are centre-of-town high, but the food is delightful: perhaps hanger steak with watercress, horseradish and beets, fish fingers with chips and mushy peas, or Blythburgh pork chop with wild fennel and Mendip snails.

The top-notch puddings range from traditional to decidedly unusual (sea buckthorn berry posset).

Koya

49 Frith Street, W1D 4SG (7434 4463, www.koya.co.uk). Tottenham Court Road tube. **Open** noon-3pm, 5.30-10.30pm Mon-Sat; 5.30-10pm Sun. £. Noodles. **Map** p112 C2 **11**

You can easily spot London's favourite Japanese noodle bar by the long queue outside. Fear not – there's a fairly rapid turnover at the shared wooden tables, and the food (authentic Japanese preparations using fresh, locally sourced vegetables, meats and fish) is well worth the wait. The menu stars udon noodles (rather than the currently hugely popular ramen) in all their glorious possibilities. Koya's own ginger tea makes an ideal accompaniment to the salty food.

Maison Bertaux

28 Greek Street, W1D 5DQ (7437 6007, www.maisonbertaux.com). Leicester Square tube. **Open** 9am-10.30pm Mon-Sat; 9am-8pm Sun. £. Café. **Map** p112 C2 **12**

Oozing arty, bohemian charm, this café dates back to 1871, when Soho was London's little piece of the Continent. Battered bentwood tables and chairs add to the feeling of being in a pâtisserie in rural France. The provisions (cream cakes, greasy pastries, pots of tea) really aren't the point.

Pitt Cue Co

1 Newburgh Street, W1F 7RB (7287 5578, www.pittcue.co.uk). Oxford Circus tube. **Open** noon-3pm, 6-10.30pm Mon-Sat; noon-4pm Sun. ££. North American. **Map** p112 A2 **13**

This tiny place has a ground-floor takeaway and standing-room-only bar, with a dining room in the basement. No bookings are taken, and there's often a queue. So what's the attraction? Slow-cooked and grilled meat, often paired with tangy, sour slaws, pickles and a dash of heat. Pulled pork, beef brisket and beef ribs are dry-rubbed and smoked for hours, over charcoal or wood. The signature ribs are slathered in sticky barbecue sauce. Eat-in meals are served in enamel dishes suggestive of prison plates, but prison food never tasted this good.

Pizza Pilgrims

NEW *11 Dean Street, W1D 3RP (7287 8964, http://pizzapilgrims.co.uk).* Tottenham Court Road tube. **Open** noon-10.30pm daily. £. Pizza. **Map** p112 C1 ⑭
The main basement dining area is intimate, with 1960s Italian film posters helping to create the feel of a retro Soho trattoria. Pizzas are chewy and soft in the Neapolitan style, the appealing, thick bases layered with on-trend toppings: 'nduja, a spicy Calabrian sausage, is paired well with simple marinara sauce, for example.

Polpo

41 Beak Street, W1F 9SB (7734 4479, www.polpo.co.uk). Piccadilly Circus tube. **Open** noon-11pm Mon-Sat; noon-4pm Sun. ££. **Italian/wine bar**. **Map** p112 A2 ⑮
In an 18th-century townhouse that was once home to Canaletto, this charming *bàcaro* (Venetian-style wine bar) was the first of a mini-chain. Here, the room has a fashionably distressed look, the wines (served in rustic jugs of 250ml or 500ml) are selected from four good importers, and the food is a procession of small dishes, all of them packed with flavour. Some choices are classic Venetian (such as the cicheti bar snack); others are more adventurous.

Shoryu Ramen

9 Regent Street, SW1Y 4LR (no phone, www.shoryuramen.com). Piccadilly Circus tube. **Open** 11am-3.30pm, 5-11.30pm Mon-Sat; 11am-3.30pm, 5-10.30pm Sun. £. **Noodles**. **Map** p112 B4 ⑯

Shoryu pips its West End tonkotsu rivals when it comes to the taste and texture of its broth. As well as Hakata-style ramen (noodles in a rich, boiled-down, pork-bone broth), the other notable feature is speed. Extra toppings such as bamboo shoots and boiled eggs are to be expected, but kaedama (plain refill noodles) are a godsend for anyone sharing soup stock between small children.

Social Eating House

58-59 Poland Street, W1F 7NR (7993 3251, www.socialeatinghouse.com). Oxford Circus or Tottenham Court Road tube. **Open** noon-2.30pm, 6-10.30pm Mon-Sat. £££. **Small plates**. Map p112 B2 ⑰
Chef-patron Jason Atherton, once sorcerer's apprentice to Gordon Ramsay, has been spreading culinary magic across the West End: his Little Social bistro opened in March 2013, opposite his fine dining Pollen Street Social. Just weeks later, chef role delegated to Paul Hood, Atherton opened Social Eating – still our favourite of his stable. The ground-floor dining room has a mirrored ceiling to create the impression of space in a low room; upstairs is a smart cocktail bar, called the Blind Pig, which also has a separate entrance. But most of the action is in the dining room, with a kitchen brigade who are clearly at the top of their game: stunning presentation and amazing flavour combinations, with great service.

Spuntino

61 Rupert Street, W1D 7PW (no phone, www.spuntino.co.uk). Piccadilly Circus tube. **Open** noon-midnight Mon-Wed; noon-1am Thur-Sat; noon-11pm Sun. ££. **North American**. Map p112 B3 ⑬
It's a challenge to find Spuntino (look for 'number 61') – when you do, it's a dark, grungy space where dim lights dangle in cages, the walls are cracked and battered, and the staff sport daring tattoos under flimsy vests. The

anti-establishment vibe trickles into the menu, which is Italian-American with plenty of 'additude'. Served mostly on all-the-rage enamelled tin dishes, food features big bold flavours packed into tiny portions: from a dinky slider (mini-burger), filled with moist pulled pork and pickled apple, to a black-edged pizzetta (mini-pizza) topped with long stems of pleasantly bitter cicoria (Italian dandelion), thin salami slices and a hit of chilli.

10 Greek Street

10 Greek Street, W1D 4DH (7734 4677, www.10greekstreet.com). Tottenham Court Road tube. **Open** noon-2.30pm, 5.30-10.45pm Mon-Sat. **£££**. Modern European. **Map** p112 C2 ⑲
10 Greek Street appears to be yet another trendy, no-bookings restaurant, but the food can be excellent: the likes of smoked eel with horseradish sauce and beetroot, followed by perfectly rendered duck breast. The look is a little spartan, with menus on blackboards, though by night the place takes on a certain low-lit ambience. You can book for lunch, but not for dinner.

Yauatcha

15-17 Broadwick Street, W1F 0DL (7494 8888, www.yauatcha.com). Piccadilly Circus or Tottenham Court Road tube. **Open** noon-11.30pm Mon-Sat; noon-10.30pm Sun. **£££**. **Dim sum/tearoom**. **Map** p112 B2 ⑳
This dim sum restaurant is a sultry lounge-like basement den, with fish tanks and starry ceiling lights, where young professionals, Chinese families and suited business people enjoy their succession of freshly prepared – and highly impressive – perennial favourites.

Shopping

& Other Stories

256-258 Regent Street, W1B 3AF (7479 7070, www.stories.com).
Oxford Circus tube. **Open** 10am-9pm Mon-Fri; 10am-8pm Sat; noon-6pm Sun. **Map** p112 A1 ㉑
Owned by high street chain H&M but designed and produced independently, & Other Stories is aimed at a more fashion savvy shopper. A large team of designers, including many from style brands like Acne and Sonia Rykiel, have worked on the brand. The capacious store offers accessories, lipsticks and lingerie to match the frocks.

Berwick Street

www.berwickstreetlondon.co.uk. Piccadilly Circus or Tottenham Court Road tube. **Map** p112 B2 ㉒
The buzzy street market (9am-6pm Mon-Sat), in an area better known for its lurid, neon-lit trades, is one of London's oldest. Dating back to 1778, it's still great for seasonal produce and cheap fabric; Chris Kerr, son of legendary 1960s tailor Eddie, still crafts bespoke suits at no.31, and there are several vintage shops. The indie record shops that used to cluster here have taken a pasting, but this is still London's vinyl destination: you'll find Sister Ray (nos.34-35), Reckless Records (no.30) and the Music & Video Exchange (no.95) on Berwick Street itself, and on adjoining streets Sounds of the Universe (7 Broadwick Street), BM Soho (25 D'Arblay Street) and Phonica (51 Poland Street). Berwick Street is also home to Gosh! (p119).

Carnaby Street

www.carnaby.co.uk. Oxford Street tube. **Map** p112 A2 ㉓
As famous as the King's Road back when the Sixties were Swinging, Carnaby Street was, until a few years ago, more likely to sell you a postcard of the Queen snogging a punk rocker than a fishtail parka. But the noughties have been kind and Carnaby is cool again. Among decent chains (Lush, Muji), Kingly Court (7333 8118) is the highlight,

'Foyled Again?'

London's iconic bookstore makes a brand-new start.

In the mid-1980s, Foyles (right) wasn't just the worst bookshop in London – it was probably the worst in the world. Founded in 1903, it was run from 1945 by charming but thoroughly autocratic Christina Foyle, daughter of the founder.

She would sack anyone who'd worked at the shop for six months, lest they acquire an improved contract. She would move staff from their areas of specialist knowledge, so they'd be less tempted to browse at work. Notoriously, to prevent too many staff having access to cash, she introduced a double queuing system – you took your book to a desk, swapped it for a ticket, paid the ticket at a second desk, then collected your purchase from a third. Foyles had massive stock, but few staff knew where books were. No wonder a competitor felt able to run a series of posters saying: 'Foyled again? Try Dillons'.

Still, she kept Foyles in operation up to her death in 1999 – the year Dillons folded. 'In her 80s,' her *Guardian* obituary noted, 'she was still reading at least a book a day, drinking only champagne and declining even to try to cook.'

Surprisingly, a decade of shrewd management later, Foyles had become the most impressive independent bookshop in London –so it decided to make things difficult again. With Central Saint Martins art school having decamped to Granary Square (p106), Foyles has reopened in the bigger, art deco premises it left behind.

CEO Sam Husain describes his new store as 'a bookshop

for the twenty-first century', with 37,000sq ft of floorspace laid out by architects Lifschutz Davidson Sandilands around an impressive central atrium, and eight levels (four actual floors) packed with more than 200,000 books. Wherever you stand, you can see every part of the building, and the place is bathed in a contemplation-inducing glow. It's light years away from the dusty nooks and crannies of the old building.

Books aside, the focus is on the social aspect of reading. A whole floor is dedicated to events, from readings by Michael Palin and Jarvis Cocker to themed reading groups, and the swish new café is run by Leafi, the people behind the Whitechapel Gallery's smart bistro. There's even a capacious art space, curated by Future City.

Foyles veterans may find the new store a smidge anodyne, but any business making such a gutsy statement in favour of ink and paper deserves to enjoy their exciting new chapter.

a three-tiered complex containing a funky mix of various chains and independents. Thus encouraged, boutiques (among them OTHER/shop, right) have been thronging to the alleys nearby, with especially strong showings for stores for lovers of hip trainers.

Foyles

NEW *107-109 Charing Cross Road, WC2H 0EB (7437 5660, www.foyles. co.uk). Tottenham Court Road tube.* **Open** 9.30am-9pm Mon-Sat, noon-6pm Sun. **Map** p112 C2 **24**
See box left.

Gosh!

1 Berwick Street, W1F 0DR (7636 1011, www.goshlondon.com). Oxford Circus tube. **Open** 10.30am-7pm daily. **Map** p112 B2 **25**
There's nowhere better to bolster your comics collection than at this Soho specialist. There's a huge selection of Manga comics, but it's graphic novels that take centre stage, from early classics such as *Krazy Kat* to the best of Alan Moore. Classic children's books, of the *This is London* vein, are also a strong point.

Liberty

Regent Street, W1B 5AH (7734 1234, www.liberty.co.uk). Oxford Circus tube. **Open** 10am-8pm Mon-Sat; noon-6pm Sun. **Map** p112 A2 **26**
A creaky mock Tudor department store masterpiece, built in the 1920s, Liberty has upped its game over the last few years – a store-wide 'renaissance' (in its own words) that introduced a raft of cool new contemporary labels and a series of inspired events. Shopping here is about more than just spending money; artful window displays, exciting new collections and luxe labels make it an experience to savour. Despite being fashion-forward, Liberty respects its dressmaking heritage with a good haberdashery department.

OTHER/shop

21 Kingly Street, W1B 5QA (7734 6846, www.other-shop.com). Oxford Circus tube. **Open** 10.30am-6.30pm Mon-Sat; noon-5pm Sun. **Map** p112 A2 **27**
Founders Matthew Murphy and Kirk Beattie are the best-turned-out stalwarts of London's fashion scene. Their now defunct b store project was one of the capital's most influential boutiques. This latest initiative draws on the pair's near-decade of experience, but with a fresh outlook. The simple, two-floor store is a pared-down, glitz free showcase for OTHER's full range of men's and women's fashion and footwear, plus books, jewellery and art. A reworked London classic.

Nightlife

Borderline

Orange Yard, off Manette Street, W1D 4JB (0844 847 2465, www.theborderline. co.uk). Tottenham Court Road tube. **Map** p112 C2 **28**
A cramped, sweaty dive bar-slash-juke joint, the Borderline has long been a favoured stop-off for touring American bands of the country and blues type, but you'll also find a variety of indie acts and singer-songwriters here.

Comedy Store

1A Oxendon Street, SW1Y 4EE (0844 871 7699, www.thecomedystore.co.uk). Leicester Square or Piccadilly Circus tube. **Map** p112 C3 **29**
The Comedy Store made its name as the home of 'alternative comedy' in the 1980s. The venue has a gladiatorial semicircle of seats, and some of the circuit's best bills.
Event highlights The legendary 'King Gong' show (last Mon of the mth).

Leicester Square Theatre

6 Leicester Place, WC2H 7BX (0844 873 3433, www.leicestersquaretheatre.com). Leicester Square tube. **Map** p112 C3 **30**
The main auditorium programmes a good mix of big-name comedy (it's a

favourite of US comics), cabaret and straight plays, but keep an eye also on the inventive little basement space, with its champagne bar.

Madame JoJo's

8-10 Brewer Street, W1F 0SD (7734 3040, www.madamejojos.com). Leicester Square or Piccadilly Circus tube. **Map p112 B3 ③**

Famed nights at this red and shabby basement club include variety – Kitsch Cabaret is every Saturday night – but its long-running Tuesday nighter, White Heat, still books up-and-coming bands and DJs.

Pizza Express Jazz Club

10 Dean Street, W1D 3RW (0845 602 7017, www.pizzaexpresslive.com). Tottenham Court Road tube. **Map p112 C1 ②**

The upstairs restaurant (7437 9595) is a straightforward jazz-free branch of the pizza chain, but downstairs the 120-capacity basement venue is one of the best modern mainstream jazz venues in town.

Ronnie Scott's

47 Frith Street, W1D 4HT (7439 0747, www.ronniescotts.co.uk). Leicester Square or Tottenham Court Road tube. **Map p112 C2 ③**

Opened (albeit on a different site) by the British saxophonist Ronnie Scott in 1959, this jazz institution was completely refurbished five years ago. The capacity was expanded to 250, the food got better and the bookings drearier. Happily, Ronnie's has got back on track, with jazz heavyweights once more dominating in place of the mainstream pop acts who held sway for a while.

Arts & leisure

Curzon Soho

99 Shaftesbury Avenue, W1D 5DY (0871 703 3988, www.curzoncinemas.com). Leicester Square tube. **Map p112 C2 ③**

All the cinemas in the Curzon group programme a superb range of shorts, rarities, double bills and mini-festivals, but the Curzon Soho is the best – not least because it has a good ground-floor café and decent basement bar.

Gielgud Theatre

35 Shaftesbury Avenue, W1D 6AR (0844 482 5130, www.curiouson stage.com). Piccadilly Circus tube. **Map p112 C3 ③**

Christopher Boone, a young Asperger Syndrome sufferer, is trying to solve the mysterious death of his neighbour's dog in this electrifying staging of Mark Haddon's novel, *The Curious Incident of the Dog in the Night-time*. Production is subject to change.

Odeon Leicester Square

Leicester Square, WC2H 7LQ (0871 224 4007, www.odeon.co.uk). Leicester Square tube. **Map p112 C3 ③**

This art deco masterpiece is London's archetypal red-carpet cinema for premieres. Catch one of the occasional silent movie screenings with live organ music if you can; otherwise, it will be a comfy viewing of a pricey current blockbuster.

Prince Charles Cinema

7 Leicester Place, off Leicester Square, WC2H 7BY (7494 3654, www. princecharlescinema.com). Leicester Square tube. **Map p112 C3 ③**

The downstairs screen here offers the best value in town (from £8) for releases that have ended their first run elsewhere. The weekend singalong screenings are very popular – *Sound of Music*, *Rocky Horror*, *Grease*….

Prince Edward Theatre

28 Old Compton Street, W1D 4HS (0844 482 5155, www.miss-saigon.com). Leicester Square tube. **Map p112 C2 ③**

This theatre is currently showing *Miss Saigon*, a welcome return for West End impresario Cameron Mackintosh (see box p123) and a brilliant night out if

Soho Theatre p122

you want spectacle, lung-power, Big Emotions and a life-size model helicopter – less so if you're after three-dimensional characters or a sense of humour. Production is subject to change.

Prince of Wales

Coventry Street, W1D 6AS (0844 482 5110, www.bookofmormonlondon.com). Leicester Square tube. **Map** p112 C3 ㊴
Broadway smash *The Book of Mormon* sees strapping young Latter Day Saints missionaries attempt to convert heathen Ugandan villagers through sheer politeness – while Trey Parker and Matt Stone's script ducks no obscene phrase. Production is subject to change.

Queen's Theatre

51 Shaftesbury Avenue, W1D 6BA (0844 482 5160, www.lesmis.com). Leicester Square tube. **Map** p112 C3 ㊵
The capital's longest running musical, *Les Misérables*, offers quasi-operatic power ballads and some bona fide classics in a gritty tale of injustice and poverty during the French Revolution. Production is subject to change.

Soho Theatre

21 Dean Street, W1D 3NE (7478 0100, www.sohotheatre.com). Tottenham Court Road tube. **Map** p112 C2 ㊶
Its cool blue neon lights, front-of-house café and occasional late-night shows attract a younger, hipper crowd than most theatres. The Soho brings on aspiring writers through regular workshops, has regular solo comedy shows and has got stuck in to cabaret.

tkts

Clocktower Building, Leicester Square, WC2H 7NA (www.tkts.co.uk). Leicester Square tube. **Open** 9am-7pm Mon-Sat; 11am-7pm Sun. **Map** p112 C3 ㊷
Avoid getting ripped off by the touts and buy tickets for West End blockbusters at much-reduced rates, either on the day or up to a week in advance. It's not uncommon to find the best seats sold at half price.

Covent Garden

Covent Garden is understandably popular with visitors. A traffic-free oasis in the heart of the city, replete with shops, cafés and bars – and the **London Transport Museum** – it centres on a restored 19th-century covered market. On the west side, the portico of **St Paul's Covent Garden** hosts jugglers and escapologists. And if you're looking for great vocal performances rather than street performances, the **Royal Opera House** is here too.

Sights & museums

Presiding over the eastern end of Oxford Street, the landmark **Centre Point** tower now has a public bar and restaurant (**Paramount**, p126).

Covent Garden Piazza

Covent Garden tube. **Map** p113 E3 ㊸
The Piazza offers a combination of gentrified shops, restaurants and cafés, and living statues and buskers. Most of the entertainment takes place under the portico of St Paul's Covent Garden (p124), while tourists are drawn to the upmarket chain stores and sometimes quirky but often twee boutiques in the 180-year-old covered market. The architecture is handsome, though – it can be best appreciated from the Amphitheatre Café Bar's terrace loggia at the Royal Opera House (p130). Much classier shops are opening here now, led by the Apple Store (p126), but the North Hall's Apple Market still has arts and crafts stalls (Tue-Sun) and antiques (Mon), while the Jubilee Market will exceed anyone's requirements for novelty T-shirts.

London Transport Museum

Covent Garden Piazza, WC2E 7BB (7379 6344, www.ltmuseum.co.uk). Covent Garden tube. **Open** 10am-6pm

Mr Saigon

The West End theatre impresario on his revival of *Miss Saigon*.

Superstar producer Cameron Mackintosh spoke to *Time Out* about the revival of his 1989 blockbuster at the **Prince Edward Theatre** (p120), and his personal investment in and love of London's West End theatres.

A musical about the Vietnam War still sounds faintly insane. Was it a gamble at the time?
'It wasn't a gamble that would have caused me any grief if I'd lost it. It came at the end of the mad '80s, Thatcherism and all that, so the public, who hadn't booked tickets upfront for *Cats*, *Les Mis* and *Phantom*, thought: we're not going to be caught out this time. So it took enormous advance sales.'

This is a new production. What has changed?
'The original was a great big operatic box full of great big pristine set pieces; this is the seething dirty streets of Bangkok and Saigon.'

Your work now revolves around your old blockbusters. Do you ever want to rip it all up and start again?
'Darling, when you're as old as I am you cherish the very few musicals that have come your way that you know are great classics. You become their guardian.'

Since the Apollo Theatre roof collapsed in 2012, there's been concern about the physical integrity of the West End. Do you have full confidence in the seven theatres you own?
'I've spent more money on my theatres since I bought them than I did buying them. I've renovated this one [the Prince Edward] three times in the 15 years I've had it. It used to be horrible. I love architecture almost as much as I love my musicals. I know that after I'm gone the buildings I leave behind are going to last another hundred years.'

LONDON BY AREA

Mon-Thur, Sat, Sun; 11am-6pm Fri.
Admission £15; free-£11.50 reductions.
Map p113 F3 **44**

Tracing the city's transport history from the horse age, this fine museum focuses on social history and design, illustrated by a superb array of buses, trams and trains, many of which the kids can climb on. The collections are in broadly chronological order, beginning with the Victorian gallery and a replica of Shillibeer's first horse-drawn bus service from 1829, while a new gallery focuses on London Transport's inspiring poster art.
Event highlights Guided tours of the museum's massive west London depot (last Fri & Sat of mth).

St Paul's Covent Garden
Bedford Street, WC2E 9ED (7836 5221, www.actorschurch.org). Covent Garden tube. **Open** 8.30am-5pm Mon-Fri; 9am-1pm Sun. Times vary on Sat, phone for details. **Admission** free; donations appreciated. **Map** p113 E3 **45**

Known as the Actors' Church, this magnificently spare building was designed by Inigo Jones for the Earl of Bedford in 1631. The thespians commemorated on its walls range from those lost in obscurity to those destined for immortality. Surely there's no more romantic tribute in London than Vivien Leigh's plaque, simply inscribed with words from Shakespeare's *Antony & Cleopatra*: 'Now boast thee, death, in thy possession lies a lass unparallel'd.'

Eating & drinking

Balthazar
4-6 Russell Street, WC2B 7BN (3301 1155, www.balthazarlondon.com). Covent Garden tube. **Open** 7.30am-midnight Mon-Fri; 10am-midnight Sat; 10am-11pm Sun. **£££. French.** **Map** p113 F3 **46**

Balthazar London is a French-style bistro that mimics its New York predecessor perfectly: red awnings, leather banquettes, giant antiqued mirrored walls, beautiful mosaic floors. Signature dishes such as the onion soup are still there – a Gruyère lid grilled over a subtantial bowl of thick country bread, immersed in a rich and sweet chicken stock – but richness pervades every dish, from duck shepherd's pie, served in a cast-iron dish, to the comforting gratin dauphinois. Portions are filling, but don't skip the bread basket – the outstanding bread can also be taken away from the boulangerie next door.

Delaunay
55 Aldwych, WC2B 4BB (7499 8558, www.thedelaunay.com). Covent Garden, Temple tube or Charing Cross tube/rail. **Open** 7am-midnight Mon-Fri; 8am-midnight Sat; 9am-11pm Sun. **£££. Brasserie. Map** p113 F2 **47**

Comparisons with the iconic Wolseley (p74) are inevitable. The Delaunay is also a 'grand café' in the Continental mould, and the same owners created and run both. The menu majors on German classics, the likes of choucroute (warm sauerkraut with sausages, salted meats and charcuterie) and a classic wiener schnitzel, along with perfectly presented desserts and cakes hailing from mittel-Europe. Breakfast is a highlight: perfect Viennoiseries, porridge, pancakes, eggs every way, muesli, full English… and of course, it also serves afternoon tea.

Dishoom
12 Upper St Martin's Lane, WC2H 9FB (7420 9320, www.dishoom.com). Covent Garden or Leicester Square tube. **Open** 8am-11pm Mon-Thur; 8am-midnight Fri; 9am-midnight Sat; 9am-10pm Sun. **££.** **Indian. Map** p113 D3 **48**

Dishoom has got the look of a Mumbai 'Irani' café spot on. Solid oak panels, antique mirrors and ceiling fans say 'retro grandeur', and there's a fascinating display of old magazine covers, adverts and fading photos of Indian families. Parts of the menu are familiar street snacks (a terrific pau bhaji), but classy cocktails and intriguingly flavoured lassis move things upmarket.

Gordon's

47 Villiers Street, WC2N 6NE (7930 1408, www.gordonswinebar.com). Embankment tube or Charing Cross tube/ rail. **Open** 11am-11pm Mon-Sat; noon-10pm Sun. **Wine bar. Map** p113 E4 ㊾

Gordon's has been serving drinks since 1890, and it looks like it – the place is a specialist in yellowing, candle-lit alcoves. Although it is surprisingly modern, the wine list doesn't bear expert scrutiny and the food is buffet-style, but atmosphere is everything, and this is a great, bustling place, redolent of romantic assignations.

Great Queen Street

32 Great Queen Street, WC2B 5AA (7242 0622). Covent Garden or Holborn tube. **Open** noon-2.30pm, 6-10.30pm Mon-Sat; 1-3pm Sun. **££. British. Map** p113 F1 ㊿

The pub-style room here thrums with bonhomie, while the outdoor tables are almost never vacant. Ranging from snacks to shared mains, the menu is designed to tempt and satisfy rather than educate or impress. The menu changes daily. Booking is essential, and the robust food is worth it. At the Sunday lunch session, diners sit and are served together. The Dive bar downstairs serves snacks and drinks.

Hawksmoor Seven Dials

11 Langley Street, WC2H 9JJ (7856 2154, www.thehawksmoor.co.uk). Covent Garden tube. **Open** noon-3pm, 5-10.30pm Mon-Thur; noon-3pm, 5-11pm Fri, Sat; noon-9.30pm Sun. **£££. Steakhouse. Map** p113 E2 (51)

Hawksmoor stands out as the benchmark for an all-round bar and grill experience. The site's a real beauty, evocative of old New York with its speakeasy feel and old brickwork. The cocktails are masterfully concocted and the steaks are sublime, with clued-up staff keen to advise on the various cuts of meat and lengthy wine list.

Homeslice *13 Neal's Yard, WC2H 9DP (7836 4604, www.homeslicepizza.co.uk). Covent Garden tube.* **Open** noon-10.30pm Mon-Sat; noon-8pm Sun. **£. Pizza. Map** p113 D2 (52)

Fresh from the wood-fired oven, Homeslice's thin-crust pizzas are available by the slice (£4) or 20-inch wheel (£20). More innovative options include one with bone marrow slivers on top; another combines white anchovy, chard and Doddington cheese. The service is impeccably attentive, and there are craft beers and prosecco on draught.

Kopapa

32-34 Monmouth Street, WC2H 9HA (7240 6076, www.kopapa.co.uk). Leicester Square tube. **Open** 8.30-11am, noon-11pm Mon-Fri; 9.30am-4pm, 4.30-11pm Sat; 9.30am-4pm Sun. **££. Fusion. Map** p113 D2 (53)

Kopapa serves breakfast, small dishes, great wines and great coffee, in a come-as-you-are café setting. Many of its bare tables are shared; around half are bookable, the rest are not. The lights are low, the seats close together. The coffees, smoothies and wines by the glass are all first rate, but it's fabulous tapas-style fusion food that really makes Kopapa stand out.

Opera Tavern

23 Catherine Street, WC2B 5JS (7836 3680, www.operatavern.co.uk). Covent Garden tube. **Open** noon-3pm, 5pm-11.30pm Mon-Fri; noon-11.30pm Sat; noon-5pm Sun. **££. Spanish-Italian. Map** p113 F2 (54)

Low-lit, on-trend and immediately appealing, this is a restaurant of real character. The grand old pub premises date from 1879, but have received a major refit. It's equally accomplished

LONDON BY AREA

as a bar and restaurant, with a menu that craftily meshes Italianate small plates and Spanish tapas.

Paramount

Centre Point, 101-103 New Oxford Street, WC1A 1DD (7420 2900, www. paramount.uk.net). Tottenham Court Road tube. **Open** 8-10.30am, noon-11pm Mon-Fri; noon-11pm Sat; noon-9.45pm Sun. **£££. Modern European**. Map p112 C1 ⑤

Located on the 32nd floor of the landmark Centre Point building, it's not surprising the Tom Dixon-designed interior of this smart restaurant is upstaged by the superb view. Still, Colin Layfield's menu tries to hold its own with carefully constructed dishes, but – except for breakfast – it's pricey. The bar on the floor above often welcomes walk-ins.

Scoop

40 Shorts Gardens, WC2H 9AB (7240 7086, www.scoopgelato.com). Covent Garden tube. **Open** Sept-May noon-10.30pm Mon-Wed, Sun; noon-11.30pm Thur-Sat. June-Aug noon-midnight daily. **£. Ice-cream**. Map p113 D2 ⑤

Frequent queues are a testament to the quality of the ice-cream, even dairy-free healthy versions, at this Italian artisan's shop. Flavours include a very superior Piedmont hazelnut type, which can be eaten in at a few tables or taken away.

J Sheekey

28-34 St Martin's Court, WC2N 4AL (7240 2565, www.j-sheekey.co.uk). Leicester Square tube. **Open** noon-3pm, 5.30pm-midnight Mon-Sat; noon-3.30pm, 6-11pm Sun. **£££. Fish & seafood**. Map p113 D3 ⑤

Sheekey's Oyster Bar opened in 2009, yet another enticement to visit this fine restaurant. Unlike many of London's period pieces (which this certainly is: it was chartered in the mid 19th century), Sheekey's buzzes with fashionable folk. Even if you opt

for the main restaurant, your party of four may be crammed on to a table for two, but the accomplished menu will take your mind off it, stretching from sparklingly simple seafood platters to dishes that are interesting without being elaborate.

Terroirs

5 William IV Street, WC2N 4DW (7036 0660, www.terroirswinebar.com). Charing Cross tube/rail. **Open** noon-3pm, 5.30-11pm Mon-Sat. **£££**. Wine bar. Map p113 E4 ⑤

Now extending over two floors, Terroirs is a superb and very popular wine bar that specialises in the new generation of organic and biodynamic, sulphur-, sugar- or acid-free wines. The list is only slightly shorter than the Bible and the food is terrific: a selection of French bar snacks and seafood.

Wahaca

66 Chandos Place, WC2N 4HG (7240 1883, www.wahaca.co.uk). Covent Garden or Leicester Square tube. **Open** noon-11pm Mon-Sat; noon-10.30pm Sun. **£. Mexican**. Map p113 E3 ⑤

Wahaca has a look as cheery as its staff, with lamps made of tomatillo cans dotted with bottle tops, wooden crates packed with fruit, and tubs of chilli plants. The menu – Mexican food, but made with British ingredients – is really designed for sharing, tapas-style, but you can also choose one of the larger plato fuertes (enchiladas, burritos or grilled dishes).

Shopping

Apple Store

1-7 The Piazza, WC2E 8HA (7447 1400, www.apple.com). Covent Garden tube. **Open** 9am-9pm Mon-Sat; noon-6pm Sun. Map p113 E3 ⑥

A temple to geekery, this is the world's biggest Apple Store, with separate rooms – set out over three storeys – devoted to each product line. The exposed brickwork, big old oak tables and stone floors make it an inviting place, and it's also the world's first Apple Store with a Start Up Room, where staff will help set up your new iPad, iPhone, iPod or Mac, or transfer files from your old computer to your new one – all for free.

Cecil Court

www.cecilcourt.co.uk. Leicester Square tube. **Map** p113 D3 ⑥

Bookended by Charing Cross Road and St Martin's Lane, picturesque Cecil Court is known for its antiquarian book, map and print dealers. Notable residents include children's specialist Marchpane (no.16), Watkins (nos.19 & 21) for occult and New Age titles, and 40-year veteran David Drummond at Pleasures of Past Times (no.11), who specialises in theatre and magic.

Coco de Mer

23 Monmouth Street, WC2H 9DD (7836 8882, www.coco-de-mer.co.uk). Covent Garden tube. **Open** 11am-7pm Mon-Wed, Fri, Sat; 11am-8pm Thur; noon-6pm Sun. **Map** p113 D2 ⑥

London's most glamorous erotic emporium sells a variety of tasteful books, toys and lingerie, from glass dildos that double as objets d'art to crotchless culottes and corsets.

Fopp

1 Earlham Street, WC2H 9LL (7845 9770, www.fopp.com). Covent Garden or Leicester Square tube. **Open** 10am-10pm Mon-Wed; 10am-11pm Thur-Sat; noon-6pm Sun. **Map** p113 D2 ⑥

Three floors of new musical releases and back-catalogue surprises, plus good selections of books and DVDs, all at competitive prices, make this a great place for bargains. Look out for world cinema, art-house masterpieces and anime – plus '80s teen classic DVDs on the ground floor and basement, with Fopp's full music selection upstairs.

Hope & Greenwood

1 Russell Street, WC2B 5JD (7240 3314, www.hopeandgreenwood.co.uk). Covent Garden tube. **Open** 11am-7.30pm Mon-Fri; 10.30am-7.30pm Sat; noon-6pm Sun. **Map** p113 F2 ⑥

This adorable 1950s-style, letter-box-red cornershop is the perfect place to find the sherbets, chews and chocolates that were once the focus of a proper British childhood. Even the staff look the part: beautifully turned out in pinnies, ready to pop your sweets in a one of those classic striped paper bags with a smile. A great pitstop for last-minute presents.

James Smith & Sons

53 New Oxford Street, WC1A 1BL (7836 4731, www.james-smith.co.uk). Holborn or Tottenham Court Road tube. **Open** 10am-6pm Mon-Sat. **Map** p113 D1 ⑥

For more than 175 years, this charming shop, its Victorian fittings still intact, has held its own in the niche market of umbrellas and walking sticks. Forget your throwaway brolly that will break at the first puff of wind, and instead invest in one of Smith's wonderful hickory-crooked City umbrellas.

Neal's Yard Dairy

17 Shorts Gardens, WC2H 9AT (7240 5700, www.nealsyarddairy.co.uk). Covent Garden tube. **Open** 10am-7pm Mon-Sat. **Map** p113 D2 ⑥

Neal's Yard buys from small farms and creameries and matures the cheeses in its own cellars until they're ready to sell. Names such as Stinking Bishop and Lincolnshire Poacher are as evocative as the aromas in the shop.

Opening Ceremony

35 King Street, WC2E 8JG (7836 4978, www.openingceremony.us). Covent Garden tube. **Open** 11am-8pm Mon-Sat; noon-6pm Sun. **Map** p113 E3 ⑥

Opening Ceremony has a winning formula that combines the owners' own zeitgeist-tapping designs with hot-off-the-press new labels and

Covent Garden

revivals of long-forgotten brands, as well as exclusives from the likes of Chloë Sevigny. The colour-popping London store is also home to one of the capital's biggest Kenzo ranges outside the designer label's flagship.

Stanfords

12-14 Long Acre, WC2E 9LP (7836 1321, www.stanfords.co.uk). Covent Garden or Leicester Square tube. **Open** 9am-8pm Mon-Fri; 10am-8pm Sat; noon-6pm Sun. **Map** p113 D3 ⑥⑧

Three floors of travel guides, literature, maps, language guides, atlases and magazines. The basement houses the complete range of British Ordnance Survey maps, and you can plan your next move over Fairtrade coffee in the café.

Nightlife

Heaven

Underneath the Arches, Villiers Street, WC2N 6NG (7930 2020, www.heaven nightdublondon.com). Embankment tube or Charing Cross tube/rail. **Map** p113 E4 ⑥⑨

London's most famous gay club is a bit like *Les Misérables* – it's camp and full of history, and tourists love it. Popcorn on Mondays has long been a good bet, but it's really all about G-A-Y on Thursdays, Fridays and Saturdays. For as long as anyone can remember, divas with an album to flog (Madonna, Kylie, Girls Aloud) have turned up to perform here at the weekend.

12 Bar Club

22-23 Denmark Street, WC2H 8NL (7240 2622, www.12barclub.com). Tottenham Court Road tube. No credit cards. **Map** p113 D1 ⑦⓪

This much-cherished hole-in-the-wall – if smoking were still allowed, it's the kind of place that would be full of it – books a grab-bag of stuff. The size (capacity 100, a stage that barely accommodates a trio) dictates a predominance of singer-songwriters.

Arts & leisure

Cambridge Theatre

32-34 Earlham Street, WC2H 9HU (0844 800 1110, www.matildathe musical.com). Covent Garden tube or Charing Cross tube/rail. **Map** p113 D2 ⑦①

Transferring to the West End in 2011, *Matilda* snatched up Olivier Awards like a sticky-fingered child in a sweetshop, and this Royal Shakespeare Company production (by Matthew Warchus, soon to take charge at the Old Vic, p64) is still a treat. With hindsight, Dennis Kelly and Tim Minchin's musical, born of the 1988 novel by Roald Dahl, is a little long, but when it's good, it's very, very good. And it's even better when it's horrid. Production subject to change.

Coliseum

St Martin's Lane, WC2N 4ES (7845 9300, www.eno.org). Leicester Square tube or Charing Cross tube/rail. **Map** p113 D4 ⑦②

Built as a music hall in 1904, the home of the English National Opera (ENO) is in sparkling condition following a renovation in 2004. All works are performed in English, and prices are generally cheaper than at the Royal Opera House – especially with reduced price tickets for their 'Undress for the Opera' scheme. The ENO has been under the youthful stewardship of music director Edward Gardner since 2006, during which time occasional duds have been offset by surprising sell-outs, but he is due to leave in 2015 and, at the time of writing, the ENO had just suffered a 30% cut in funding.

Donmar Warehouse

41 Earlham Street, WC2H 9LX (0844 871 7624, www.donmarwarehouse.com). Covent Garden or Leicester Square tube. **Map** p113 E2 ⑦③

The Donmar isn't actually a warehouse but a 251-seat boutique theatre. Successive artistic directors – Sam Mendes, Michael Grandage and now Josie Rourke – have kept it on a fresh, intelligent path. The venue's combination of artistic integrity and intimate size has proved hard to resist, with many high-profile film actors appearing, among them Nicole Kidman, Gwyneth Paltrow and Ewan McGregor, but tickets sell out in a flash. Join the traditional morning queue for £7.50 standing tickets – or the £10 Barclays Front Row tickets, released at 10am every Monday morning.

Lyceum Theatre

21 Wellington Street, WC2E 7RQ (www. lyceum-theatre.co.uk). Charing Cross tube/rail. **Map** p113 F3 ⓴

Nothing prepares you for the impact of *The Lion King*'s opening sequence: with the surge of 'Circle of Life' reverberating through your chest, a cacophonous cavalcade of species marches on as if Noah's Ark had emptied onto the stage. The plot is paper thin, but the show's global range of theatrical techniques create an explosive spectacle. Production is subject to change.

New London Theatre

166 Drury Lane, WC2B 5PQ (0844 412 2708, www.warhorseonstage.com). Holborn tube. **Map** p113 E1 ⓯

With a Spielberg film adaptation under its belt, *War Horse* is now a truly global phenomenon, but Handspring's astonishing life-size puppets – skeletally modernist in form but utterly, magically alive thanks to their talented army of puppeteers – remain the true stars of this National Theatre (p65) production. Michael Morpurgo's story is simple: Devon-dwelling teen Albert Narracott signs up for World War I – in order to track down his beloved horse Joey. Production is subject to change.

Novello Theatre

Aldwych, WC2B 4LD (0844 482 5137, www.mamma-mia.com). Covent Garden or Holborn tube. **Map** p113 F3 ⓰

Judy Craymer's bold idea of turning the insanely catchy songs of ABBA into a musical is a winner. Given the music, a story just about solid enough to stay on its platform heels, and a Greek island setting, it's impossible not to fall for *Mamma Mia!*'s twinkling charms. Production subject to change.

Royal Opera House

Bow Street, WC2E 9DD (7304 4000, www.roh.org.uk). Covent Garden tube. **Map** p113 E2 ⓱

The Royal Opera House was founded in 1732 on the profits of a production of John Gay's *Beggar's Opera*; the current building, built roughly 150 years ago but extensively remodelled, is the third on the site. Organised tours explore the massive eight-floor building, taking in the main auditorium, the costume workshops and sometimes a ballet rehearsal. The glass-roofed Floral Hall, the Crush Bar and the Amphitheatre Café Bar (with its terrace over the market) are open to the general public. Critics argue the programming can be a little spotty, especially above the famously elevated ticket prices at the top end. Never mind: there are still fine productions, many of them under the baton of Antonio Pappano. This is also home to the Royal Ballet.

Theatre Royal Drury Lane

Catherine Street, WC2B 5JF (7492 9930, www.charlieandthechocolatefactory.com). Covent Garden tube. **Map** p113 F2 ⓲

Roald Dahl might not have liked the whiz-popping rave that Sam Mendes has created from his addictive kids' book *Charlie and the Chocolate Factory*, but what a show this is: a deliciously twisted anti-talent contest in which young Charlie finds a golden ticket and enters the factory of mysterious confectioner, Wonka, to battle four revoltingly spoiled brats for a lifetime's supply of chocolate. Production is subject to change.

The City

The City

Holborn to Clerkenwell

The City of London collides with the West End in Clerkenwell and Holborn. Bewigged barristers inhabit the picturesque **Inns of Court**, while City boys head from their loft apartments to the latest restaurant in what is one of London's foodiest areas.

Sights & museums

Courtauld Gallery

Strand, WC2R 1LA (7848 2526, www.courtauld.ac.uk/gallery). Temple tube. **Open** 10am-6pm daily. **Admission** £6; free-£5 reductions; £3 Mon. **Map** p132 A4 **1**

In the north wing of Somerset House (p136), the Courtauld's collection of paintings has several works of world importance. There are outstanding pre-19th century works (don't miss

Lucas Cranach's fine *Adam & Eve*), but the strongest suit is Impressionist and post-Impressionist paintings, such as Manet's astonishing *A Bar at the Folies-Bergère* and numerous works by Cézanne. Downstairs, the sweet little gallery café shouldn't be overlooked.

Dr Johnson's House

17 Gough Square, EC4A 3DE (7353 3745, www.drjohnsonshouse.org). Chancery Lane tube or Blackfriars tube/ rail. **Open** *May-Sept* 11am-5.30pm Mon-Sat. *Oct-Apr* 11am-5pm Mon-Sat. **Admission** £4.50; free-£3.50 reductions; £10 family. No credit cards. **Map** p132 B4 **2**

Author of one of the first – surely the most significant and certainly the wittiest – dictionaries of the English language, Dr Johnson (1709-84) also wrote poems, a novel and one of the earliest travelogues. You can tour the stately Georgian townhouse where he came up with his inspired definitions: 'far-fetch: A deep stratagem. A ludicrous word'.

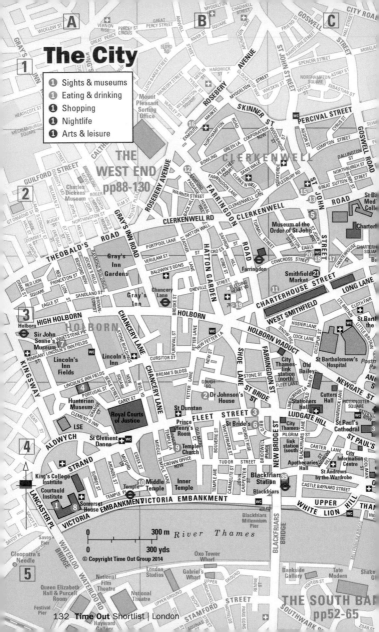

The City

A   **B**   **C**

1. Sights & museums
2. Eating & drinking
3. Shopping
4. Nightlife
5. Arts & leisure

THE WEST END
pp88-130

Charles Dickens Museum

CLERKENWELL

Mount Pleasant Sorting Office

ROSEBERY AVENUE

SKINNER ST

PERCIVAL STREET

GOSWELL ROAD

Museum of the Order of St John

Gray's Inn Gardens

Gray's Inn

CLERKENWELL RD

CLERKENWELL

HATTON GARDEN

FARRINGDON ROAD

Farringdon

Smithfield Market

THEOBALD'S ROAD

Chancery Lane

HOLBORN

CHARTERHOUSE STREET

LONG LANE

WEST SMITHFIELD

HIGH HOLBORN

Sir John Soane's Museum

Holborn

Lincoln's Inn Fields

Lincoln's Inn

HOLBORN VIADUCT

FARRINGDON ST

St Bartholomew's Hospital

City Thameslink station (north)

Old Bailey

NEWGATE ST

Cutters Hall

Stationers Hall

Hunterian Museum

SHOE LANE

Dr Johnson's House

FLEET STREET

St Bride's

St Dunstan

LUDGATE HILL

St Paul's Cathedral

ST PAUL'S

Royal Courts of Justice

St Clement Danes

Prince Henry's Room

Temple Church

NEW BRIDGE ST

City Thameslink station (south)

Apothecaries Hall

St Andrews by the Wardrobe

City Information Centre

King's College Institute

Courtauld Institute

Somerset House

Middle Temple

Inner Temple

Blackfriars Station

Blackfriars

CASTLE BAYNARD STREET

VICTORIA EMBANKMENT

UPPER THAMES ST

WHITE LION HILL

Cleopatra's Needle

WATERLOO BRIDGE

VICTORIA EMBANKMENT

Blackfriars Millennium Pier

BLACKFRIARS BRIDGE

0   300 m   *River Thames*

0   300 yds

© Copyright Time Out Group 2014

Oxo Tower Wharf

Savoy Pier

Queen Elizabeth Hall & Purcell Room

Festival Pier

London Studios

Gabriel's Wharf

National Film Theatre

National Theatre

Hayward Gallery

UPPER GROUND

STAMFORD STREET

Bankside Gallery

Tate Modern

THE SOUTH BANK
pp52-65

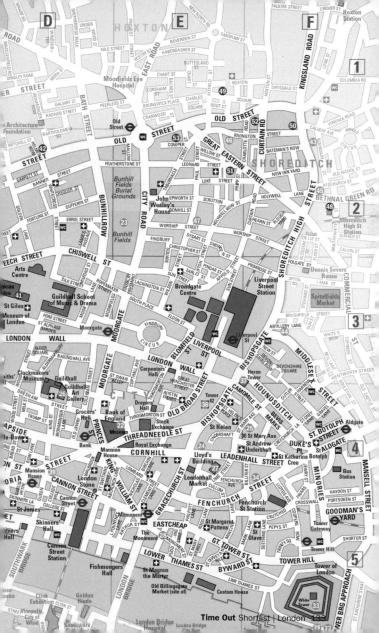

The other underground

Ride the long-mothballed postal train.

Most theme parks will let you loop-the-loop your teeth out of their sockets. But what about the understated thrill of a pootle on a postal train? Here at Time Out, we were able to find out for ourselves when we took a trip on one of the driverless electric trains of the old Post Office Underground Railway (the 'Mail Rail'). The disused railway is set to be turned into an underground ride in time for the opening of the new British Postal Museum & Archive in 2016.

With the help of £4.5m from the Heritage Lottery Fund, the museum will combine existing Post Office Museum & Archive collections in repurposed premises near the old Royal Mail sorting office at Mount Pleasant, with more exhibition space and entry to the Mail Rail within the old depot itself.

Museum exhibitions will curate almost 400 years of records and objects to highlight how British postal services have helped to shape the modern world, with notable artefacts including a first edition of James Joyce's *Ulysses*, original evidence from the Great Train Robbery trial and flintlock pistols used to defend Mail Coaches in the 19th century. Stories told will range from that of the 'human letter' suffragettes who posted themselves to the prime minister, to the world's first programmable computer, Colossus, heralding the digital revolution.

The Mail Rail is the world's only purpose-built underground postal rail system, a narrow-gauge system running from Paddington to Whitechapel with six stations, in operation from 1927 to 2003. At its peak it was operating for 22 hours daily, moving around four million letters a day.

The exhibition at the Mount Pleasant depot, where engines across the Mail Rail network were brought for maintenance, will highlight the industrial heritage of the railway and relate it to wider stories of moving the mail by rail. Part of the tunnel network will be opened for public access too, and from here visitors will be able to join a train for a ride along a one-kilometre loop of track through Mount Pleasant station. All aboard!

For more information, see http:// postalmuseum.wordpress.com.

Fleet Street
Chancery Lane or Temple tube.
Map p132 B4 ❸
The first printing press on this legendary street of newspapers was installed behind St Bride's Church (below) in 1500 by William Caxton's assistant, Wynkyn de Worde, but it wasn't until 1702 that the UK's first daily newspaper, the *Daily Courant*, rolled off the presses. By the end of World War II, half a dozen newspaper offices were churning out scoops, but they all moved away after Rupert Murdoch won his bitter war with the print unions in the 1980s, leaving only grand buildings including Reuters (no.85), the *Daily Telegraph* (no.135) and the jet-black art deco classic *Daily Express* (nos.121-128).

Hunterian Museum
Royal College of Surgeons, 35-43 Lincoln's Inn Fields, WC2A 3PE (7869 6560, www.rcseng.ac.uk/ museums). Holborn tube. **Open** 10am-5pm Tue-Sat. **Admission** free. No credit cards. **Map** p132 A4 ❹
John Hunter (1728-93) was a pioneering surgeon and anatomist, and physician to King George III. His huge collection of medical specimens can be viewed in this two-floor museum. The grisly exhibits include various bodily mutations and the brain of 19th-century mathematician Charles Babbage.

Museum & Library of the Order of St John
St John's Gate, St John's Lane, EC1M 4DA (7324 4005, www.museumstjohn. org.uk). Farringdon tube/rail. **Open** 10am-5pm Mon-Sat. *Tours* 11am, 2.30pm Tue, Fri, Sat. **Admission** free; suggested donation £5, £4 reductions. **Map** p132 C2 ❺
Now known for its ambulance service, the Order of St John started with Christian medical practices during the Crusades of the 11th to 13th centuries. In a Tudor gatehouse are gathered artefacts relating to the Hospitaller Knights, from Jerusalem, Malta and the Ottoman Empire, and a separate collection explaining the evolution of the modern ambulance service. Across St John's Square, the Priory Church, its pretty garden and its 12th-century crypt open regularly to the public.

St Bride's Church
Fleet Street, EC4Y 8AU (7427 0133, www.stbrides.com). Temple tube or Blackfriars tube/rail. **Open** 9am-6pm Mon-Fri; 10am-6.30pm Sun. Times vary Sat, so phone ahead. **Admission** free. **Map** p132 B4 ❻
St Bride's, 'the journalists' church', contains a shrine to hacks killed in action. The interior was rebuilt after Blitz bombing. Down in the crypt, a quietly excellent museum displays fragments of the churches that have existed on this site since the sixth century and tells the story of the newspapers on Fleet Street. According to local legend, the spire was the inspiration for the classic tiered wedding cake.

Sir John Soane's Museum
13 Lincoln's Inn Fields, WC2A 3BP (7405 2107, www.soane.org). Holborn tube. **Open** 10am-5pm Tue-Sat; 10am-5pm, 6-9pm 1st Tue of mth. *Tours* 11am Sat. **Admission** free; donations appreciated. *Tours* free-£5. **Map** p132 A3 ❼
Architect Sir John Soane (1753-1837) was an obsessive collector of art, furniture and architectural ornamentation, partly for enjoyment and partly for research. He turned his house into an amazing museum to which 'amateurs and students' should have access. Much of the museum's appeal derives from the domestic setting and ingenious contrivances, but the real wow is the Monument Court. At its lowest level is a 3,000-year-old sarcophagus of alabaster so fine that it's almost translucent, as well as the cell

LONDON BY AREA

of Soane's fictional monk Don Giovanni. The first phase of a long-term programme of renovation saw the expansion of the museum into the next-door house; next in line is the restoration of Sir John Soane's private apartments and his former Model Room, for his collection of architectural models, on the second floor of No.13 Lincoln's Inn Fields. The entire floor will be reopen in 2016. Event highlights Monthly candlelit tours – always book in advance.

Somerset House

Strand, WC2R 1LA (7845 4600, www.somersethouse.org.uk). Temple tube or Charing Cross tube/rail. **Open** 10am-6pm daily. **Admission** free. *Embankment Galleries prices vary; see website for details.* **Map** p132 A4 **8**

Architect Sir William Chambers spent the last 20 years of his life, from 1775, working on this neoclassical edifice overlooking the Thames. Effectively the first purpose-built office block in the world, it was built to accommodate learned societies such as the Royal Academy, and also the Inland Revenue. The Inland Revenue is still here, but the rest of the building is open to the public. It houses the lovely Courtauld (p131) and has a beautiful courtyard with choreographed fountains, a river-view café and other restaurants. It also hosts temporary art and fashion exhibitions, and has a history display – with ceremonial barge – downstairs.

Temple Church & Inner Temple

Fleet Street, EC4Y 7HL (7353 8559, www.templechurch.com). Temple tube. **Open** times vary; check website for details. **Admission** £4; free reductions. No credit cards. **Map** p132 B4 **9**

The quiet, beautiful quadrangles of Middle Temple (7427 4800, www.middletemple.org.uk) and Inner Temple (7797 8250, www.innertemple.org.uk) have been home to lawyers since medieval times, with Temple Church – private chapel of the mystical Knights Templar order, its structure inspired by Jerusalem's Church of the Holy Sepulchre – serving both. The rounded apse contains the worn gravestones of several Crusader knights, but the church was refurbished by Wren and Victorians, and damaged in the Blitz. Event highlights Organ recitals in Temple Church (Wed lunchtimes).

Two Temple Place

2 Temple Place, WC2R 3BD (7836 3715, www.twotempleplace.org). Temple tube. **Open** *Late Jan-mid Apr* 10am-4.30pm Mon, Thur-Sat; 10am-9pm Wed; 11am-4.30pm Sun. **Admission** free. **Map** p132 B4 **10**

Two Temple Place's Portland stone exterior and oriel windows are handsome – but the interior is extraordinary: the Three Musketeers adorn a fine staircase, intricately carved literary characters crowd the first floor, 54 apparently random busts – Voltaire and Marlborough, Anne Boleyn enjoying the company of Mary Queen of Scots – stare down from the medieval-style Great Hall. Built for William Waldorf Astor in 1895, Two Temple Place opens to the public three months a year with superb exhibitions.

Eating & drinking

Le Comptoir Gascon

61-63 Charterhouse Street, EC1M 6HJ (7608 0851, www.comptoirgascon.com). Farringdon tube/rail. **Open** noon-2.30pm, 6-10pm Tue-Sat. **££**. **French**. **Map** p132 C3 **11**

Comptoir is the modern rustic cousin (dainty velour chairs, exposed pipes, open brickwork, pottery dishes) of the more serious-minded Club Gascon (57 West Smithfield, 7796 0600, www.clubgascon.com), but exudes as much class and confidence as its forebear in the presentation of delectable regional specialities of Gascony. The posh café vibe is enhanced by capable and amiable French staff.

Eagle

159 Farringdon Road, EC1R 3AL (7837 1353). Farringdon tube/rail. **Open** noon-11pm Mon-Sat; noon-5pm Sun. **££**. **Gastropub.** Map p132 B2 ⑫

Widely credited with being the first gastropub (it opened in 1991), this is still recognisably a pub that serves big-flavoured, quality food: noisy, often crowded, with no-frills service and dominated by an open range where T-shirted cooks toss earthy grills in theatrical bursts of flame.

Foxlow

NEW *69-73 St John Street, EC1M 4AN (7014 8070, www.foxlow.co.uk). Farringdon tube/rail.* **Open** noon-3pm, 5.30-10.30pm Mon-Sat; noon-5.30pm Sun. **££. International.** Map p132 C2 ⑬

Will Beckett and Huw Gott, the duo behind the Hawksmoor steakhouses (p125), have scored again with this newcomer. It has a cosily masculine vibe (warm woods, low lighting and comfy retro-themed furniture) and a compact menu of meaty dishes to comfort and soothe, plus impeccably sourced steaks. The youthful staff are a marvel, with beaming smiles and a nothing-too-much-trouble attitude.

Look Mum No Hands

49 Old Street, EC1V 9HX (7253 1025, www.lookmumnohands.com). Barbican tube or Old Street tube/rail. **Open** 7.30am-10pm Mon-Fri; 9am-10pm Sat; 9.30am-10pm Sun. **£. Café.** Map p133 D2 ⑭

Look Mum is a cycle-friendly café-bar with cycle parking in a courtyard, a one-person workshop and plenty of space to hang out, snack, use the Wi-Fi, and – in the evenings – drink bottled beer or well-priced wine. Live afternoon screenings of cycle races take place in the big main room. The food is simple – cured meat

platters, baked tarts, pastries and cakes. Another branch has opened in Hackney (125-127 Mare Street, E8 3RH, 07985 200 472).

Modern Pantry

47-48 St John's Square, EC1V 4JJ (7250 0833, www.themodernpantry.co.uk). Farringdon tube/rail. **Open** 8am-10pm Mon; 8am-11pm Tue-Fri; 9am-4pm, 6-10.30pm Sat; 10am-4pm, 6-10pm Sun. **£££. International.** Map p132 C2 ⑮

A culinary three-parter in a pair of Georgian townhouses that feels savvy and still of the moment a few years after opening. Both pantry (takeaway) and café are at street level; upstairs are adjoining, informal dining rooms. Service is spot on and the menu brilliantly fuses all kinds of ingredients. Weekend brunch is special – and busy.

Moro

34-36 Exmouth Market, EC1R 4QE (7833 8336, www.moro.co.uk). Farringdon tube/rail or bus 19, 38, 341. **Open** 12.30-10.30pm Mon-Sat; 12.30-2.45pm Sun. **£££. Spanish/North African tapas.** Map p132 B2 ⑯

A meal at Sam and Sam Clark's Moro is a delight. For a restaurant with a deservedly big reputation, its decor is unpretentious, the centrepiece being a simple view of the kitchen's wood-fired oven. You can enjoy tapas at the bar or dine at leisure on the likes of chargrilled sea bass with spiced rice and fried okra in yoghurt with pomegranate from the regularly changing Moorish menu. Next door, Morito (no.32, EC1R 4QE, 7278 7007, closed Sun) is a fine no-booking offshoot.

St John

26 St John Street, EC1M 4AY (7251 0848, www.stjohnrestaurant.com). Barbican tube or Farringdon tube/rail. **Open** noon-2.45pm, 6-10.45pm Mon-Fri; 6-10.45pm Sat; 1-2.30pm Sun. **£££. British.** Map p132 C2 ⑰

Leading light of the modern British cooking revival, St John is an austere-looking place, opened in 1995 in the shell of a smokehouse by chef-patron Fergus Henderson. Its spirit hasn't changed: the focus is on unusual seasonal British ingredients, simply cooked and presented. Less expensive is the short menu at the boisterous no-reservations bar.

Vinoteca

7 St John Street, EC1M 4AA (7253 8786, www.vinoteca.co.uk). Farringdon tube/rail. **Open** noon-11pm Mon-Sat. **Wine bar. Map** p132 C3 ⓳

Inspired by the Italian *enoteca* (a blend of off-licence and wine bar, with bar snacks), Vinoteca is in fact more of a gastropub in spirit. But even if you want no more to eat than bread and olive oil, come here for the impressive 200-bottle wine list, of which 25 labels are available by the glass.

Ye Old Mitre

1 Ely Court, at the side of 8 Hatton Gardens, EC1N 6SJ (7405 4751). Chancery Lane tube or Farringdon tube/rail. **Open** 11am-11pm Mon-Fri. **Pub. Map** p132 B3 ⓳

The secluded location requires you to slink down an alleyway just off Hatton Garden, where you'll be transported to a parallel pub universe, where the clientele are friendly and the staff (in pristine black and white uniforms) briskly efficient. There's even the remains of a tree within the front room. Open only during the week, it's an atmospheric, pint-sized pub that's earned its top-notch reputation.

Zetter Townhouse

49-50 St John's Square, EC1V 4JJ (7324 4545, www.thezettertownhouse. com). Farringdon tube/rail. **Open** 7am-midnight Mon-Wed, Sun; 7am-1am Thur-Sat. **Bar. Map** p132 C2 ⓴

Spread across the ground floor of the Zetter hotel's (p180) sister site, this cosy cocktail lounge is a collaboration with the founders of 69 Colebrooke Row (p151). Colebrooke's head barman Tony Conigliaro is an expert alcohol alchemist, renowned for creating leftfield liquids and libations in his laboratory. Here the drinks list is unique, experimental yet refreshingly uncomplicated. Switched-on staff are delighted to talk you through your tipple. You can turn up unannounced, but book ahead to be sure of a seat.

Nightlife

Fabric

77A Charterhouse Street, EC1M 3HN (7336 8898, www.fabriclondon.com). Farringdon tube/rail. **Open** 10pm-6am Fri; 11pm-8am Sat; 11pm-6am Sun. **Map** p132 C3 ㉑

Fabric is the club most party people come to see in London: the main room has the stomach-wobbling Bodysonic dancefloor, the second is a rave-style warehouse, the third is where the cool stuff happens. Fridays belong to the bass: highlights include DJ Hype, who takes over all three rooms once a month for his drum 'n' bass, and dubstep night Playaz. Saturdays rock to techy, minimal, deep house sounds. Stellar DJs – and big queues – are a given.

The City

Fewer than 10,000 souls are resident within the Square Mile (1.21 square miles, in fact), but every working day the population increases tenfold, as bankers, brokers, lawyers and traders storm into their towering office blocks. The City still holds to boundaries set by the second-century walls of Roman Londinium (a few sections of which remain), although it then had six times more inhabitants than it does now. The streets are full of historic gems, but the real crowd-pullers are **St Paul's** and the **Tower of London**.

Clockwise from top left: Gherkin p140; Postman's Park p141; Tower of London p143

Sights & museums

The art gallery at the **Barbican** (£12, free-£10 reductions; p164) has good exhibitions of art, design and architecture, while the free Curve space shows excellent commissions. Of the three classic skyscrapers in the City – **Lloyd's** (below), the **'Gherkin'** (30 St Mary Axe, right) and **Tower 42** ('NatWest Tower') – only the latter is open to the public. However, its **City Social** bar-restaurant (p144) has increasing numbers of high-rise rivals, including in what is, for now, the City's tallest building: **Heron Tower** (Duck & Waffle, p144); for more, see box p145.

Bank of England Museum

Entrance on Bartholomew Lane, EC2R 8AH (7601 5545, www.bankofengland. co.uk/museum). Bank tube/DLR. **Open** 10am-5pm Mon-Fri. **Admission** free. **Map** p133 E4 ㉒

Housed in the bank's former Stock Offices, this museum explores the history of the national bank. As well as a chance to lift a 13kg gold bar (albeit one encased in a secure box you poke your hand into), there are ancient coins and original artwork for British banknotes, and a display on former employee Kenneth Grahame, author of *The Wind in the Willows*.

Bunhill Fields

Old Street tube/rail. **Admission** free. **Map** p133 E2 ㉓

The importance of this nonconformist burial ground was recognised in 2011, when it was protected from development by a Grade I listing. It's a moving little place, hemmed in by office walls and crammed with memorials to dead dissenters, such as John Bunyan, Daniel Defoe and William Blake.

'The Cheesegrater' (122 Leadenhall Street)

www.122leadenhallstreet.com. Liverpool Street tube/rail. **Map** p133 E4 ㉔

There's no public access to Lord Rogers' latest eye-catching skyscraper, but you can wander underneath the 737ft steel-and-glass wedge between trees in the 'landscaped' area there.

'The Gherkin' (30 St Mary Axe)

www.30stmaryaxe.com. Liverpool Street tube/rail. **Map** p133 F4 ㉕

Completed almost a decade ago, Lord Foster's distinctively curved skyscraper has become a cherished icon of modern London, its 'Gherkin' nickname plainly apt. There's no regular public access.

Guildhall Art Gallery

Guildhall Yard, EC2P 2EJ (7332 3700, www.guildhallartgallery.cityoflondon. gov.uk). St Paul's tube or Bank tube/DLR. **Open** 10am-5pm Mon-Sat; noon-4pm Sun. **Admission** free. *Temporary exhibitions* £5; free-£3 reductions. **Map** p133 D4 ㉖

The City of London's gallery (free to enter since spring 2011) contains dull portraits of royalty and some former mayors, and plenty of wonderful surprises, including a brilliant Constable, high-camp Pre-Raphaelite works and various absorbing paintings of historic London. A sub-basement has the scant remains of a 6,000-seat Roman amphitheatre, built around AD 70.

Lloyd's of London

1 Lime Street, EC3M 7HA (www.lloyds. com). Monument tube. **Map** p133 E4 ㉗

Lord Rogers' high-tech building has all its mechanical services (ducts, stairwells, lift shafts) on the outside, a design that still looks modern after 25 years. The original Lloyd's Register, decorated with bas-reliefs of sea monsters and nautical scenes, is on nearby Fenchurch Street. No public access.

Monument

Monument Street, EC3R 8AH (7626 2717, www.themonument.info).

Monument tube. **Open** *Oct-Mar* 9.30am-5pm daily. *Apr-Sept* 9.30am-5.30pm daily. **Admission** £3; free-£2 reductions. No credit cards. **Map** p133 E5 ㉓

The Monument, the world's tallest free-standing stone column, was designed by Sir Christopher Wren and his (often overlooked) associate Robert Hooke as a memorial to the Great Fire of London. It measures 202ft from the ground to the tip of the golden flame on the orb at its top, exactly the distance east to Farriner's bakery in Pudding Lane, where the fire is supposed to have begun on 2 September 1666. Reopened after a glorious £4.5m refurbishment, the Monument can again be climbed, by a spiral interior staircase, for fine views.

Museum of London

150 London Wall, EC2Y 5HN (7001 9844, www.museumoflondon.org.uk). Barbican or St Paul's tube. **Open** 10am-6pm daily. **Admission** free; suggested donation £3. **Map** p133 D3 ㉙

This expansive museum (set in the middle of a roundabout) tells the whole history of London – with help from east London's Museum of London Docklands (p163). Themes include 'London Before London' – flint axes, fossils, grave goods – and 'Roman London', which has a reconstructed dining room complete with mosaic floor. Also on the ground floor, sound effects and audio-visual displays illustrate the medieval city, along with cases of shoes and armour, and there's a moving exhibit on the Black Death. Rush downstairs for the outstanding galleries on modern London, opened in 2010. Among many fine exhibits are an unexploded Blitz bomb, a reconstruction of the Vauxhall Pleasure Gardens, an actual 18th-century debtors' prison cell and, in a new gallery since summer 2014, Thomas Heatherwick's delicate flower cauldron from the 2012 Olympics (see box p60).

Postman's Park

St Paul's tube. **Map** p132 C3 ㉚

This peaceful, fern-filled park near St Paul's contains the Watts Memorial to Heroic Sacrifice: a wall of Victorian ceramic plaques, each of which commemorates a fatal act of bravery.

St Paul's Cathedral

Ludgate Hill, EC4M 8AD (7236 4128, www.stpauls.co.uk). St Paul's tube. **Open** 8.30am-4pm Mon-Sat. *Galleries, crypt & ambulatory* 9.30am-4.15pm Mon-Sat. **Admission** £16; free-£14 reductions; £36 family. **Map** p132 C4 ㉛

A £40m restoration a few years ago left the main façade of St Paul's looking as brilliant as it must have when the first Mass was celebrated here in 1710. The vast open spaces of the interior contain memorials to national heroes such as Wellington and Lawrence of Arabia, as well as superb mosaics and gilt added by the Victorians. And the cathedral comes bang up to date with *Martyrs (Earth, Air, Fire, Water)*, the first of two permanent video installations by Bill Viola, showing four individuals, being martyred by the four classical elements. The Whispering Gallery, inside the dome, is reached by 259 steps from the main hall (the acoustics are so good a whisper can be clearly heard across the dome). Stairs continue up to first the Stone Gallery (119 steps), with its high external balustrades, then outside to the Golden Gallery (152 steps), with its giddying views. Head down to the crypt to see Nelson's grand tomb and the small tombstone of Sir Christopher Wren himself, inscribed: 'Reader, if you seek a monument, look around you.'

Tower Bridge Exhibition

Tower Bridge, SE1 2UP (7403 3761, www.towerbridge.org.uk). Tower Hill tube or Tower Gateway DLR. **Open** *Apr-Sept* 10am-6.30pm daily. *Oct-Mar* 9.30am-6pm daily. **Admission** £8; free-£5.60 reductions; £12.50-£18 family. **Map** p133 F5 ㉜

City Social p144

Opened in 1894, this is the 'London Bridge' that wasn't sold to America. Originally powered by steam, the drawbridge is now opened by electric rams when big ships need to venture this far upstream (check when the bridge is next due to be raised on the website). An entertaining exhibition on the history of the bridge is displayed in the old steamrooms and on the west walkway, which provides a crow's-nest view along the Thames.

Tower of London

Tower Hill, EC3N 4AB (0844 482 7777, www.hrp.org.uk). Tower Hill tube or Tower Gateway DLR. **Open** *Mar-Oct* 10am-5.30pm Mon, Sun; 9am-5.30pm Tue-Sat. *Nov-Feb* 10am-4.30pm Mon, Sun; 9am-4.30pm Tue-Sat. **Admission** £21.45; free-£18.15 reductions; £55 family. **Map** p133 F5 ㉝

Despite exhausting crowds and long climbs up narrow stairways, this is one of Britain's finest historical sites. Who wouldn't be fascinated by a close-up look at the crown of Queen Victoria or the armour (and mighty codpiece) of Henry VIII? The buildings of the Tower span 900 years of history and the bastions and battlements house a series of interactive displays on the lives of monarchs – and excruciatingly painful deaths of traitors.

The highlight has to be the Crown Jewels, viewed from a slow-moving travelator (get there early to minimise queuing), but the other big draw is the Royal Armoury in the White Tower: four floors of swords, armour, pole-axes, halberds and other gruesome tools for chopping people up. Executions of noble prisoners were carried out on the green in front of the Tower. Also in the White Tower, the Line of Kings is a collection of arms and armour, some belonging to monarchs, life-sized wooden horses and carved heads of kings. It was first displayed here after the Restoration as a propaganda tool for the legitimacy of the monarchy. Dispersed over the years, the collection is now back in its entirety.

Tickets are sold in the kiosk just west of the palace and visitors enter through the Middle Tower, but there's a free audio-visual display in the Welcome Centre outside the walls. There's plenty enough to do to fill a day, but skip to the highlights using the audio tour (which takes an hour), or by joining the highly entertaining free tours led by the Yeoman Warders (Beefeaters), who also care for the Tower's ravens.

'The Walkie-Talkie' (20 Fenchurch Street)

www.20fenchurchstreet.co.uk. Liverpool Street tube/rail. **Map** p133 F4 ㉞

Rafael Viñoly's distinctively top-heavy officeblock – nicknamed the 'Fryscraper' in September 2013, after reflected sunlight melted a Jaguar parked in the street below – is one new building that can be enjoyed by ordinary joes: levels 35-37 will be a 'Sky Garden' viewing area, and public terrace, served by a restaurant, café and bar. It's all due to open in late 2014.

Eating & drinking

For drinks with a view, see box p145.

Black Friar

174 Queen Victoria Street, EC4V 4EG (7236 5474). Mansion House tube or Blackfriars tube/rail. **Open** 10am-11pm Mon-Thur, Sat; 10am-11.30pm Fri; noon-10.30pm Sun. **Pub.** **Map** p132 C4 ㉟

This wedge-shaped pub at the north end of Blackfriars Bridge offers a handful of real ales, wine by the glass, standard lagers and some decent pub nosh, but it's the extraordinary Arts and Crafts interior, resplendent with carvings of monks and odd mottos, that makes the place worth a visit.

City Social

NEW *Tower 42, 25 Old Broad Street, EC2N 1HQ (7877 7703, http:// citysociallondon.com). Bank tube/DLR or Liverpool Street tube/rail.* **Open** *Restaurant* noon-3pm, 6-11.30pm Mon-Fri; 6-10.30pm Sat. *Bar* noon-10.30pm Mon-Fri; 5-10.30pm Sat. **££££. Modern European/ cocktail bar** Map p133 E4 ⑯

Chef Jason Atherton has taken over the 24th floor restaurant in Tower 42, with an attached bar that anyone can just show up to (via two lots of security, an escalator and at least one lift, that is). In the bar, the food and drink is of a far higher standard than you might reasonably expect up a skyscraper. Cocktails have just enough invention to make them worth the lofty prices. The Pea-lini, for example, comprises 'salted pea cordial', spearmint, absinthe, citric acid, prosecco – and an edible flower. Bar snacks carry Atherton's recognisably idiosyncratic details, like a 'ploughman's basket', which came with cheese, bread and things in little jars, laid out picnic-style in front of us on a checked cloth.

Duck & Waffle

40th floor, 110 Bishopsgate, EC2N 4AY (3640 7310, www.duckandwaffle.com). Liverpool Street tube/rail. **Open** 24hrs daily; limited menu served midnight-4.30am daily. **£££. International.** Map p133 E3 ⑰

The 755ft-tall Heron Tower (radio mast included) opened in 2011. On top of all the so-called office 'villages', a bit under 600ft up in the distinctive stepped roof, are two restaurants: the expensive Brazilian-Peruvian-Japanese fusion restaurant-bar Sushisamba (floors 38-39; 3640 7330, http://sushi samba.com), with its open terraces (bookings required for the restaurant), and the newer Duck & Waffle, which lacks the terraces but is open 24/7 – a real London rarity. The waffles come out at night, duck is served during the day, and a full English breakfast comes in at £13.

Perkin Reveller

The Wharf at the Tower of London, EC3N 4AB (3166 6949, www.perkin reveller.co.uk). Tower Hill tube. **Open** 10am-11pm Tue-Sat; 10am-5pm Sun. **££. Modern European.** Map p133 F5 ⑱

This dining room of sparse glass and white walls serves a seasonal mix of classic British and Modern European dishes, done with a bit of imagination: a clever starter of venison 'cottage pie' – tender chunks of juniper-scented venison topped with a creamy potato purée foam scattered with crisp ham pieces – served in a glass teacup, for instance, or an equally nicely presented and flavoured Cornish fish stew. Quality cooking among the tourist trap options around the Tower.

Sweetings

39 Queen Victoria Street, EC4N 4SA (7248 3062). Mansion House tube. **Open** 11.30am-3pm Mon-Fri. **£££. Fish & seafood.** Map p133 D4 ⑲

In these days of makeovers and global menus, Sweetings is that rare thing – a traditional British restaurant that clings to its traditions as if the Empire depended on it. It opens only for lunch, takes no bookings, and is full soon after noon with City gents, so order a silver pewter mug of Guinness and enjoy the wait.

Shopping

One New Change

1 New Change, EC4M 9AF (7002 8900, www.onenewchange.com). St Paul's tube or Bank tube/DLR. Map p132 C4 ⑳

Designed by Pritzker Prize-winning French starchitect Jean Nouvel, this dark, low-slung 'groundscraper' mall isn't immediately lovable – and even the shops (Reiss, Topshop, Swarovski) and eateries (Eat, Nando's, a champagne bar) feel a little predictable. But take the glass elevators up to the top floor and you'll be rewarded with superb views – on a level with the dome of St Paul's – which can be enjoyed for

LONDON BY AREA

Cocktails with altitude

London has sprouted a plethora of sky bars.

For swish cocktails, plush lounges and gourmet snacks galore, not to mention a front-row seat to the sexiest skyline on the planet, head to some of London's favourite sky bars and rooftop bars.

The grand art deco edifice that is now the ME by Meliá London was once Marconi House. From here, the first BBC programming was broadcast in 1922. Hence the name of the **Radio Rooftop Bar** (336-337 The Strand, WC2R 1HA, 0845 601 8980, www.melia.com), ten storeys up. Equipped with a retractable roof, big sofas and space heaters, the bar mainly faces south (oh look – there's the Oxo Tower and Big Ben). It's a sleek, glammed-up destination; a DJ keeps things upbeat.

To go higher, head to **Paramount** (p126), on an upper storey of the landmark Centre Point building, which has dominated the area at the east end of Oxford Street since 1967. The 360-degree wraparound viewing gallery, with floor-to-ceiling glass and cocktails, on the 33rd floor is dramatic and glamorous. The main bar and restaurant on the floor below are glitzy too.

But for real 21st-century altitude drama, take the express lift – faster than a bullet train – up the side of the Heron Tower to the 39th floor, and **Sushisamba** (p144). Occupying the top floors of one of the highest buildings in the City, it offers breathtaking views down over the adjacent Gherkin; further afield you can see the Thames, St Paul's Cathedral and much else besides. As well as a restaurant, Sushisamba has two small bars, plus an outdoor

Sushisamba

roof terrace bar. Cocktails are pricey and the list is short, but this is still a destination bar par excellence, with a blinged-up crowd.

The high life continues at **Ting** on the 35th floor of the Shard (p59), London's newest icon. We'd give the £18-a-starter restaurant bit a swerve. Instead, book Ting's more affordable neighbouring 'lounge'. This shares its statement toilets, with glass-walled cubicles and heated seats. Oh, and there are the stunning views too, of course.

And there's more! Take the lift higher still, to the 52nd floor, to find **Gong**, London's highest bar. At this altitude, it's actually not so easy to pick out landmarks. But you'll have views stretching to the South Downs, or Canary Wharf and beyond, or the hills of north Middlesex. Be warned: you'll pay a premium for drinking in such an elevated location, although on a Sunday, Monday or Tuesday – when the usual minimum spend of £30 a head is waived – you could get away with a nursing a £7 bottle of beer for your stay. And you are on top of the world.

free or accompanied by a pricey drink or tapas from Madison's (8305 3088, www.madisonlondon.net).

Arts & leisure

Barbican Centre

Silk Street, EC2Y 8DS (7638 4141, 7638 8891 box office, www.barbican.org.uk). Barbican tube or Moorgate tube/rail. **Map** p133 D3 ❹

The Barbican is a prime example of 1970s brutalism, softened by square ponds of friendly resident ducks. The complex has a concert hall, theatre, cinema and art galleries, a labyrinthine array of spaces that isn't at all easy to navigate. Programming, however, is first class. At the core of the classical music roster, performing 90 concerts a year, is the brilliant London Symphony Orchestra (LSO), supplemented by top rock, jazz and world-music gigs. The annual BITE season cherry-picks exciting theatre and dance from around the globe, and the cinema shows a good mixture of mainstream, art-house and international films.

A new concert hall, Milton Court (1 Milton Street, EC2Y 9BH 7638 8891, www.gsmd.ac.uk), has opened just outside the Barbican's main entrance, with a 608-seat auditorium and two smaller theatres.

Event highlights Architecture tours (£10.50; £8.40 reductions); the Conservatory opens once a fortnight (check the website for details).

LSO St Luke's

161 Old Street, EC1V 9NG (7588 1116, 7638 8891 box office, www.lso.co.uk/lsostlukes). Old Street tube/rail. **Map** p133 D2 ❷

The London Symphony Orchestra's conversion of this Grade I-listed Hawksmoor church (note the distinctive spire: a fluted obelisk) into a 370-seat concert hall some years ago cost £20m, but the classical concerts and sheer variety of pop/rock gigs prove it was worth every penny.

Shoreditch

Just north-east of the City proper, this scruffy pleasure zone soaks up bankers' loose change. The area's edginess and artiness have followed cheaper rents north and east into Dalston and Hackney (pp156-163), but in and around the triangle made by Shoreditch High Street, Great Eastern Street and Old Street the many bars and remaining clubs are still lively – on a Friday or a Saturday night, often unpleasantly so.

Eating & drinking

Hoi Polloi

Ace Hotel, 100 Shoreditch High Street, E1 6JQ (8880 6100, www.hoi-polloi. co.uk). Shoreditch High Street rail. **Open** 7am-midnight Mon-Wed, Sun; 7am-1am Thur-Sat. **££. Brasserie**. **Map** p133 F2 ❸

The Ace Hotel's (p178) large restaurant has retro and contemporary styling reminiscent of a 1950s Scandinavian cruise ship. The casual, sneaker-clad service is notably smooth and well informed, and the menu looks like a college music paper. It covers breakfast, lunch, snacks, cocktails and dinner. The dishes are British, very seasonal and juxtapose flavours in modern but not outlandish ways that leave you craving more. Excellent.

Mayor of Scaredy Cat Town

12-16 Artillery Lane, E1 7LS (7078 9639, www.themayorofscaredycattown. com). Liverpool Street tube/rail or Shoreditch High Street rail. **Open** 5pm-midnight Fri, Sat; noon-10.30pm Sun. **Cocktail bar**. **Map** p133 F3 ❹

Part of the trend for 'secret' speakeasies, this one is a basement bar beneath Breakfast Club. The entrance is the one that looks like the big Smeg fridge door. Inside, you'll find a quirky, dimly lit cocktail bar in exposed brick and wood: a bit *Twin*

Peaks. The drinks menu makes an amusing mockery of more self-conscious 'underground' venues, and the cocktails are well crafted.

Pizza East

56 Shoreditch High Street, E16JJ (7729 1888, www.pizzaeast.com). Shoreditch High Street rail. **Open** noon-midnight Mon-Wed; noon-1am Thur; noon-2am Fri; 10am-2am Sat; 10am-midnight Sun. **£. Pizza. Map** p133 F2 ⓯

Pizza East is in a big space that used to be a club and still looks like one floor of an old factory. There's more than pizza on the Italian-American menu (calamari with caper aioli, polenta with deep-fried chicken livers), but the pizzas are well-made and adventurous (witness clam pizza, a New England speciality, which comes garnished with cherry tomatoes). This place is noisy, but the welcome friendly.

Tramshed

32 Rivington Street, EC2A 3LX (7749 0478, www.chickenandsteak.co.uk). Old Street tube/rail. **Open** 11.30am-11pm Mon, Tue; 11.30am-midnight Wed-Sat; 11.30am-9.30pm Sun. **£££. Steak & chicken. Map** p133 E2 ⓰

Chef Mark Hix has always had a thing for meat, and his latest venture takes things to extremes. To be precise, you can have roast chicken for one or to share, steak, chicken salad, or steak salad. (A few 'bar snax' include ox cheek croquettes and – the sole veggie option – radishes with celery salt.) All this happens in a turn-of-the-century Grade II-listed industrial building, a vast room with a soaring ceiling. In pride of place is a work by Damien Hirst: a formaldehyde-filled tank containing a bullock and rooster.

Worship Street Whistling Shop

63 Worship Street, EC2A 2DU (7247 0015, www.whistlingshop.com). Old

Street tube/rail. **Open** 5pm-midnight Mon-Wed; 5pm-1am Thur; 5pm-2am Fri, Sat. **Cocktail bar. Map** p133 E2 ⓱

Semi-secret location, Victoriana, re-interpretations of classic British drinks: it's all here. The cellar room is darkly Dickensian, full of cosy corners and leather armchairs. In the back is a windowed laboratory crammed with equipment modern and antiquated, used to create wondrously described ingredients that constitute the cocktails. You may find 'chip pan bitters', 'Hereford soil distillate', or 'high pressure hydrosol' used as ingredients for the original and stimulating drinks.

Shopping

Just east of Shoreditch is one of the city's trendiest – and best – shopping areas, now increasingly sleek and grown-up. We've listed key boutiques in the vicinity of **Redchurch Street**, **Old Spitalfields Market** and **Brick Lane** on pp159-162.

Boxpark

2-4 Bethnal Green Road, E1 6GY (7033 9441, www.boxpark.co.uk). Shoreditch High Street rail. **Open** 1-8pm Mon-Wed, Fri-Sun; 11am-10pm Thur. **Map** p133 F2 ⓳

Refitted shipping containers plonked underneath the elevated Shoreditch High Street Overground station make up this contemporary 'shopping mall'. Installed in 2011, the units of Boxpark are full of labels (Puma, Nike, North Face), but also contain an impressive array of independents, cafés and pop-ups (Wah Nails, Bukowski burgers, University College London's Launch-box).

Goodhood Store

41 Coronet Street, N1 6HD (7729 3600, http://goodhoodstore.com). Old Street tube/rail. **Open** 11am-6.30pm Mon-Sat; noon-5pm Sun. **Map** p133 E1 ⓴

Boxpark p147

Stock for this boutique-like store is selected by streetwear obsessives/ owners Kyle and Jo, with items that are weighted towards Japanese independent labels. There are also shirts and tops from men from Norse Projects, womenswear from APC Madras, and covetable pieces for both men and women from Wood Wood. A cabinet full of watches, sunglasses and jewellery makes this a great place for presents for hard-to-please boyfriends and girlfriends.

House of Hackney

NEW *131 Shoreditch High Street, E1 6JE (7739 3901, www.houseof hackney.com). Old Street tube/rail.* **Open** 10am-7.30pm Mon-Sat; 11am-5pm Sun. **Map** p133 F1 ⑩
House of Hackney is one of the most gorgeous retail establishments to land in London in years – bedecked in the deliberately over-the-top juxtapositions of print on print on print that is its signature. Upstairs, you'll find rolls of wallpaper, fabric, trays, mugs, fashion and collaborative designs with brands like Puma; downstairs are generously proportioned sofas and plump armchairs in more-is-more combinations of print and texture.

Nightlife

Although some people still associate Shoreditch with cutting-edge nightlife, few of those live in London: most Friday and Saturday nights the place is a mess of City drunks and hen parties. The handful of cool venues that remain are terrific, but the hipsters – for better and worse – congregate a bus or Overground ride north in **Dalston** and **Hackney** (box p157).

Book Club

100-106 Leonard Street, EC2A 4RH (7684 8618, www.wearetbc.com). Old Street tube/rail or Shoreditch High Street rail. **Open** 8am-midnight Mon-Wed; 8am-2am Thur, Fri; 10am-2am Sat; noon-midnight Sun. **Admission** free-£5. **Bar/café**. **Map** p133 E2 ⑪
The lovely-looking, open and airy Book Club fuses lively creative events with late-night drinking seven nights of the week. Locally themed cocktails include the Shoreditch Twat, and food is served all day. There's also free Wi-Fi, a pool table, ping pong and lots of comfy seats. The programme might include street poets or a Thinking & Drinking science lecture.

Plastic People

147-149 Curtain Road, EC2A 3QE (7739 6471, www.plasticpeople.co.uk). Old Street tube/rail. **Open** 9.30pm-2am Thur; 10pm-4am Fri, Sat. **Map** p133 F1 ⑫
The ever-popular Plastic People subscribes to the old-school line that all you need for a kicking party is a dark basement and a sound system – but then it has been putting on parties since the old-school was new. The programming remains true to form: deep techno to house, all-girl DJ line-ups and many a secret gig from a star DJ (Thom Yorke, anyone?).

XOYO

32-37 Cowper Street, EC2A 4AP (7729 5959, www.xoyo.co.uk). Old Street tube/rail. **Open** varies; check website for details. **Map** p133 E2 ⑬
Relaunched in 2012 under the management of Andy Peyton, 800-capacity XOYO is first and foremost a nightclub. This former printworks is a bare concrete cell, defiantly taking the 'chic' out of 'shabby chic'. The open space means the atmosphere is always buzzing, as the only place to escape total immersion in the music is the small smoking courtyard outside. The Victorian loft-style space provides the sort of effortlessly cool programming you might – foolishly – expect to be prevalent in Shoreditch.

Old Royal Naval College p164

Neighbourhoods

LONDON BY AREA

Camden & Islington

The key north London destination is the partly gentrified Camden. Famous for its **market** and close to Regent's Park and **London Zoo**, it's one of London's liveliest nightlife areas. West of Camden, snooty **St John's Wood** is the spiritual home of cricket. To the east, Islington has some fine bars and restaurants, as well as excellent small arts venues.

Sights & museums

Lord's & MCC Museum

St John's Wood Road, NW8 8QN (7616 8595, www.lords.org). St John's Wood tube. **Open** *Museum* 10am-4.30pm daily (non-match days). *Tours* phone or see website for details. **Admission** *Museum* £7.50; £5 reductions. *Tours* £18; free-£12 reductions; £40 family.

The opposite side of Regent's Park from Camden, Lord's is more than just a famous cricket ground – as the HQ of the Marylebone Cricket Club (MCC), it is the official guardian of the rules of cricket. As well as staging international matches, the ground is home to the Middlesex County Cricket Club (MCCC). Visitors can see the museum (with such curiosities as a stuffed sparrow with the ball that killed it), or take a tour round the futuristic NatWest Media Centre pod and portrait-bedecked Long Room.

ZSL London Zoo

Regent's Park, NW1 4RY (7722 3333, www.zsl.org/london-zoo). Baker Street or Camden Town tube then 274, C2 bus. **Open** check website for details. **Admission** £21-£26; free-£23.40 reductions.

London Zoo has been open in one form or another since 1826. Spread over 36 acres and containing more than 600 species, it cares for many of the endangered variety – as well as your nippers at the children's zoo. The emphasis throughout is on upbeat education. Exhibits are always entertaining – we especially like the recreation of a kitchen overrun with cockroaches – but sometimes the zoo sensibly just lets the animals be the stars: witness the expanded Penguin Beach, Gorilla Kingdom and new Tiger Territory.

Eating & drinking

For top-quality craft beer, there's a Camden branch of **Brewdog** (see box p160).

Made in Camden
Roundhouse, Chalk Farm Road, NW1 8EH (7424 8495, www.madeincamden. com). Chalk Farm tube. **Open** noon-2.30pm, 6-10.30pm Mon-Fri; 10.30am-3pm, 6-10.30pm Sat; 10.30am-3pm Sun. **£. Brasserie**.
A note-perfect mix of concert posters, panoramic windows, dark wood and red seating is the setting for confident fusion dishes. Small plates – Moroccan spiced lamb with green salsa houmous and flatbread, miso-marinated aubergine with lime and chilli salsa, or soy glazed salmon with potato mash and sprouting broccoli – are consistently good. The weekend brunch menu features a global mix of eggy and cheesy things.

Market
43 Parkway, Camden, NW1 7PN (7267 9700, www.marketrestaurant.co.uk). Camden Town tube. **Open** noon-2.30pm, 6-10.30pm Mon-Sat; 11am-3pm Sun. **££. British**.
Stripped-back hardly covers the decor here: brick walls are ragged and raw; zinc-topped tables are scuffed; wooden chairs look as if they were once used in a classroom. Food is similarly pared down, reliant on the flavours of high-quality seasonal produce.

Ottolenghi
287 Upper Street, Islington, N1 2TZ (7288 1454, www.ottolenghi.co.uk).

Angel tube or Highbury & Islington tube/rail. **Open** 8am-10.30pm Mon-Sat; 9am-7pm Sun. **££. Bakery-café**.
This is more than an inviting bakery. Behind the pastries piled in the window is a slightly prim deli counter with lush salads, available day and evening, eat-in or take away. As a daytime café, it's brilliant, but people also flock here for fine fusion food at dinner.

69 Colebrooke Row
69 Colebrooke Row, Islington, N1 8AA (07540 528593 mobile, www.69colebrookerow.com). Angel t ube. **Open** 5pm-midnight Mon-Wed, Sun; 5pm-1am Thur; 5pm-2am Fri, Sat.
Cocktail bar.
With just a handful of tables plus a few stools at the bar, 69 may be smaller than your front room, but the understated, intimate space proves a fine environment in which to enjoy pristine cocktails (liquorice whisky sours, perhaps), mixed with quiet ceremony. Impeccably attired staff, handwritten bills and tall glasses of water poured from a cocktail shaker mark out this lovely enterprise.

Trullo
300-302 St Paul's Road, Islington, N1 2LH (7226 2733, www.trullorestaurant. com). Highbury & Islington tube/rail. **Open** 12.30-3pm, 6-10.30pm Mon-Sat; 12.30-3pm Sun. **££. Italian**.
A super-popular local serving some of the best food in Islington. The menu packs a lot of interest into a short space, and changes daily: a sprightly salad of broad beans, pecorino, little gem lettuce and mint, say, followed by pappardelle with beef shin ragù. Desserts run from melon granita to caprese chocolate torte.

Shopping

Camden Market
Camden Lock *Camden Lock Place, off Chalk Farm Road, NW1 8AF (www.camdenlockmarket.com).*

LONDON BY AREA

Open 10am-6pm Mon-Thur, Sun; 10am-6.30pm Fri, Sat (reduced stalls Mon-Fri).

Camden Lock Village *east of Chalk Farm Road, NW1 (www.camdenlock. net).* **Open** 10am-6pm daily.

Stables Market *off Chalk Farm Road, opposite Hartland Road, NW1 8AH (7485 5511, www.stablesmarket. com).* **Open** 10.30am-6pm Mon-Fri (reduced stalls); 10am-6pm Sat, Sun.

All *Camden Town or Chalk Farm tube.*

'Camden Market' can refer to several markets in Camden, as listed above; weekends are by far the busiest time to visit, although some stalls are open all week. Zoom past Camden Market (neon sunglasses, pseudo-witty slogan garments), perhaps popping into the Electric Ballroom, which sells vinyl and CDs at weekends and is also a music venue, to the railway bridge. There you'll find Camden Lock, with numerous stalls selling crafts, home furnishings, jewellery, toys and gifts, increasingly sophisticated street food, and youngsters lolling around the canal lock whenever the weather's half decent. Camden Lock Village, which runs along the towpath, opened after major fire damage in 2009; there are funky moped seats to sit on. North along Chalk Farm Road is the Stables Market, noted for its new and vintage fashion, and always packed with shoppers. The Horse Hospital area is good for second-hand clothing, food stands and designer furniture.

Nightlife

Koko

1A Camden High Street, NW1 7JE (0870 432 5527, 0844 847 2258 box office, www.koko.uk.com). Mornington Crescent tube.

Avoid standing beneath the sound-muffling overhang downstairs and you may find that this one-time music hall is one of London's finest venues. The 1,500-capacity hall stages weekend club nights and gigs by indie rockers, from cultish to those on the up.

Lock Tavern

35 Chalk Farm Road, NW1 8AJ (7482 7163, www.lock-tavern.co.uk). Chalk Farm tube. **Open** noon-midnight Mon-Thur; noon-1am Fri, Sat; noon-11pm Sun.

A tough place to get into at weekends, with queues of artfully distressed rock urchins and one of Camden's most arbitrary door policies. It teems with aesthetic niceties inside (cosy black couches and warm wood panelling downstairs, open-air terrace on the first floor), but it's the unpredictable after-party vibe that packs in the punters.

Roundhouse

Chalk Farm Road, NW1 8EH (7424 9991 information, 0844 482 8008 box office, www.roundhouse.org.uk). Chalk Farm tube.

A one-time railway turntable shed, the Roundhouse was used for experimental theatre and hippie happenings in the 1960s before becoming a rock venue in the '70s. The venue reopened a few years ago, and now mixes arty rock gigs with dance, quality theatre and multimedia events. Sightlines can be poor, but acoustics are good.

Arts & leisure

Almeida

Almeida Street, N1 1TA (7359 4404, www.almeida.co.uk). Angel tube.

A well-groomed 325-seat venue with a funky bar attached, the Almeida is turning out increasingly wonderful theatre (*Chimerica* was many critics' favourite play of 2013) under new artistic director Rupert Goold.

Sadler's Wells

Rosebery Avenue, EC1R 4TN (0844 412 4300, www.sadlerswells.com). Angel tube.

Camden

Worth the trip

London is huge – more than eight million people live in Greater London's 600 square miles – so covering even must-sees is a challenge. We've thus focused this guidebook on central London and areas with particular character. But here are some one-off treats we couldn't leave out.

Hampstead Heath

Hampstead tube or Hampstead Heath rail.

On a summer's day or a crisp afternoon of autumn, many Londoners head north of Camden (p150) to Hampstead Heath. The trees and grassy hills of the heath make it a surprisingly wild patch of the metropolis. Aside from the pleasure of walking, sitting, taking in the fine views over London or even swimming in the ponds, there's also stately pile Kenwood House (Hampstead Lane, NW3 7JR, 8348 1286, www.english-heritage.org.uk). Built in 1616 (and reopening in 2014 after extensive refurbishment), it contains a superb art collection, given to the nation as the Iveagh Bequest in 1927: we can't get enough of the Rembrandt self-portrait. The café – with lots of outdoor seating – is good.

Hampton Court Palace

East Molesey, Surrey KT8 9AU (0844 482 7777, www.hrp.org.uk). Hampton Court rail, or riverboat from Westminster to Hampton Court Pier (Apr-Oct). **Open** *Apr-Oct* 10am-6pm daily. *Nov-Mar* 10am-4.30pm daily. **Admission** £16.95; free-£14.30 reductions; £43.46 family. *Maze* £3.85; £2.75 reductions. *Gardens* Apr-Oct £5.50; free-£4.70 reductions; Nov-Mar free.

A half-hour train ride south-west of central London, this is a spectacular palace, once owned by Henry VIII. It was built in 1514 and for 200 years was at the focal point of English history: Shakespeare gave his first performance to James I here in 1604; and, after the Civil War, Oliver Cromwell was so besotted by the building he moved in. Centuries later, the rosy walls of the palace still dazzle. Its vast size can be daunting, so take advantage of the costumed guided tours. The Tudor Kitchens are fun, with their giant cauldrons and fake pies, the Great Hall has beautiful tapestries and stained glass, and the landscaped gardens contain fine topiary and the famous maze.

Royal Botanic Gardens (Kew Gardens)

Kew, Richmond, Surrey TW9 3AB (8332 5655, www.kew.org). Kew Gardens tube/rail, Kew Bridge rail or riverboat to Kew Pier. **Open** *Sept, Oct* 9.30am-6pm daily. *Nov, Jan* 9.30am-4.15pm daily. *Feb, Mar* 9.30am-5.30pm daily. *Apr-Aug* 9.30am-6.30pm Mon-Fri; 9.30am-7.30pm Sat, Sun. **Admission** £16; free-£14 reductions.

This half square mile of horticultural wonders is a joy to amble around in – surely the finest botanic gardens anywhere in the world. The unparalleled collection of plants was begun by Queen Caroline, wife of George II, with exotic plants brought back by voyaging botanists (Charles Darwin among them). In 1759, 'Capability' Brown was employed by George III to improve on the work of his predecessors, setting the template for a garden

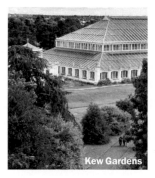
Kew Gardens

that has long attracted thousands of visitors each year. Head straight for the 19th-century greenhouses, filled to the roof with tropical plants, and next door the Waterlily House's quiet and pretty indoor pond (closed in winter). Brown's Rhododendron Dell is at its best in spring, while the Xstrata Treetop Walkway, some 60ft above the ground, is terrific fun in autumn.

Wembley Stadium

Stadium Way, Wembley, Middx HA9 0WS (0844 980 8001, www. wembleystadium.com). Wembley Park tube or Wembley Stadium rail. Few Englishmen avoid dewy eyes on seeing Wembley, even if the vast steel arch of Lord Foster's 2007 redesign fails to generate the nostalgic rush of the twin towers of the 1920s stadium. Still, the new 90,000-seater stadium is impressively designed, and the guided tours give a fantastic flavour of the venue's history: here England won their only World Cup in 1966, and the crossbar from which Hurst's disputed goal bounced is in one of the cafés.

Wimbledon Lawn Tennis Museum

Museum Building, All England Lawn Tennis Club, Church Road, SW19 5AE (8946 6131, www.wimbledon.org/museum). Southfields tube or bus 493. **Open** 10am-5pm daily; ticket holders only during championships. **Admission** (incl tour) £20; free-£17 reductions.
The spiritual home of tennis really comes alive for the grass-court tournament each year, but if you haven't already applied for tickets on the showcourts, you're too late. You can queue on the day for the outer courts, come late for returns, or watch highlights on TV and visit the museum. It covers the history of tennis, with interactives such as a 200° screen that simulates playing on Centre Court and a recreation of a 1980s men's dressing room with the 'ghost' of John McEnroe; Andy Murray's kit from his Wimbledon victory in 2013 has also been acquired. The ticket price includes a behind-the-scenes tour.

WWT Wetland Centre

Queen Elizabeth's Walk, Barnes, SW13 9WT (8409 4400, www.wwt. org.uk). Hammersmith tube then bus 283, Barnes rail, or bus 33, 72, 209. **Open** *Mar-Oct* 9.30am-6pm daily. *Nov-Feb* 9.30am-5pm daily. **Admission** £9.99; free-£7.45 reductions; £27.82 family.
Reclaimed from industrial reservoirs a decade ago, the 43-acre wetland reserve is four miles from central London, but feels a world away. Quiet ponds, rushes, rustling reeds and wildflower gardens all teem with bird life – some 150 species – as well as the now very rare water vole.

The key London venue for dance is this dazzling complex, home to an impressive line-up of local and international contemporary dance performers, and with a pleasantly compact auditorium.

The East End

What we refer to here as the **East End** isn't exactly the East End: definitions vary, but no one would exclude Shoreditch (p146). But the term is a useful catch-all for an area that is still London's hippest zone for clubs, shops and, increasingly, food and drink. On the doorstep of the City, **Spitalfields** is known for its covered market, surrounded by restaurants and bars. To its east, **Brick Lane** may be world-famous for its curries, but it is increasingly home to excellent boutiques. Slightly north, **Hoxton** begins where the City overspill into Shoreditch comes to an end: it does boisterous late drinking and pile-'em-in clubs. Further east, **Bethnal Green** has the Museum of Childhood; to the north, once unheralded **Dalston** is now shorthand for cool London, with a fine cluster of music and arts venues.

Sights & museums

Dennis Severs' House

18 Folgate Street, E1 6BX (7247 4013, www.dennissevershouse.co.uk). Liverpool Street tube/rail or Shoreditch High Street rail. **Open** 6-9pm Mon, Wed; noon-4pm Sun; noon-2pm 1st & 3rd Mon of the mth. **Admission** £7 Mon daytime; £10 Sun daytime; £14 evening.

The ten rooms of this original Huguenot house have been decked out to recreate vivid snapshots of daily life in Spitalfields between 1724 and 1914. A tour through the compelling 'still-life drama', as American creator Dennis Severs dubbed it, takes you through the cellar, kitchen, dining room, smoking room and upstairs to the bedrooms. With hearth and candles burning, smells lingering and objects scattered apparently haphazardly, it feels as though the inhabitants have deserted the building only moments before you arrived.

Geffrye Museum

136 Kingsland Road, E2 8EA (7739 9893, www.geffrye-museum.org.uk). Hoxton rail. **Open** 10am-5pm Tue-Sun. **Admission** free; donations appreciated.

In a set of 18th-century almshouses, the Geffrye offers a vivid physical history of the English interior. Displaying original furniture, paintings, textiles and decorative arts, the museum recreates a sequence of typical middle-class living rooms from 1600 to the present – a fascinating take on domestic history.

V&A Museum of Childhood

Cambridge Heath Road, E2 9PA (8983 5235, www.museumofchildhood.org.uk). Bethnal Green tube/rail or Cambridge Heath rail. **Open** 10am-5.45pm daily. **Admission** free; donations appreciated.

Home to one of the world's finest collections of kids' toys, dolls' houses, games and costumes, the Museum of Childhood shines brighter than ever after extensive refurbishment, which has given it an impressive entrance. Part of the Victoria & Albert (p80), the museum has been amassing child-related objects since 1872, with Barbie Dolls complementing Victorian praxinoscopes. There are plenty of interactive exhibits and a decent café.

Eating & drinking

For craft beer in east London, see box p160.

Albion

2-4 Boundary Street, E2 7DD (7729 1051, www.albioncaff.co.uk). Shoreditch High Street rail. **Open** 8am-11pm Mon-Sat; 8am-10pm Sun. **£. Café.**

Almost every new London restaurant seems to be mining the vein of nostalgia for traditional British cuisine these days, but few have pulled it off as well as Terence Conran's stand-out 'caff', shop and bakery in the Boundary hotel, with its platters of cupcakes and doorstop-thick slices of battenberg baked on-site, and mains such as toad in the hole or devilled kidneys.

Brick Lane Beigel Bake

159 Brick Lane, E1 6SB (7729 0616). Liverpool Street tube/rail, Shoreditch High Street rail or bus 8. **Open** 24hrs daily. **£.** No credit cards. **Bakery**.

This little East End institution produces perfect bagels, both plain and filled (cream cheese, brilliant salt beef), superb bread and moreish cakes. Even at 3am, fresh baked goods are being pulled from the ovens; no wonder the queue trails out the door when local bars and clubs begin to close.

Poppies

6-8 Hanbury Street, E1 6QR (7247 0892, www.poppiesfishandchips.co.uk). Liverpool Street tube/rail or Aldgate East tube. **Open** 11am-11pm Mon-Sat; 11am-10.30pm Sun. **££. Fish & chips**.

A worthy replacement for the East End caff that preceded it, Poppies serves perfectly fried fish from Billingsgate Market (cod, haddock, rock, scampi, halibut) with hand-cut chips, home-made tartare sauce and mushy peas. You can sit in – service is by sharply dressed, authentically amiable Italian chaps. The location between Brick Lane and Spitalfields is handy.

Song Que

134 Kingsland Road, E2 8DY (7613 3222, www.songque.co.uk). Hoxton rail. **Open** noon-3pm, 5.30-11pm Mon-Sat; 12.30pm-11pm Sun. **£. Vietnamese**.

North-east London holds its monopoly on the best Vietnamese restaurants in the city, with Song Que the benchmark. It's a canteen-like operation to which diners of all types are attracted – be

Northern nights

There's a new addition to north-east London's nightlife venues. But this one isn't a basement dive bar, dilapidated pub or too-cool-for-school danceteria. Nope, **Oslo** (1A Amhurst Road, E8 1LL, 3553 4831, www.oslohackney.com) is a proper music venue with a decent-sized stage, proper sound system and light rig. The former railway building hosts bands most nights, with an impressive selection of weekend club nights.

Of course, the era of the dive venue is far from over, but its heartland is over in Dalston. Even long-established Shoreditch nights, like the influential bass night FWD>>, now take place in Dalston: FWD>> is in the **Dance Tunnel** (95 Kingsland High Street, E8 2PB, www.ilovefwd.com) on Thursday fortnights. The **Shacklewell Arms** (71 Shacklewell Lane, E8 2EB, 7249 0810, www.shacklewellarms. com), meanwhile, a pub that's clung on to its original tropical-mural decor, has become a Dalston staple with its edgy programming. Equally exciting is the **Nest** (36-44 Stoke Newington Road, N16 7XJ, 7354 9993, www. ilovethenest.com). The basement club hosts weekend parties crammed with cool electro, disco, house and rock 'n' rave tunes. But it was the more sophisticated **Dalston Superstore** (117 Kingland High Street, E8 2PB, 7254 2273, http://dalstonsuperstore.com) that spearheaded the area's boogie renaissance back in 2009 – it still pulls huge crowds on to its intense pitch-black dancefloor.

LONDON BY AREA

I am here to please you

White Lyan

prepared to share tables at busy times. Beef pho and barbecued quail with citrus dipping sauce are superb.

Tayyabs

83 Fieldgate Street, E1 1JU (7247 9543, www.tayyabs.co.uk). Aldgate East or Whitechapel tube. **Open** noon-11.30pm daily. **£. Pakistani.**

A bit of a walk south-east of Brick Lane, Tayyabs is the East End equivalent of the caffs favoured by truckers in South Asia. It has been around since the 1970s, and although the interior has been extended, it's a challenge to bag a table. Cooking is big, bold and sassy. When it's just too busy, try Needoo Grill, round the corner (87 New Road).

Typing Room

NEW *Town Hall Hotel Patriots Square, E2 9NF (020 7871 0461, www.typing room.com). Bethnal Green tube or Cambridge Heath rail.* **Open** noon-2.30pm, 6-10.30pm Wed-Sat; noon-3.30pm Sun. **££££. Modern European.**

Jason Atherton, current toast of the capital's dining scene, is behind this lauded new restaurant. There are plenty of 'modernist' food trends on chef Lee Westcott's plates, such as all-the-rage New Nordic: a bit of dehydration here, some smoking there, plus sprigs, twigs and petals. Dishes are so intricate and exquisite it seems a pity to eat them: a pigeon arrived entombed in a wooden box, tendrils of smoke curling up from the edges – the contents had been gently smoked on a fragrant 'nest' of pine needles. Crisp-skinned chunks with tender, ruby-red middles were then carved and teamed with an intense jus, chewy barley and chunks of mellow, salt-baked celeriac.

White Lyan

NEW *153 Hoxton Street, N1 6PJ (3011 1153, www.whitelyan.com). Hoxton rail.* **Open** 6pm-1am Mon-Wed, Sun;

6pm-2am Thur; 6pm-3am Fri, Sat. **Cocktail bar.**

The first solo venue from Ryan Chetiyawardana is a genuine pioneer in a new cocktail movement. The former White Horse pub in the untrendy bit of Hoxton isn't much from the outside, but once inside it's clear this is no standard operation. Instead of a back bar stacked with spirits there are big fridges holding the pre-made products of hours of labour by Ryan and his team. Spirits are made to order, or refined and 'rebuilt' using filtered water and distillations. You can't order off menu, and there's only one of each colour of wine and one lager, but the cocktails are unusual and outstanding.

Shopping

On Sundays, the whole area from **Old Spitalfields Market** (p161) east to Brick Lane is hectic. Follow our Itinerary (pp48-50) to get the best out of it.

Blitz

55-59 Hanbury Street, E1 5JP (7377 0730, www.blitzlondon.co.uk). Shoreditch High Street rail. **Open** 11am-7pm Mon-Wed; 11am-8pm Thur-Sat; 11am-7pm Sun.

Blitz puts the other vintage shops in the capital to shame. This is a vintage department store, covering all floors of a glorious old furniture factory. There's a furniture selection from Broadway Market's the Dog & Wardrobe, an accessories floor, a book collection and rails and rails of neatly presented fashion. The selection is all killer and no filler – and cleaned, steamed and folded before it hits the shop floor.

Broadway Market

www.broadwaymarket.co.uk. London Fields rail or bus 236, 394.

Broadway Market has huge fashion kudos, but it's high-quality produce (this is primarily a specialist food market), well-edited vintage clothing

New brews

Where the people pulling your pint crafted the booze.

Cock Tavern

The traditional London pub is under threat, with dread warnings about closures regularly in the news. For many pubs, the answer has been evolve to survive. The first wave was gastrofication: pubs reopening as 'gastropubs', places where the focus was providing restaurant-quality food. Currently, salvation is being sought in 'craft beer' – the artisanal cousin of the more tightly defined real ale – which brings a more diverse, less macho touch to the world of beer. While many London pubs now serve impressive selections of craft beer, on handpull and bottled, increasing numbers have gone a step further, making their own beer in their own microbreweries.

As with all things hipster, east London is the heartland of the new brewers. Decorated with no more than a few beer signs, and with comfortably scuffed furniture, Hackney's **Cock Tavern** (315 Mare Street, E8 1EJ, www.thecocktavern. co.uk) has seemed a timeless classic since it opened. The pub cellar is home to Howling Hops

microbrewery, the output of which is mostly drunk in the Cock. Try the lively Pale XX, or the rich and black Smoked Porter. With a terrific setting by the River Lea in Hackney Wick, the **Crate Brewery** (White Building, Unit 7, Queens Yard, E9 5EN, 07834 275687, www. cratebrewery.com) is a hip canalside pizzeria-cum-microbrewery, with high vaulted ceilings hung with bare lightbulbs, benches made from recycled coffee sacks and a bar pulled together using railway sleepers. Crate's own brews – a pale ale, a bitter and a strong stout were available on our visit – aren't the best in town, but its selection of world beers is hard to beat. In Bethnal Green, the beautifully preserved Victorian **Kings Arms** (11A Buckfast Street, E2 6EY, 7729 2627, http://the kingsarmspub.com) has a classic wood-panelled interior and an impressive beer board, supplying a toasty brown ale called Earl's Broken Biscuits.

East London also holds a slender majority in the even newer trend of 'open breweries' – where small-scale breweries open up a taproom. Check out the **Cygnet** (60 Dace Road, E3 2NQ, www.trumansbeer. co.uk), also in Hackney Wick, which is open daily. The brewery behind it started making Truman's beer again in 2010 – the original brewery ran from 1666 to 1989, and Truman's pubs (some in use under different owners, many derelict) are scattered all over east London). There's also the **London Fields Brewery** (365-366 Warburton

Street, E8 3RR), a big space that serves Allpress coffee in the morning, and its own ales at night, along with food and entertainment.

There's microbrewed life elsewhere in London, of course. The Kings Arms' sister pub, for instance, sits among the gracious Georgian townhouses of Islington. The **Earl of Essex** (25 Danbury Street, N1 8LE, 7424 5828, www.earlofessex. net) has kept its island back bar and its Watney's beer barrel signage – but its board details a changing list of around 18 beers and ciders, from as far afield as the USA and as local as the pub's own on-site Earls Brewery. Bigger craft producers include the **Camden Town Brewery**, with railway arch premises at Kentish Town West (55-59 Wilkin Street Mews, NW5 3NN, 7485 1671, www.camdetownbrewery.com/ brewery-bar). And the London outposts of Scottish craft brewery **Brewdog** (www.brewdog.com) in Camden (113 Bayham Street, NW1 0AG), Shoreditch (51-55 Bethnal Green Road, E1 6LA) and Shepherd's Bush (15-19 Goldhawk Road, W12 8QQ) offer a fine initiation into the world of craft beer. Admit to a bartender you've no idea where to start and they'll gladly guide you through the list, offering tasters. And what a list it is – every one of Brewdog's groundbreaking beers on keg draught and bottle, from the smooth, amber 5am Saint to the quadruple IPA 'Sink the Bismarck' at 41 per cent.

and independent boutiques (Artwords, Black Truffle) that make it really worth a visit. The market wasn't always like this: after years of decline, in 2004 the local traders' and residents' association set about transforming their ailing fruit and veg market. Now, it's one of the city's most successful local markets.

Columbia Road Market

Columbia Road, E2. Hoxton rail or bus 26, 48, 55. **Open** 8am-2pm Sun.
On Sunday mornings, this unassuming East End street is transformed into a swathe of fabulous plant life and the air is fragrant with blooms. But it's not just about flora: alongside the market is a growing number of shops selling everything from pottery and Mexican glassware to cupcakes and perfume. Get there early for the pick of the crop, or around 2pm for the bargains; refuel at Jones Dairy (23 Ezra Street).

Old Spitalfields Market

Commercial Street, between Lamb Street & Brushfield Street, E1 6AA (7247 8556, www.spitalfieldsoldmarket. com). Liverpool Street tube/rail or Shoreditch High Street rail. **Open** 9.30am-5pm Thur, Fri, Sun. *Antiques* 8.30am-4.30pm Thur. *Food* 10am-5pm Fri-Sun. *Fashion* 9.30am-5pm Fri. *Records & books* 10am-4pm 1st & 3rd Fri of the mth. No credit cards.
Since the 2003 renovation and total overhaul of the much-loved Spitalfields Market, it's a leaner, cleaner affair, bulked out with slightly soulless boutiques. A pitch here is expensive, so expect gastro-nibbles, wittily sloganed baby T-shirts and leather bags. If you want to avoid the crowds and make more idiosyncratic finds, forget the busy Sunday market and come on a Thursday for heaps of vintage fashion.

Redchurch Street

Shoreditch High Street rail.
A shabby Shoreditch cut-through, Redchurch is a strong contender for

LONDON BY AREA

London's best shopping street. As one of Redchurch Street's first new residents, Caravan (no.3) helped redefine the street with its eccentric vintage-style homewares and gifts. Aussie botanical beauty shop Aesop (no.5A) and classic menswear brand Sunspel (no.7) can be found at one end. Further up are darkly lit menswear store Hostem (nos.41-43), decadent interiors at Maison Trois Garçons (no.45), vintage-style up-dos and manicures at the Painted Lady (no.65) and even 1990s, er, vintage at grungy thrift shop Sick (no.105). Highlights are concept store Aubin & Wills (nos.64-66), where you can buy men's, women's and homeware lines or catch a film in the small cinema, and an expansive Labour & Wait (no.85), selling aesthetically pleasing mops, enamel bread bins, stylish ladles and other simple essentials.

Rough Trade East
Dray Walk, Old Truman Brewery, 91 Brick Lane, E1 6QL (7392 7788, www.roughtrade.com). Liverpool Street tube/rail. **Open** 8am-9pm Mon-Thur; 8am-8pm Fri; 10am-8pm Sat; 11am-7pm Sun.
Since opening here in 2007, the indie music store has never looked more upbeat. This 5,000sq ft record store, café and gig space offers a dizzying range of vinyl and CDs, spanning punk, indie, dub, soul, electronica and more. With 16 listening posts and a stage for live sets, this is close to musical nirvana.

Vintage Emporium
14 Bacon Street, E1 6LF (7739 0799, www.vintageemporiumcafe.com). Shoreditch High Street rail. **Open** 11am-7pm Mon-Fri; 10am-7pm Sat, Sun.
We love this relaxed vintage store and café (complete with bright yellow 1960s coffee machine). Partners Jess Collins and Oli Stanion opened it on a shoestring on a Brick Lane back alley, selling clothes from the Victorian era

through to the 1950s. Oh, and it hosts naked life-drawing classes – a sight to behold as you sip your herbal tea.

Nightlife

For a round-up of the key Dalston nightlife venues, see box p156.

Bethnal Green Working Men's Club
42-44 Pollard Row, E2 6NB (7739 7170, www.workersplaytime.net). Bethnal Green tube/rail. **Open** hrs vary; check website for details.
The sticky red carpet and broken lampshades perfectly suit the programme of quirky lounge, retro rock 'n' roll and fancy-dress burlesque parties from spandex-lovin' husband-and-wife dance duos and the like. The mood is friendly, the playlist upbeat and the air always full of artful, playful mischief.

Café Oto
18-22 Ashwin Street, E8 3DL (7923 1231, www.cafeoto.co.uk). Dalston Junction or Dalston Kingsland rail. **Open** 8.30am-5.30pm Mon-Fri; 9.30am-5.30pm Sat; 10.30am-5.30pm Sun. *Shows* 8pm. No credit cards.
This 150-capacity Dalston café and music venue can't easily be categorised, though it offers the tidy definition: 'creative new music that exists outside of the mainstream'. That means Japanese noise rockers, electronica pioneers, free improvisers and artists from the weird fringes of the rock, folk and classical music.

Vortex Jazz Club
Dalston Culture House, 11 Gillet Street, N16 8JN (7254 4097, www.vortexjazz. co.uk). Dalston Kingsland rail.
The Vortex is on the first floor of a handsome new-build, with a restaurant on the ground floor. The space can feel a bit sterile, but the programming has been superb for years, packed with left-field talent from Britain, Europe

and the United States. This is London's most exciting jazz venue.

Arts & leisure

Whitechapel Gallery

77-82 Whitechapel High Street, E1 7QX (7522 7888, www.whitechapelgallery. org). Aldgate East tube. **Open** 11am-6pm Tue-Sun. **Admission** free.

This East End stalwart has enjoyed a major redesign that saw the Grade II-listed building expand into the equally historic former library right next door – cleverly, the architects left the two buildings stylistically distinct rather than smoothing out their differences. The gallery gave itself an archive centre, restaurant and café, and tripled its exhibition space, improving a reputation as an art pioneer that was built on shows of Picasso (in 1939, his *Guernica* was shown here), Pollock and Kahlo.

Docklands & the Olympic Park

The flagship for finance-led urban redevelopment under the last Tory government in an area that was once thriving docks to the east of the City, Docklands was for many years barely populated tower blocks awaiting economic revival. Nowadays, the northern end of the Thames peninsula known as the Isle of Dogs is all shiny megabanks, with **One Canada Square** ('Canary Wharf Tower') a well-known London landmark almost lost between them. It seems Mayor Boris Johnson has taken note of its eventual success, setting up inward investment opportunities for the neglected areas around the Royal Docks to the east of Canary Wharf.

To the north of Docklands, the **Olympic Park** (p164) is the major highlight of an area that increasingly

of interest to visitors. For a walk up the Lea River, starting at Three Mills, passing the Olympic Park, and finishing in hipster-ville Hackney Wick, see pp46-47.

Sights & museums

Emirates Air Line

North terminal *27 Western Gateway, E16 4FA. Royal Victoria DLR.* **South terminal** *Edmund Halley Way, SE10 0FR. North Greenwich tube.* **Both Open** 7am-9pm Mon-Fri; 8am-9pm Sat; 9am-9pm Sun. **Tickets** £4.30 single; £2.20 5-15s, free under-5s.

Arguments for a cable car across the Thames as a solution to any of London's many transport problems are, at best, moot, but as a tourist thrill it's superb. The pods zoom 295ft up elegant stanchions at a gratifying pace. Suddenly there are brilliant views of the expanses of water that make up the Royal Docks, the ships on the Thames, Docklands and the Thames Barrier. Good fun and good value – but note that the cable car may not run in high winds. Tickets are cheaper if you use an Oyster card – plus you avoid the ticket desk queues.

Museum of London Docklands

No.1 Warehouse, West India Quay, Hertsmere Road, E14 4AL (7001 9844, www.museumindocklands.org. uk). Canary Wharf tube or West India Quay DLR. **Open** 10am-6pm daily. **Admission** free.

Housed in a 19th-century warehouse (itself a Grade I-listed building), this huge sibling of the Museum of London (p141) provides an excellent introduction to the complex history of London's docks and the river. Displays over three storeys take you from the arrival of the Romans all the way to the docks' 1980s closure and the area's redevelopment. There are temporary exhibitions on the ground floor, along with a café and play area.

LONDON BY AREA

Queen Elizabeth Olympic Park

www.queenelizabetholympicpark.co.uk.
Stratford tube/rail/DLR, West Ham tube/
rail. **Open** 24hrs daily.

The post-Games Olympic Park, now officially renamed the Queen Elizabeth Olympic Park, reopened in 2014. The immaculate parkland to the north was launched in 2013, its paths and waterways enhanced by the new Timber Lodge, with its café. Next came the Zaha Hadid-designed Aquatics Centre, open for public swimming (£3.50-£4.50 adults, £2-£2.50 reductions), followed by the Velopark, used for road, track, BMX and mountain biking. South of this is all the remaining parkland, with children's play areas, walking trails, a couple of dozen public artworks plus the 274ft ArcelorMittal Orbit, designed by Anish Kapoor (£15 adults, £7-£12 reductions). Only the Olympic Stadium remains under refurbishment: it is due to open in 2015 for the Rugby World Cup, before being handed over to West Ham football club in 2016. In the meantime, the stadium continues to host music events Hard Rock Calling and Wireless Festival. For a good vantage point on the park, head to the Moka East café in the View Tube (Marshgate Lane, E15 2PJ, www.theviewtube.co.uk).

Trinity Buoy Wharf

64 Orchard Place, E14 0JW (www.
trinitybuoywharf.com). East India
DLR. **Open** *Long Player* 11am-4pm
(11am-5pm in summer) Sat, Sun.

In the 1860s, London's only lighthouse was built here to train lighthouse keepers. The former repairs yard – which has great views of the O2 Arena (p166) on the far bank – now hosts regular art events, and the lighthouse is a permanent home for the meditative sounds of the *Long Player* art installation. There's also a 1940s diner car (7987 4334, www.fatboysdiner.co.uk, 10am-4pm daily)

and a café (8am-5.30pm Mon-Fri, 10am-5.30pm Sat, Sun).

Greenwich

South of the Thames, but east of the City, Greenwich is laden with royal and maritime heritage. Most easterly of London's UNESCO World Heritage sites – the riverside colonnades of the Old Royal Naval College make it one of the most breathtaking – it merits a day's exploration by itself. The **Emirates Air Line** (p163) crosses the river from the **O2 Arena** (p166).

Sights & museums

Cutty Sark

King William Walk, SE10 9HT (8858 2698, www.cuttysark.org.uk). Cutty Sark DLR. **Open** 10am-6pm daily.
Admission £13.50; free-£11.50 reductions; £20-£29 family.

Built in Scotland in 1869, this graceful tea clipper was the quickest in the business when it was launched – renovation was rather slower, especially after the ship went up in flames in 2007. Fortunately, most of the timbers had already been put in storage, and the vessel is now once more a great visitor attraction – controversially raised 10ft above the ground, so that you can admire the copper keel, and with the entrance punched through one side. The interactives within the ship are informative, but the best fun is clambering around the decks and cabins.

Discover Greenwich & the Old Royal Naval College

2 Cutty Sark Gardens, SE10 9LW (8269 4799, www.oldroyalnaval college.org.uk). Cutty Sark DLR. **Open** 10am-5pm daily. **Admission** free.

Designed by Wren in 1694, with Hawksmoor and Vanbrugh helping to complete it, the Old Royal Naval College was originally a hospital for seamen, with pensioners living here from 1705 to 1869, when the complex became the Royal Naval College. The public are allowed into the impressive rococo chapel, where there are free organ recitals, and the Painted Hall, a tribute to William and Mary that took Sir James Thornhill 19 years to complete. In 2010, the Pepys Building (the block of the Naval College nearest the *Cutty Sark*, the pier and Cutty Sark DLR) reopened as the excellent Discover Greenwich. It's full of focused, informative exhibits on the surrounding buildings, the life of the pensioners, Tudor royalty and so forth, delivered with a real sense of fun: while grown-ups read about scagliola (a fake stone building material), the kids can try on a knight's helmet.

National Maritime Museum

Romney Road, SE10 9NF (8858 4422, 8312 6565 information, www.nmm.ac.uk). Cutty Sark DLR or Greenwich DLR/rail. **Open** 10am-5pm Mon-Wed, Fri-Sun; 10am-8pm Thur. **Admission** free; donations appreciated.

The world's largest maritime museum contains a huge store of maritime art, cartography, models, interactives and regalia – and it's even bigger since the impressive expansion in 2011 into the new Sammy Ofer Wing. Centred on 'Voyagers: Britons and the Sea' – a collection of 200 artefacts, accompanied by an audio-visual installation called the Wave – this extension also has the Compass Lounge (with free Wi-Fi), where you can explore the collection using computers, and a brasserie, café and shop. Other ground-level galleries include 'Explorers' (great sea expeditions back to medieval time) and 'Maritime London' (the city as a port). Here, too, you'll find Nelson's Trafalgar uniform, blood-stained and

with fatal bullet-hole – until it moves to the new 'Nelson, Navy, Nation' gallery, due in October 2013. Level two holds the interactives: the Bridge is a ship simulator, All Hands lets children load cargo, and you can try your hand as a ship's gunner. 'The Ship of War' is the museum's superb collection of models, dating from 1660 to 1815, and the 'Atlantic: Slavery, Trade, Empires' gallery looks at the brutal trade between Britain, Africa and the Americas during the 17th to 19th centuries. More recent additions include the Great Map, a large interactive floor map of the oceans, and a Nelson Navy, Nation Gallery, which recalls the sea-borne battles of the 18th century.

From the museum, a colonnaded walkway leads to the Queen's House (8312 6565, 10am-5pm daily, free admission), designed by Inigo Jones and holding art by Hogarth and Gainsborough. At the top of the hill, the Royal Observatory and Planetarium (8312 6565, www.rog.nmm.ac.uk; £10, reductions vary) are also part of the museum – make sure you allow some time to photograph yourself straddling the Prime Meridian Line.

Eating & drinking

Old Brewery

Pepys Building, Old Royal Naval College, SE10 9LW (3327 1280, www.oldbrewerygreenwich.com). Cutty Sark DLR or Maze Hill rail. **Open** 11am-11pm daily. **££.** **Beer bar/restaurant.**

By day, the Old Brewery is a café; by night, it becomes a restaurant. There's a small bar, with tables outside in a large walled courtyard – a lovely spot in which to test the 50-strong beer list – but most of the action is in the vast, high-ceilinged main space, beneath a wave-like structure of empty bottles and a handsome wall of shiny copper vats. The short menu highlights provenance and seasonality, with matching beers suggested for each dish.

Nightlife

O2 Arena & IndigO2

Millennium Way, SE10 0BB (8463 2000 information, 0844 856 0202 box office, www.theo2.co.uk). North Greenwich tube.

Since its launch in 2007, this conversion of the Millennium Dome has been a huge success. The O2 Arena – a state-of-the-art, 23,000-capacity enormo-dome with good acoustics and sightlines – hosts headline rock and pop acts. Its little brother, Indigo2, isn't actually that little (capacity 2,350) but is a good fit for big soul, funk and pop-jazz acts (Roy Ayers, Stacey Kent), old pop stars (Gary Numan, Ultravox) and all points between. Thames Clippers (p184) run half hourly back into town.

Notting Hill

Notting Hill Gate, Ladbroke Grove and Westbourne Park tube stations make a triangle that contains lovely squares, grand houses and fine gardens, along with shops, bars and restaurants that serve the kind of bohemian who can afford to live here. Off Portobello Road are the boutiques of Westbourne Grove and Ledbury Road.

Eating & drinking

Ledbury

127 Ledbury Road, W11 2AQ (7792 9090, www.theledbury.com). Westbourne Park tube. **Open** 6.30-10.15pm Mon; noon-2.15pm, 6.30-10.15pm Tue-Sat; noon-2.30pm, 7-10pm Sun. **£££. French.**

Notting Hillites flock to this elegant gastronomic masterpiece, where the food is as adventurous and accomplished as any, but less expensive than many. Expect to enjoy flavours that are both delicate but intense, often powerfully earthy. There's a well-priced, top-quality wine list too. Booking is highly recommended.

Mazi

12-14 Hillgate Street, W8 7SR (7229 3794, www.mazi.co.uk). Notting Hill Gate tube. **Open** 6.30-10.30pm Mon, Tue; noon-3pm, 6.30-1.30pm Wed-Sat; noon-3pm, 6.30-10.30pm Sun. **££.**
Greek.

As properly Greek as you'll find in London, this newcomer showcases traditional and progressive cooking. The wine list is entirely Greek, sourced from new-wave producers as well as classic appellations. Even Mazi's retsina is modern style: lightly resinated and very palatable. Dishes such as Greek salad (horiátiki) are near-perfect; matsata – rabbit stew with fresh pasta – also had correctly rustic flavours. Simply but attractively furnished, with eager, attentive service.

Shopping

Honest Jon's

278 Portobello Road, W10 5TE (8969 9822, www.honestjons.com). Ladbroke Grove tube. **Open** 10am-6pm Mon-Sat; 11am-5pm Sun.

Honest Jon's found its way to Notting Hill in 1979, and the owner helped James Lavelle set up Mo'Wax records. Expect to find a fine selection of jazz, hip hop, soul, broken beat, reggae and Brazilian music on the shelves.

Portobello Road Market

Portobello Road, W10 (www.portobelloroad.co.uk). Ladbroke Grove or Notting Hill Gate tube. **Open** *General* 9am-6pm Mon-Wed; 9am-1pm Thur; 7am-7pm Fri, Sat. *Antiques* 6am-4pm Fri, Sat. No credit cards.

Portobello is always busy, but fun. Antiques start at the Notting Hill end; further down are food stalls, and emerging designer and vintage clothes congregate under the Westway and along the walkway to Ladbroke Grove on Fridays (usually marginally quieter) and Saturdays (invariably manic). Continue to Golborne Road for more shops and junk stalls.

Essentials

Shangri-La at the Shard p171

Hotels

The 2012 Games initiated a frenzy of hotel-building in London that still hasn't yet abated. In fact, more luxury hotels seem to have opened over the last year than in the run-up. The most eye-catching new hotel is clearly the **Shangri-La** (p171), looming over London from the 34th to 52nd floors of the Shard (p59), but it isn't the hottest opening. That accolade belongs to André Balazs' first hotel in the UK, the celeb-haunted **Chiltern Firehouse** (p172). And our favourite of the new luxe brigade? Firmdale's gigantic but exquisitely detailed and charmingly staffed **Ham Yard Hotel** (p175).

There's ongoing refurbishment of well-established grand hotels, notably the **Lanesborough** (1 Lanesborough Place, Knightsbridge, SW1X 7TA, 7259 5599, www.lanesborough.com), which is due to reopen after extensive renovations in late 2014, while several highly anticipated new hotels will be with us soon, not least the **Beaumont**, the first hotel from ace restaurateurs Corbin and King, with one suite *inside* an Antony Gormley sculpture.

Room prices are high. Chic hotels offering self-described 'tiny' rooms at lower-than-you-might-fear rates – notably **Dean Street** (p173) and its sibling **Shoreditch Rooms** (p180) – is one solution.

No-frills hotels are another good option, although we prefer to stay at what we're tempted to call 'no-frills boutique': **citizenM** (p169), **QBic** (p179) and the **Z Soho** (p177), places that pair good rates with a bit of style. The pioneer in this category, the **Hoxton** (p179), is planning new premises in Holborn.

In truth, although there are few bargains in London, there is plenty of good value to be found. If you need something that's genuinely

cheap, expect to book months ahead, lower your standards, or go online and gamble on a last-minute deal.

Money matters

When visitors moan about London prices (you know you do), their case is strongest when it comes to hotels. We reckon any decent double under £120 a night is good value here: hence, £ in the listings is a rack rate of around £100 and less. Hotels do offer special deals, though, notably at weekends; check their websites or ask when you book, and also look at discount websites such as **www.lastminute. com**, **www.alpharooms.com** or **www.trivago.co.uk**.

The South Bank

citizenM London Bankside

20 Lavington Street, SE1 0NZ (3519 1680, www.citizenm.com). Southwark tube or Blackfriars tube/rail. **££.**
This Dutch hotel is affordable, stylish, buzzy, and right in the thick of the arty action: right behind Tate

Modern (p59). The ground floor is a slick and cosy café-bar and reception area: self-check-in, but with brilliant staff on hand to offer help and, when higher-grade rooms are free, upgrades. Guests are invited to use it as their 'living room' and – thanks to the neat but welcoming design – do so. The rooms are tiny, comfy and well thought out: automatic blackout blinds, free Wi-Fi, a drench shower with removable sidehead, storage under the bed, and free movies.

Premier Inn London County Hall

County Hall, Belvedere Road, SE1 7PB (0871 527 8648, www.premierinn.com). Waterloo tube/rail. **££**.
A position right by the London Eye (p56) and friendly, efficient staff make this refurbished chain hotel the acceptable face of budget convenience. Check in is quick; rooms are spacious, clean and warm, with comfortable beds and decent bathrooms with good showers, although some are quite dark. Buffet-style breakfast is extra and wireless internet access costs £3 a day (guests get half an hour free).

Shangri-La at the Shard

NEW *31 St Thomas Street, SE1 9QU (7234 8000, www.shangri-la.com/london). London Bridge tube/rail.* **££££**.
You won't have any problem finding your accommodation if you book here: it's in the Shard (p59), which can be seen from pretty much anywhere in London. Check in at the high-ceilinged but rather sterile lobby, from which you'll be guided by smoothly efficient staff to the superfast lifts, which whisk you in seconds to rooms spread over floors 34-52 (the hotel opened with 59 rooms and suites; more than 200 will be added in the coming months). The views are magnificent (especially from the more expensive rooms, which have 180° views), but the expensive-looking, Asian decor is blandly cosmopolitan.

South Kensington & Chelsea

B+B Belgravia

64-66 Ebury Street, Belgravia, SW1W 9QD (7259 8570, www.bb-belgravia. com). Victoria tube/rail. **££**.
B+B Belgravia has taken the B&B experience to a new level, although you pay a bit more for the privilege of staying somewhere with a cosy lounge that's full of white and black contemporary furnishings. It's sophisticated and fresh without being hard-edged, and there are all kinds of goodies to make you feel at home: an espresso machine for 24/7 caffeine, an open fireplace, newspapers and DVDs.

Morgan House

120 Ebury Street, Belgravia, SW1W 9QQ (7730 2384, www.morganhouse.co.uk). Pimlico tube or Victoria tube/rail. **£**.
The Morgan has the understated charm of the old family home of a posh, unpretentious English friend: a pleasing mix of nice old wooden or traditional iron beds, pretty floral curtains and coverlets in subtle hues, the odd chandelier or big gilt mirror over original mantelpieces, padded wicker chairs and sinks in every bedroom. Though there's no guest lounge, guests can sit in the little patio garden. Free Wi-Fi is provided.

Number Sixteen

16 Sumner Place, South Kensington, SW7 3EG (7589 5232, www.firmdale hotels.com). South Kensington tube. **£££**.
This may be Firmdale's most affordable hotel, but there's no slacking in style – witness the fresh flowers and origami-ed birdbook decorations in the comfy drawing room, with its inviting fireplace. Bedrooms are generously sized, bright and light, and carry the Kit Kemp trademark mix of bold and traditional. By the time you finish breakfast in the calming conservatory,

ESSENTIALS

which looks out on the delicious back garden with its central water feature, you'll have forgotten you're in the city.

West End

Charlotte Street Hotel

15-17 Charlotte Street, Fitzrovia, W1T 1RJ (7806 2000, www.firmdalehotels. com). Goodge Street or Tottenham Court Road tube. **££££**.

This gorgeous Firmdale hotel is a fine exponent of Kit Kemp's fusion of traditional and avant-garde – you won't believe it was once a dental hospital. Public rooms contain Bloomsbury Set paintings (Duncan Grant, Vanessa Bell), while the bedrooms mix English understatement with bold decorative flourishes. The huge beds and trademark polished granite bathrooms are suitably indulgent, and some rooms have very high ceilings. The bar-restaurant buzzes with media types, for whom the screening room must feel like a home comfort.

Chiltern Firehouse

NEW *1 Chiltern Street, Marylebone, W1U 7PA (7073 7676, www.chilternfirehouse. com). Baker Street tube.* **££££**.

This Grade II-listed red-brick former fire station was for years the secret location of London's most-anticipated new hotel. The key factor was André Balazs who, as the man behind the celeb-friendly Chateau Marmont in LA and the Mercer in New York, has the gift for creating exclusive hotels with incredible buzz. The see-and-be-seen restaurant (p91) opened first, under visionary chef Nuno Mendes, and was immediately block-booked; ditto the 26 refined suites, each a model of intelligent, comforting design.

Claridge's

55 Brook Street, Mayfair, W1K 4HR (7629 8860, www.claridges.co.uk). Bond Street tube. **££££**.

Claridge's is sheer class and pure atmosphere, its signature art deco

redesign still dazzling. Photographs of Churchill and sundry royals grace the grand foyer, as does an absurdly over-the-top Dale Chihuly chandelier. Without departing too far from the traditional, Claridge's bars and restaurant are actively fashionable – particularly with the arrival of Simon Rogan, who opened his Fera restaurant in 2014. The rooms divide evenly between deco and Victorian style, with period touches balanced by high-tech bedside panels.

Clink78

78 King's Cross Road, WC1X 9QG (7183 9400, www.clinkhostels.com). King's Cross tube/rail. **£**.

In a former courthouse, the Clink sets the bar high for hosteldom. There's the setting: the original wood-panelled lobby and courtroom where the Clash stood before the beak (now filled with backpackers surfing the web). Then there's the urban chic ethos, with new graffiti-styled decor and a refurbished bar. The smaller, quieter Clink261 (261-265 Gray's Inn Road, 7833 9400) is nearby.

Connaught

Carlos Place, Mayfair, W1K 2AL (7499 7070, www.the-connaught.co.uk). Bond Street tube. **££££**.

It isn't the only London hotel to provide butlers, but there can't be many that offer 'a secured gun cabinet room' for hunting season. This is traditional British hospitality for those who love 23-carat gold leaf and stern portraits in the halls, but all mod cons in their room, down to free Wi-Fi and flatscreens in the en suite. Both of the bars – gentleman's club cosy Coburg and cruiseship deco Connaught – and the Hélène Darroze restaurant are impressive. There's also a less atmospheric new wing, with a terrific spa and swimming pool.

Covent Garden Hotel

10 Monmouth Street, WC2H 9HB (7806 1000, www.firmdalehotels.com). Covent

Garden, Leicester Square or Tottenham Court Road tube. **££££**.

On the ground floor, the 1920s Paris-style Brasserie Max and its retro zinc bar continues to buzz – testament to the deserved popularity of Firmdale's snug and stylish 1996 establishment. Its Covent Garden location and tucked-away screening room ensure it still attracts starry customers, and guests needing a bit of privacy can retreat upstairs to the lovely panelled private library, with honesty bar. In the individually styled guest rooms, pinstriped wallpaper and floral upholstery are mixed with bold, contemporary elements. It's a stunner.

Dean Street Townhouse & Dining Room

69-71 Dean Street, Soho, W1D 3SE (7434 1775, www.deanstreettownhouse. com). Leicester Square or Piccadilly Circus tube. **£££**.

This is another winning enterprise from the people behind Soho House members' club. To one side of a buzzy ground-floor restaurant are four floors of bedrooms that run from full-size rooms with early Georgian panelling and reclaimed oak floors to half-panelled 'Tiny' rooms barely bigger than their double beds – but available from £100. The atmosphere is gentleman's club cosy (there are cookies in a cute silver Treats container in each room), but modern types are reassured by rainforest showers, 24hr room service, DAB radios, free wireless internet and big flatscreen TVs.

Dorchester

53 Park Lane, Mayfair, W1K 1QA (7629 8888, www.thedorchester.com). Hyde Park Corner tube. **££££**.

A Park Lane fixture since 1931, the Dorchester's interior is opulently classical, but its attitude is cutting-edge, with a terrific level of personal service. The hotel employs no fewer than 90 chefs at the Grill Room, Alain Ducasse and China Tang. With one of the best lobbies in town, amazing park views, state-of-the-art mod cons and a magnificently refurbished spa containing an angelic tearoom, it's small wonder the hotel has always welcomed film stars (from the departed Liz Taylor to Tom Cruise) and political leaders (Eisenhower planned D-Day here).

Generator p174

Ham Yard Hotel

45 Park Lane

45 Park Lane, Mayfair, W1K 1PN (7493 4545, www.45parklane.com). Hyde Park Corner tube. **£££**.

Offspring of the Dorchester, which it faces across a twinkly-treed forecourt, 45 Park Lane has translated the high standards of the Dorchester into a buzzier, boutiquier, even blingier form. Where the Dorchester offers liveried concierges, 45 allocates guests a sharply suited personal host; where the Dorchester can arrange a limo, so can 45 – or lend you a folding bike. Wolfgang Puck brings high-end steaks to the Cut restaurant, and Bar 45 has the UK's largest collection of American wines. Rooms are standard rectangles given character by well-chosen art, quality furnishings, great views (ask for an upper floor) and considered touches such as a yoga mat and in-safe electrical outlet.

Generator

NEW *37 Tavistock Place, Bloomsbury, WC1H 9SE (7388 7666, http://generator hostels.com/en). Russell Square tube.* **£**.

With a handily central Bloomsbury location, the Generator is a good option for those on ultra-tight budgets. It has been part of a global refit of the chain, creating private rooms for £25 a night. Throughout there's free Wi-Fi, plus the familiar attributes of a lively hotel: 24hr lounge that hosts regular gigs and DJs, 24hr laundry, 24hr luggage store and 24hr reception.

Great Northern Hotel

King's Cross St Pancras Station, Pancras Road, N1C 4TB (3388 0800, www.gnhlondon.com). King's Cross tube/rail. **£££**.

Designed by Lewis Cubitt, the city's first railway hotel (take that, St Pancras Renaissance!) opened in 1854. The furniture is, in many cases, bespoke: witness the Couchette rooms, each with a double bed snugly fitted into the window to echo overnight train carriages, or ceiling lights raised and lowered by steam-punk pulleys. You're not expected to suffer the privations of a Victorian traveller: free wireless internet and film and music libraries on the 40-inch TV, Egyptian cotton sheets, free water in the fridge, and walk-in showers are all standard. USB ports for recharging are placed by the beds, as well as being strategically located (with laptop plug sockets) in the public areas. There's no room service: instead, each floor has a pantry, full of jars of vintage sweeties, a stand of cakes, tea and coffee, newspapers and books – even a USB printer. There's also a grand restaurant on the first floor, plus a busy ground-floor bar.

Ham Yard Hotel

NEW *1 Ham Yard, Soho, W1D 7DT (3642 2000, www.firmdalehotels.com). Piccadilly Circus tube.* **££££**.
We're fans of all the Firmdale hotels – and co-owner Kit Kemp's trademark splashy, clashy colours, winningly teamed with antique and distressed furniture – but Ham Yard has immediately leapt to the top of our list. It's partly just a matter of scale: here Firmdale took over a whole yard in central London, and have built there a grandly proportioned hotel, a separate block of hotel apartments, and a cluster of curated shops around a central courtyard. But guests won't feel lost, due to unusually friendly service, and Kemp's ability to combine conversation-starter decor (witness the deconstructed loom over reception) with intimate, arty details. There's a library and drawing room, A big ground-floor bar and restaurant, with rear conservatory, an exquisite basement bowling alley, and, of course, fabulously well-appointed rooms (marble and flatscreens in the bathrooms, bespoke toiletries, tech that actually works first time).

Harlingford Hotel

61-63 Cartwright Gardens, Bloomsbury, WC1H 9EL (7387 1551, www. harlingfordhotel.com). Russell Square tube or Euston tube/rail. **££**.
An affordable hotel with bundles of charm in the heart of Bloomsbury, the Harlingford has light airy rooms with boutique aspirations. Decor is lifted from understated sleek to quirky with the help of vibrant colour splashes from the glass bathroom fittings and the mosaic tiles. The crescent it's set in has a lovely, leafy private garden.

Hazlitt's

6 Frith Street, Soho, W1D 3JA (7434 1771, www.hazlittshotel.com). Tottenham Court Road tube. **£££**.
Four Georgian townhouses comprise this charming place, named after William Hazlitt, a spirited 18th-century essayist who died here in abject poverty (he's buried at nearby St Anne's). With flamboyance and staggering attention to detail, the rooms evoke the Georgian era, all fireplaces, heavy fabrics, free-standing tubs and exquisitely carved half-testers, yet modern luxuries – air-con, TVs in antique cupboards, free Wi-Fi and triple-glazed windows – have also been attended to. It gets creakier and more crooked the higher you go, culminating in enchanting garret single rooms.

Jenkins Hotel

45 Cartwright Gardens, Bloomsbury, WC1H 9EH (7387 2067, www. jenkinshotelbloomsbury.com). Russell Square tube or Euston tube/rail. **£**.
This well-to-do Georgian beauty has been a hotel since the 1920s. It still has an atmospheric, antique air, although the rooms have mod cons enough – TVs, mini-fridges, tea and coffee, as well as free Wi-Fi. Its looks have earned it a role in *Agatha Christie's Poirot*, but it's not chintzy, with a sober but perfectly pleasant recent refurb. The breakfast room is handsome.

London Edition

NEW *10 Berners Street, Fitzrovia, W1T 3NP (7781 0000, http://edition-hotels. marriott.com/london). Oxford Circus or Tottenham Court Road tube.* **£££**.
The London Edition makes a big impact as you walk into its grand hall of a lobby, with double-height rococo ceilings, floor-to-ceiling windows and marble pillars. It's the setting for the lobby bar, with a mix of comfortable, snazzy seating: sofas with faux-fur throws and wing-backed chairs, plus a blackened steel bar, a real fire and a colossal silver egg-shaped object

where you might expect a chandelier; off to one side is the excellent Berners Tavern (p102), while hidden away at the back is the clubby, wood-panelled Punch Room bar. Bedrooms are a contrast: akin to dachas, with matte oak floors, wood-panelled walls and more faux-fur throws tossed on luxurious beds. Larger rooms come with sofas, some have large furnished terraces and all have rainforest showers, Le Labo toiletries (with the hotel's woody signature scent), iPod docks and free Wi-Fi.

Montagu Place

2 Montagu Place, Marylebone, W1H 2ER (7467 2777, www.montagu-place.co.uk). Baker Street tube. **£££**.
At this stylish small hotel, in a pair of Grade II-listed Georgian townhouses, all guestrooms have pocket-sprung beds, as well as cafetières and flatscreen TVs (DVD players are available from reception). The look here is boutique-hotel sharp, except for an uneasy overlap of bar and reception – though you can instead simply get your drink and retire to the graciously modern lounge.

Morgan

24 Bloomsbury Street, Bloomsbury, WC1B 3QJ (7636 3735, www.morganhotel.co.uk). Tottenham Court Road tube. **££**.
This brilliantly located, comfortable budget hotel looks better than it has for a while after renovations. The rooms have ditched floral for neutral, and are equipped with free wireless, voicemail, air-con and flatscreen televisions with Freeview. A slap-up English breakfast is served in a good-looking room with wood panelling, decorated with London prints and blue-and-white china plates.

Sanderson

50 Berners Street, Fitzrovia, W1T 3NG (7300 1400, www.morganshotelgroup. com). Oxford Circus tube. **££££**.
This Schrager/Starck statement creation takes clinical chic to new heights. The only touch of colour in our room was a naïve landscape painting nailed to the ceiling over the silver sleigh bed. Otherwise, it's all flowing white net drapes, glass cabinets and retractable screens. The residents-only Purple Bar sports a button-backed purple leather ceiling and fabulous cocktails; the 'billiard room' has a purple-topped pool table and weird tribal adaptations of classic dining-room furniture.

Savoy

Strand, WC2R 0EU (7836 4343, www. fairmont.com/savoy-london). Covent Garden or Embankment tube, or Charing Cross tube/rail. **££££**.
The superluxe, Grade II-listed Savoy reopened in 2010 after more than £100m of renovations – recreating a listed building, loved by generations of visitors for its discreet mix of Edwardian neoclassical and art deco, as a modern luxury hotel. Built in 1889 to put up theatregoers from Richard D'Oyly Carte's Gilbert & Sullivan shows in the attached theatre, the Savoy is the hotel from which Monet painted the Thames, where Vivien Leigh met Laurence Olivier, where Londoners met the martini. There's topiary at the famous cul-de-sac entrance, a fitness centre with jet-stream swimming pool in its own atrium, and a new tearoom with glass-roofed conservatory, and the leather counter of the new Beaufort champagne bar is set on a former stage for big bands, but the Savoy Grill and American Bar have barely changed. Seamless service whisks you to your room almost before you arrive.

Sumner

54 Upper Berkeley Street, Mayfair, W1H 7QR (7723 2244, www.thesumner.com). Marble Arch tube. **££**.
The Sumner's cool, deluxe looks have earned it many fans – and several awards. You won't be at all surprised: from the soft dove and slatey greys of the lounge and halls, you move up to glossily spacious accommodation

Ace Hotel London Shoreditch p178

with walk-in showers. The breakfast room feels soft and sunny, with a lovely, delicate buttercup motif and vibrant Arne Jacobsen chairs, whereas the stylishly moody front sitting room is a cosy gem.

22 York Street

22 York Street, Marylebone, W1U 6PX (7224 2990, www.22yorkstreet.co.uk). Baker Street tube. **££**.

Imagine one of those bohemian French country houses you see in *Elle Decor* – all pale pink limewashed walls, wooden floors and quirky antiques. That's the feel of this graceful, unpretentious bed and breakfast. There's no sign on the door and the sense of staying in a hospitable home continues when you're offered coffee in the spacious breakfast room-cum-kitchen with its curved communal table. The rooms have en suite baths, guests are given free rein with hot beverages, and there's free Wi-Fi.

YHA London Central

104 Bolsover Street, Fitzrovia, W1W 5NU (0845 371 9154, www.yha.org.uk). Great Portland Street tube. **£**.

The Youth Hostel Association's newest hostel is one of its best – as well as being one of the best hostels in London. The friendly and well-informed receptionists are stationed at a counter to the left of the entrance, in a substantial café-bar area. The basement contains a well-equipped kitchen and washing area; above it are five floors of clean, neatly designed rooms, many en suite. You get 24hr access (by individual key card), there's free Wi-Fi and the quiet location is an easy walk from Soho.

Z Soho

17 Moor Street, Soho, W1D 5AP (3551 3700, www.thezhotels.com). Leicester Square or Tottenham Court Road tube. **£**.

For the money, the Z is a cast-iron bargain. First, the location is superb: it really means Soho – the breakfast room/bar exits on Old Compton Street. Then there's the hotel itself, which is surprisingly chic – especially the unexpected interior courtyard, with open 'corridors' stacked above it, and room to sit and drink or smoke at the bottom – and very cheerfully run, down to free wine and nibbles of an evening. The rooms have everything you need, from a little desk to free Wi-Fi, but not much more. Including space: expect beds (perhaps a little short for anyone over 6ft) to take up

ESSENTIALS

Saving or scrimping?

How to keep to budget.

First there was the **Hoxton** (p179), back in 2009, a hip hotel that offered all mod cons in small, stylish rooms – at competitive prices. We loved it, and sat back to watch for a splurge of copy-cats.

Even after five years, the splurge is no more than a trickle: first **Z Soho** (p177) and **citizenM** (p169), were joined in 2013 by **QBic** (p179). All three are great little hotels, not blessed with much space, but done with flair. citizenM and QBic are savvier, but Z Soho is central and perfectly fine for anyone who thinks a hotel bedroom is just that: a bed in a room. The trickle may yet become – if not a flood – at least a spate: the Hoxton has a new branch nearing completion; citizenM has two branches in the pipeline.

Chains are another good option: **Premier Inn London County Hall** (p171) is right on the South Bank, and you can often find double rooms for around £100 at reasonably central locations through **Holiday Inn** and **Holiday Inn Express** (www. ichotelsgroup.com), **Ibis** (www. ibishotel.com) or **Travelodge** (www.travelodge. co.uk).

There's also the 'no-frills' approach – very low rates, with nothing inessential included. Airline-offshoot **EasyHotel** (www. easyhotel.com) was the first, but a growing number of **Tune** hotels (www.tunehotels.com) are joining them, including good Liverpool Street and King's Cross locations.

most of the room, a feeble shower, and no wardrobe or phone. A great little hotel – in both senses.

The City

Ace Hotel London Shoreditch

NEW *100 Shoreditch High Street, E1 6JQ (7613 9800, www.acehotel.com/london). Liverpool Street tube/rail or Shoreditch High Street rail.* **££**.

Ace – previously of New York, Palm Springs, Portland, Seattle and Panama – has arrived in Shoreditch, taking over an old Crowne Plaza hotel. The look of the spacious rooms is comfortable, a bit bohemian, like a modern urban apartment, with wall-to-wall daybeds/ sofas, sturdy oak or metal storage units, round oak tables and beds (and sofas too) covered in luxury denim. Furniture and accessories reflect the Ace appreciation of artisanship. You might find an Ally Capellino leather change box (her shop is just down the road) or a CF Martin & Co guitar. The lobby vibe is egalitarian and informal, with a long communal table with computers and DJs every night. There's a cute juice bar, Lovage, a nook of a coffee shop, a bar tucked into another nook, and a flower shop. And, of course, the wood-clad midcentury-look brasserie Hoi Polloi (p146).

Boundary

2-4 Boundary Street, E2 7DD (7729 1051, www.theboundary.co.uk). Liverpool Street tube/rail or Shoreditch High Street rail. **£££**.

In a converted warehouse, Conran's latest combines restaurant, rooftop bar, ground-floor café (Albion, p156) and excellent hotel rooms, the whole establishment clearly a labour of love. Each room has a wet room and handmade bed, but all are otherwise coolly individual, with classic furniture and original art. The five split-level suites range in style from the bright and sea-salt fresh Beach to a new take on

Victoriana; the remaining rooms are themed by design ethos: Mies van der Rohe, Shaker and so on.

Fox & Anchor

115 Charterhouse Street, EC1M 6AA (0845 347 0100, www.foxandanchor. com). Barbican tube or Farringdon tube/ rail. **££.**

No more than a few atmospheric, well-appointed and luxurious rooms above a bustling, darkly panelled pub, this has been one of our most enjoyable stays in London. Each en suite room differs, but the high-spec facilities (big flatscreens, clawfoot bath, drench shower) and quirky attention to detail (bottles of ale in the minibar, 'Nursing hangover' signs to hang out if you want some privacy) are common throughout. Expect some clanking market noise in the early mornings.

Hoxton Hotel

81 Great Eastern Street, EC2A 3HU (7550 1000, www.hoxtonhotels.com). Old Street tube/rail. **££.**

Everything you've heard is true. First, there's the hip location. Then there are the great design values: the foyer is a sort of postmodern country lodge (with stag's head) and rooms are small, well thought-out and full of nice touches (Frette linens, free Wi-Fi, free fresh milk in the mini fridge, free mini breakfast hung on your door handle in the morning). Above all, there's the budget-airline pricing, by which you might catch a £1-a-night ultra-bargain – but, assuming you can book far enough ahead to beat demand, ensures you get a great-value room. The addition of a handful of individually designed 'suites' a few years back, and a lively social roster, have kept the place fresh, and a new branch is planned for Holborn before the end of 2014.

QBic Hotel London City

NEW *42 Adler Street, E1 1EE (no phone, www.qbichotels.com). Aldgate East or Whitechapel tube.* **£.**

QBic is a Dutch chain of stylish budget hotels with an admirable focus on community (here they're working with local cycling charity Bikeworks and Food Cycle) and sustainability: in fact, the hotel was created at the end of 2013 by the incredibly rapid fit-out of a former office building using modular 'Cubi' bedrooms. Rooms are sold at four levels – starting at £59 a night for no view, and increasing in price if you want to see the Whitechapel Road,

QBic Hotel London City

ESSENTIALS

the inner courtyard or Altab Ali Park. Prices are pegged by keeping down the numbers of staff, which means self check-in and no cash – even vending machines are credit card only. Still, the essentials are covered: TVs in each room, free wireless internet throughout, free snack breakfast or £7.50 for a continental in the space downstairs.

Rookery

12 Peter's Lane, Cowcross Street, EC1M 6DS (7336 0931, www.rookeryhotel. com). Farringdon tube/rail. **£££**.
The front door of the Rookery is satisfyingly hard to find, especially when the streets are teeming with Fabric (p138) devotees (the front rooms can be noisy on these nights). Once inside, guests enjoy a warren of creaky rooms, individually decorated in the style of a Georgian townhouse – clawfoot baths, elegant four-posters – but also furnished with free Wi-Fi. The split-level Rook's Nest suite has views of St Paul's Cathedral. At the rear, a cosy honesty bar opens on to a sweet little patio.

Shoreditch Rooms

Ebor Street, E1 6AW (7739 5040, www. shoreditchhouse.com). Shoreditch High Street rail. **££**.
The more recent hotel from the Soho House members' club (see also Dean Street Townhouse, p173) might be the best, perfectly catching the local atmosphere with its unfussy, slightly retro design. The rooms feel a bit like urban beach huts, with pastel-coloured tongue-and-groove walls and swing doors to the en suite showers. They feel fresh and comfortable, even though they're furnished with little more than a bed, a DAB radio and old-fashioned phone, and a solid dresser (minibar, hairdryer and treats within, flatscreen TV on top). Guests get access to the eating, drinking and fitness facilities on the premises (there's an excellent rooftop pool) in

the members' club next door. 'Tiny' rooms start from just £105.

South Place Hotel

3 South Place, EC2M 2AF (3503 0000, www.southplacehotel.com). Moorgate or Liverpool Street tube/rail. **£££**.
D&D runs some of the swankiest restaurants in London, so much was expected of its first hotel. South Place delivers. It manages the difficult balance of sufficient formality to keep expense-accounters satisfied, with enough levity for you to want to spend the evening indoors. The muted top-floor Angler restaurant is a superbly oiled operation, there's a pretty interior courtyard garden bar, and the ground-floor 3 South Place bar-diner segues neatly from smooth breakfast operation to boisterous bar. The attention to detail impresses: from conversation-piece art to touch controls in the rooms or the Bond-themed pool room and library, complete with vinyl turntable.

Zetter

86-88 Clerkenwell Road, EC1M 5RJ (7324 4444, www.thezetter.com). Farringdon tube/rail. **£££**.
Zetter is a fun, laid-back, modern hotel with interesting design notes, a refreshing lack of attitude, friendly staff and firm eco-credentials (such as occupancy detection systems in the bedrooms). The rooms, stacked up on five galleried storeys overlooking the intimate bar area, are smoothly functional, but cosied up with choice home comforts like hot-water bottles and old Penguin paperbacks, as well as having walk-in showers with REN smellies. There are even folding Brompton bikes available to guests for free. Bistrot Bruno Loubet is excellent, and the 13-room Townhouse – a beautifully decorated Georgian house on the rear square – has an ace cocktail bar (p138). We're looking forward to the opening of the new Zetter Seymour Street, in Marylebone, in late 2014.

Getting Around

Airports

Gatwick Airport

0844 892 0322, www.gatwickairport. com. About 30 miles south of central London, off the M23.

The quickest rail link to London is the **Gatwick Express** (0345 850 1530, www.gatwickexpress.com) to Victoria; it runs 3.30am-12.32am daily and takes 30mins. Tickets cost £19.90 single or £34.90 open return (valid for 30 days).

Southern (0845 127 2920, www. southernrailway.com) also runs trains to Victoria, roughly every 5-10mins (every 30mins 1am-4am). It takes about 35mins, and costs £15 single.

Thameslink trains (0345 026 4700, www.firstcapitalconnect.co.uk) run to St Pancras. Tickets cost £10 sin gle or £19 for a 30-day open return.

A taxi to central London takes a bit over an hour and costs £70-£100.

Heathrow Airport

0844 335 1801, www.heathrowairport. com. About 15 miles west of central London, off the M4.

The **Heathrow Express** (0845 600 1515, www.heathrowexpress. co.uk) runs to Paddington every 15mins (5.10am-11.50pm daily) and takes 15-20mins. The train can be boarded from Terminals 1 and 3 (Heathrow Central tube station) or Terminal 5 (which has its own tube station); from Terminal 4, get a shuttle to Heathrow Central. Tickets are £21 single, £34 return (£5 more on board).

The journey by **tube** into central London is longer but cheaper. The 50-60min Piccadilly Line ride into central London costs £5.07 one way (less with Oyster, p182). Trains run every few minutes from about 5am to 11.57pm daily (6am-11pm Sun).

The **Heathrow Connect** (0845 678 6975, www.heathrowconnect.com) rail service offers direct access to stations including Ealing Broadway and Paddington. The trains run every half-hour, terminating at Heathrow Central; from there to Terminal 4 get the free shuttle; between Central and Terminal 5, there's free use of the Heathrow Express. A single to Paddington is £9.90, an open return £19.80.

By road, **National Express** (0871 781 8181, www.nationalexpress.com) runs coaches daily to London Victoria (90mins, 5am-9.35pm daily) from Heathrow Central bus terminal every 20-30mins. It's £8 for a single or £14 for a return. A **taxi** to central London costs £60-£80 and takes 30-60mins.

London City Airport

7646 0088, www.londoncityairport.com. About 9 miles east of central London.

The **Docklands Light Railway** has a stop for London City Airport, which is often less chaotic than the city's other airports. The journey to Bank station in the City takes around 20mins, and trains run 5.30am-12.30am Mon-Sat or 7.30am-11.30pm Sun. A **taxi** costs roughly £30 to central London, but less to the City or Canary Wharf.

Luton Airport

01582 405100, www.london-luton.com. About 30 miles north of central London, J10 off the M1.

A short bus ride links the airport to Luton Airport Parkway station, from which **Thameslink** trains (0345 026 4700, www.firstcapitalconnect.co.uk) depart for stations including St Pancras and City, 35-45mins. Trains leave every 15mins (hourly through the night) and cost £15.50 single and £31 return.

By coach, Luton to Victoria takes 60-90mins. **Green Line** (0344 800 4411, www.greenline.co.uk) runs a 24hr service (£10 single, £15 return). A **taxi** to central London costs £70-£80.

Stansted Airport

0844 335 1803, www.stanstedairport. com. About 35 miles north-east of central London, J8 off the M11.

The **Stansted Express** (0345 600 7245, www.stanstedexpress.com) runs to Liverpool Street station, taking 40-45mins and leaving every 15mins. Tickets are £23.40 single, £33.20 return. **National Express** (0871 781 8181, www.nationalexpress.com) is one of several coach services running to Victoria Coach Station; the journey takes at least 80 minutes, with coaches roughly every 30mins (24hrs daily), more often at peak times. A single is £10, a return £18. A **taxi** to central London is around £70-£100.

Arriving by coach

Coaches run by National Express (0343 222 1234, www.national express.com), Britain's largest coach company, arrive at **Victoria Coach Station** (164 Buckingham Palace Road, SW1W 9TP, www.tfl.gov.uk).

Arriving by rail

Trains from mainland Europe run by Eurostar (01777 777879, www. eurostar.com) arrive at **St Pancras International** station (7843 7688, www.stpancras.com).

For all train times and prices, call 0845 748 4950 or visit www. nationalrail.co.uk.

Public transport

Travel Information Centres give help with the tube, buses and Docklands Light Railway. Call 0843 222 1234 or http://journeyplanner.tfl. gov.uk for more information.
Heathrow Terminals 1, 2 & 3 tube station Open 7.15am-7.30pm daily.
King's Cross rail station Open 7.15am-8pm Mon-Sat; 8.15am-7pm Sun.
Liverpool Street tube station Open 7.15am-7pm Mon-Thur; 7.15am-8pm Fri, Sat; 8.15am-7pm Sun.

Piccadilly Circus tube station Open 7.45am-7pm Mon-Fri; 9.15am-7pm Sat; 9.15am-6pm Sun.
Victoria rail station Open 7.15am-8pm Mon-Sat; 8.15am-7pm Sun.

London Underground

Trains are hot and crowded in rush hour (8-9.30am, 4.30-7pm Mon-Fri). Even so, the colour-coded lines of the Underground ('the tube') are the quickest way to get about. Underground, Overground and DLR lines are shown on the **tube map** on the back flap.

Using the Underground

Tube and DLR fares are based on a system of six zones, which stretch 12 miles out from from central London. A flat **cash fare** of £4.70 per journey applies across zones 1-3 on the tube, £5.70 for zones 1-6. However, customers save up to £2.80 per journey with a pre-pay Oyster card (below).

To enter and exit the tube using an **Oyster card**, touch it to the yellow reader, which opens the gate. You must also touch the card to the reader when you exit, or you'll be charged a higher fare when you next use your card. On certain lines, you'll see a pink reader (the 'validator') – touch it in addition to the yellow entry/exit readers and on some routes it will reduce your fare.

To enter using a **paper ticket**, place it in the slot with the black magnetic strip facing down, then pull it out of the top to open the gates. Exit in the same way; tickets for single journeys will be retained by the gate on final exit.

Oyster cards

A pre-paid smartcard, Oyster is the cheapest way of getting around on buses, tubes and the DLR. You can get Oyster cards from www.tfl.gov.

uk/oyster, Travel Information
Centres (left), tube stations, and some
newsagents and rail stations. A £5
refundable deposit is payable on new
cards. A tube journey in zone 1 using
Oyster pay-as-you-go costs £2.20;
single journeys from zones 1-6 using
Oyster are £5 (6.30am-9.30am, 4-7pm
Mon-Fri) or £3 (all other times,
including public holidays).

Travelcards

If you're only taking the tube, DLR,
buses and trams, using Oyster to pay
as you go will always be capped at the
same price as an equivalent Day
Travelcard. However, if you're also
using National Rail services, Oyster
may not be accepted: opt instead for a
Day Travelcard, a ticket that allows
travel across all the London networks.

Anytime Day Travelcards
can be used all day. They cost £9 for
zones 1-2, up to £17 for zones 1-6.
Tickets are valid for journeys started
by 4.30am the next day. The **Off-
Peak Day Travelcard** is only for
travel after 9.30am Mon-Fri (all day
for weekends and public holidays).
It costs £8.90 for zones 1-6.
Travelcards are also available for
longer periods, in which case they
can be put on to your Oyster. If you're
staying in London for a week, a
weekly Travelcard will probably
be cheaper than pay-as-you-go.

Travelling with children

Under-5s travel free on buses and
trams. Those aged **5-10** also travel
free, but need to obtain a 5-10 Zip
Oyster photocard if not travelling
with an adult. An 11-15 Oyster
photocard is needed by **under-16s**
to pay as they go on the tube/DLR and
to buy child-fare 7-day, monthly or
longer period Travelcards. The card
allows them to travel free on buses
and trams. Those aged **16-18** can
get child fares with a 16+ Zip Oyster

photocard. For details, see www.tfl.
gov.uk/fares or call 0345 602 3813.
Visitors can apply for a
photocard (http://photocard.tfl.
gov.uk) in advance. Photocards are
not required for adult rate 7-day
Travelcards, Bus Passes or for any
adult rate Travelcard or Bus Pass
charged on an Oyster card.

Underground timetable

Tube trains run daily from around
5am (except Sunday, when they start
an hour or so later depending on the
line, and Christmas Day, when there's
no service). You shouldn't have to
wait more than ten minutes for a
train; during peak times, services
should run every two or three
minutes. Times of last trains vary;
they're usually around 12.30am
(11.30pm on Sun).

Docklands Light Railway

DLR trains (7363 9700, www.tfl.gov.
uk/dlr) run east from Bank station
(on the Central tube line) or Tower
Gateway, close to Tower Hill tube
(Circle and District lines). Stations
are shown on the Underground map.
Trains run 5.30am-12.30am daily.
With very few exceptions, adult
single **fares** on the DLR are the
same as the Underground (p182).

Rail & Overground

Independently run commuter
services coordinated by National Rail
(0845 748 4950, www.nationalrail.
co.uk) leave from the city's main
rail stations. Visitors heading to
south London, or to more remote
destinations such as Hampton
Court (p154), will need to use these
services. Travelcards are valid within
the right zones, but not all routes
accept Oyster pay-as-you-go.
The orbital **London
Overground** has patched together

a route around the whole of London. Coloured orange on the Underground map, handy sections run through north London, connecting Stratford in the east to Richmond in the south-west, and north–south through east London, connecting New Cross via Shoreditch High Street and Dalston Junction to Highbury & Islington. Trains run about every 10mins. We've listed Overground stations as 'rail', but Overground trains all accept Oyster and prices are, almost always, the same as the Underground (p182).

Buses

All London buses are now low-floor vehicles accessible to wheelchair-users and passengers with buggies. The only exception is Heritage Route 15 Routemasters (p70). Modern, redesigned 'Routemasters' run on routes: 8, 9, 10, 11, 38, 148 and 390. In 2013, route 24 (Hampstead–Pimlico) became the first route entirely run by the new bus. Using Oyster-as-you-go costs £1.45 a trip; your total daily payment, regardless of how many journeys you make, will be capped at £4.40. Fares can be paid by Oyster card, Day Travelcard, Bus & Tram pass or contactless payment card only; **cash is not accepted**. Under-16s travel for free (but must use an Oyster photocard, p183). A seven-day Bus & Tram Pass gives unlimited bus and tram travel for £20.20. Inspectors patrol buses at random; if you don't have a ticket, you may be fined £80.

Many buses operate 24hrs a day, seven days a week. There are also **night buses** with an 'N' prefix, which run from 11pm to 6am. Most night services run every 15-30mins, but busier routes run around every 10mins. They feel a lot less frequent after a heavy night.

Water transport

Most river services operate every 20-60mins from 7am to 9pm, more often and later in the summer months; see the website www.tfl.gov.uk. **Thames Clippers** (0870 781 5049, www.thamesclippers.com) runs a service between Embankment Pier and Royal Arsenal Woolwich Pier, boarded at Blackfriars, Bankside, London Bridge, Canary Wharf and Greenwich. The cheapest single costs £6.80; there are reductions if you hold an Oyster or travelcard.

Taxis & minicabs

If a **black cab**'s orange 'For Hire' sign is lit, it can be hailed. If it stops, the cabbie must take you to your destination if it's within seven miles. It can be hard to find an empty cab, especially just after the pubs close. Fares rise after 8pm on weekdays and at weekends. You can book black cabs from the 24hr **One-Number Taxi** (0871 871 8710; a £2 booking fee applies, plus 12.5% on credit cards), **Radio Taxis** (7272 0272) and **Dial-a-Cab** (7253 5000; credit cards only, booking fee £2 plus 12% handling charge), or use the **Hailo** or **Uber** app.

Minicabs (saloon cars) are often cheaper than black cabs, but only use licensed firms (look for a disc in the front and rear windows), and avoid anyone who illegally touts for business in the street: such drivers may be unlicensed, uninsured and dangerous. Fully licensed firms include **Addison Lee** (7387 8888), and **Ladycars** (8558 8510), which employs only women drivers. Otherwise, text HOME to 60835 ('60tfl'; 35p plus standard text rate) for the numbers of the two nearest licensed minicab operators and the number for None-Number Taxi, which provides licensed black cabs. If you choose a minicab, always ask the price when you book and confirm it with the driver.

Driving

Congestion charge

Driving into central London
7am-6pm Mon-Fri costs £11.50
(£10.50 by Auto Pay); the restricted
area is shown at http://tfl.gov.uk/
modes/driving/congestion-charge,
but watch out for signs and roads
painted with a white 'C' on a red
circle. Expect a fine of £65 if you fail
to pay (£130 if you fail to pay within
14 days). You can pay at http://tfl.
gov.uk/modes/driving/congestion-
charge, on 0343 222 2222 or (after
pre-registering on the website) by
SMS. You can pay any time during
the day or, for £2.50 more, until
midnight on the next charging day.

Parking

Parking on a single or double yellow
line, a red line or in residents' parking
areas during the day is illegal, and you
may be fined, clamped or towed. In the
evening (from 7pm in much of central
London) and at various weekend times
parking on single yellow lines is legal
and free. If you find a clear spot on a
single yellow during the evening, look
for a sign giving local regulations.
During the day meters cost upwards of
£1 for 15mins, limited to two hours, but
they are free at certain evening and
weekend times. Parking on double
yellows and red routes is always illegal.
NCP 24hr **car parks** (0845 050 7080,
www.ncp.co.uk) are numerous but cost
around £8/hr.

Vehicle removal

If your car has disappeared, it's
either been stolen or, if it was
illegally parked, towed to a car
pound. A release fee of £200 is levied
for removal, plus upwards of £21
per day from the first midnight after
removal. You'll also probably get a
parking ticket of £80-£150 when
you collect the car (reduced by 50%
if paid within 14 days). To find out
how to retrieve your car, call the
Trace Service hotline (0845 206 8602).

Vehicle hire

Alamo (0871 384 1086, www.alamo.
co.uk), **Budget** (0844 544 3439, www.
budget.co.uk) and **Hertz** (0843 309
3099, www.hertz.co.uk) all have
airport branches.

Cycling

London isn't the friendliest town
for cyclists, but the **London Cycle
Network** (www.londoncycle
network.org.uk) and **London Cycling
Campaign** (7234 9310, www.lcc.org.
uk) help to keep things improving, and
Transport for London (0843 222
1234, www.tfl.gov.uk) provides online
and printable route-finders.

Cycle hire

A City Hall-sponsored bike rental
scheme allows you to rent chunky
Barclays-sponsored bikes from self-
service stands across the city. You pay
£2 for 24hrs of access. After this,
rides less than 30 minutes are free,
those up to 1hr incur £1 on top of
the £2 already paid, with additional
charges for longer amounts of time
(£2/hr, £10/week); www.tfl.gov.uk/
BarclaysCycleHire has further details.
Longer-term rental is cheaper with
conventional firms, such as London
Bicycle Tour Company (7928 6838,
www.londonbicycle.com) on the
South Bank.

Walking

The best way to see London is
on foot, but the street layout is
complicated. There are street maps
in the central By Area chapters
(pp52-149); www.tfl.gov.uk/
gettingaround has route advice.

ESSENTIALS

CASS ART MANIFESTO

LET'S FILL THIS NATION WITH ARTISTS

ART IS FREEDOM. CASS ART BELIEVES IN ART. WE KNOW THE FREEDOM AND CREATIVE PLEASURE IT BRINGS. SO WE WANT EVERYONE TO REALISE THEY CAN DO IT - AND AFFORD IT.

BEST MATERIALS. ARTISTS NEED THE CHOICE OF ALL THE BEST MATERIALS. WE STOCK THE TOP BRANDS FROM AROUND THE WORLD, AS FAVOURED BY THE UK'S ARTISTS.

BEST PRICES. WE NEGOTIATE DIRECTLY WITH ALL THE FAMOUS SUPPLIERS. THEY HELP US, SO WE CAN HELP YOU. THAT'S WHY OUR PRICES ARE AS LOW AS THEY CAN GO.

OUR SHOPS. THE SPACE IS DESIGNED TO HELP YOU AND INSPIRE YOU. MATERIALS ARE ORGANISED AND DISPLAYED JUST THE WAY YOU WANT THEM. THE EFFECT IS THOUGHTFUL AND CONTEMPORARY.

OUR PEOPLE. OUR STAFF ARE ARTISTS. THEY KNOW ART. THEY ENJOY WORKING WITH WHAT THEY KNOW. THEY GIVE YOU INTELLIGENT AND THOUGHTFUL ADVICE — NO BLUFFING, NO HIDDEN AGENDA.

OUR NATION. WE ESTABLISHED OUR FIRST SHOP NEXT TO THE NATIONAL GALLERY IN 1984 AND REMAIN INDEPENDENTLY OWNED. FOR 30 YEARS WE HAVE BEEN ON A MISSION TO FILL THIS COUNTRY (ITS CITIES, TOWNS AND VILLAGES) WITH ARTISTS.

CASS PROMISE: BEST QUALITY, BEST BRANDS, BEST PRICES

ISLINGTON FLAGSHIP CHARING CROSS SOHO HAMPSTEAD KENSINGTON KINGSTON

ONLINE @ CASSART.CO.UK

Resources A-Z

See http://europa.eu/travel for information on travelling to the UK from within the EU, including visas and healthcare provision.

Accident & emergency

If you are so seriously ill or injured you need emergency care fast, call **999** or **112** free from any phone. For other medical emergencies, use the 24hr A&E departments at:

Chelsea & Westminster *369 Fulham Road, Chelsea, SW10 9NH (3315 8000, www.chelwest.nhs.uk). South Kensington tube.*
Royal London *Whitechapel Road, Whitechapel E1 1BB (7377 7000, www.bartsandthelondon.nhs.uk). Whitechapel tube/rail.*
St Thomas's *Lambeth Palace Road, Waterloo, SE1 7EH (7188 7188, www.guysandstthomas.nhs.uk). Westminster tube or Waterloo tube/rail.*
University College *235 Euston Road, Bloomsbury, NW1 2BU (3456 7890, www.udh.nhs.uk). Euston Square or Warren Street tube.*

If you require treatment for an illness or injury that is not critical or life-threatening, go to a minor injury unit or walk-in centre. For non-urgent police enquiries, call **101** (costing 15p per call).

Guy's Minor Injury Unit *Great Maze Pond, SE1 9RT (3049 8970). London Bridge tube/rail.*
St Barts Minor Injury Unit *West Smithfield, EC1A 7BE (3465 5869). St Paul's or Barbican tube.*
Soho Walk-In Centre *1 Frith Street, W1D 3HZ (7534 6500). Tottenham Court Road tube.*

Credit card loss

American Express *01273 696 933, www.americanexpress.com.*
Diners Club *0845 862 2937, www.dinersclub.co.uk.*
MasterCard *0800 964 767, www.mastercard.com.*
Visa *0800 891 725, www.visa.com.*

Customs

For allowances, see **www.hmrc.gov.uk/customs**.

Dental emergency

Dental care is free for the under-18s, students resident in this country and people on benefits, but all other patients must pay (NHS-eligible patients at a subsidised rate).

Disabled

Legislation is slowly improving access and general facilities. The bus fleet is now low-floor for easier wheelchair access, but most tube stations still have escalator-only access; those with lifts are marked with a wheelchair symbol on tube maps. A step-free tube guide is available in pdf form on the Transport for London website (https://www.tfl.gov.uk).

Most major attractions and hotels have good accessibility, though provisions for the hearing- or sight-disabled are patchier. The Inclusive London website (www.inclusivelondon.com) gives details about accessibility. The Access Project (www.accessinlondon.org) also has information on its website and, at the time of writing, was preparing an update on its invaluable reference book to include the Olympic legacy.

ESSENTIALS

Electricity

The UK uses 220-240V, 50-cycle AC voltage and three-pin plugs.

Embassies & consulates

American Embassy *24 Grosvenor Square, Mayfair, W1A 2LQ (7499 9000, http://london.usembassy.gov). Bond Street or Marble Arch tube.* **Open** 8.30am-5.30pm Mon-Fri.
Australian High Commission *Australia House, Strand, Holborn, WC2B 4LA (7379 4334, www.uk.embassy.gov.au). Holborn or Temple tube.* **Open** 9am-5pm Mon-Fri.
Canadian High Commission *38 Grosvenor Street, Mayfair, W1K 4AA (7258 6600, www.canada.org.uk). Bond Street or Oxford Circus tube.* **Open** 9.30am-4pm Mon-Fri.
Embassy of Ireland *17 Grosvenor Place, Belgravia, SW1X 7HR (7235 2171, 7225 7700 passports & visas, www.embassyofireland.co.uk). Hyde Park Corner tube.* **Open** 9.30am-5pm Mon-Fri.
New Zealand High Commission *New Zealand House, 80 Haymarket, St James's, SW1Y 4TQ (7930 8422, www.nzembassy.com). Piccadilly Circus tube.* **Open** 9am-5pm Mon-Fri.

Internet

Most hotels have broadband and/or wireless access, and many cafés offer free Wi-Fi, but some high-end hotels still charge for wireless access.

Insurance

There's access to free or reduced-cost healthcare for residents in the European Economic Area and Switzerland (bring a valid European Health Insurance Card, www.nhs.uk), as well as some countries with bilateral agreements with the UK. We still recommend you take out appropriate travel insurance – it's essential for all visitors from any other country.

Left luggage

Bus and rail stations have left-luggage desks rather than lockers; call 0343 222 1234 for details.

Gatwick Airport *01293 503 162.*
Heathrow Airport *0844 824 3115.*
London City Airport *7646 0000.*
Stansted Airport *0844 824 3109.*

Opening hours

Banks 9am-4.30pm (some close at 3.30pm, some 5.30pm) Mon-Fri; sometimes also Saturday mornings.
Businesses 9am-5pm Mon-Fri.
Post offices 9am-5.30pm Mon-Fri; 9am-noon Sat.
Pubs & bars 11am-11pm Mon-Sat; noon-10.30pm Sun; some open later.
Shops 10am-6pm Mon-Sat; many also open noon-6pm Sun.

Pharmacies

For advice on over-the-counter medication, visit a pharmacist. You can do a postcode search for your nearest pharmacist at www.nhs.uk, but there are chain pharmacists on most shopping streets.

Police

Call **999** in emergencies, or **101** for non-urgent crimes. Stations across London can be contacted on 0300 123 1212, while the following stations are usefully located:
Charing Cross *Agar Street, Covent Garden, WC2N 4JP. Charing Cross tube/rail.*
Chelsea *2 Lucan Place, SW3 3PB. South Kensington tube.*
West End Central *27 Savile Row, Mayfair, W1S 2EX. Piccadilly Circus tube.*

ESSENTIALS

Post

For general enquiries, call 0345 774 0740 or consult www.royalmail.com. Post offices are usually open 9am-6pm Mon-Fri and 9am-noon Sat, although the **Trafalgar Square Post Office** (24-28 William IV Street, WC2N 4DL, 0845 722 3344) opens all day Saturday.

Smoking

Smoking is banned in enclosed public spaces, such as clubs, hshops, restaurants and public transport.

Telephones

London's dialling code is 020; standard landlines have eight digits after that. If you're calling from outside the UK, dial your international access code (Australia 61, Canada 1, New Zealand 64, Republic of Ireland 353, South Africa 27, USA 1), then the UK code, 44, then the full London number, omitting the first 0. **US cellphone users** need a tri- or quad-band handset.

Public payphones take coins and/or credit cards, but aren't widely distributed. International calling cards are widely available.

Tickets

It's usually worth booking ahead – even obscure acts sell out, while major gigs and sport events do so in seconds. Agencies include **Ticketmaster** (0844 844 0444, www.ticketmaster. co.uk) and **See Tickets** (0871 220 0260, www.seetickets.com); they charge booking fees, so it's usually cheaper to go direct to the venue's box office. For West End shows, use the **tkts** booth in Leicester Square.

Time

Greenwich Mean Time (GMT) is five hours ahead of US Eastern Standard time. In autumn (26 Oct 2014, 25 Oct 2015) clocks go back an hour to GMT; they go forward one hour to British Summer Time in spring (30 Mar 2014, 29 Mar 2015).

Tipping

Tip in taxis, minicabs, restaurants, hotels, hairdressers and posh bars (but never pubs). Ten per cent is normal, with some restaurants adding a service charge of as much as 15%. Always check whether service has already been included in your bill – if it has there's no need to add a tip.

Tourist information

Piccadilly Circus Travel Information Centre *Piccadilly Circus Underground Station, W1D 7DH (www.visitlondon. com).* **Open** 9.15am-7pm daily.
City of London Information Centre *St Paul's Churchyard, EC4M 8BX (7332 1456, www.cityoflondon.gov.uk). St Paul's tube.* **Open** 9.30am-5.30pm Mon-Sat; 10am-4pm Sun.
Greenwich Tourist Information Centre *Discover Greenwich, Pepys House, 2 Cutty Sark Gardens, SE10 9LW (0870 608 2000, www.visit greenwich.org.uk). Cutty Sark DLR.* **Open** 10am-5pm daily.

Visas

EU citizens don't require a visa to visit the UK; for limited tourist visits, citizens of the USA, Canada, Australia, New Zealand and South Africa can also enter the UK with only a passport. But *always* check the current situation at **www.ukvisas. gov.uk well before you travel.**

What's on

Time Out is London's only quality listings magazine – free every Tuesday across the city; further listings are at www.timeout.com.

ESSENTIALS

Index

Sights & Areas

ESSENTIALS